The Lucky Ones

The Lucky Ones

a memoir

Zara Chowdhary

cntxt

Published in India by Context, an imprint of Westland Books, a division of Nasadiya Technologies Private Limited, in 2024

This edition published by arrangement with Crown, an imprint of The Crown Publishing Group, a division of Penguin Random House LLC

No. 269/2B, First Floor, 'Irai Arul', Vimalraj Street, Nethaji Nagar, Alapakkam Main Road, Maduravoyal, Chennai 600095

ISBN: 9789360455262

10 9 8 7 6 5 4 3 2 1

Printed at Manipal Technologies Limited, Manipal

For Sufi, so you may know the land you come from and its infinite love.

And for Amma, who is that infinite love made human.

Contents

The Lucky Ones

On Twenty-seventh February

in 837 C.E., Halley's comet is recorded on its fifteenth passage. It is a perihelion one, which means at this point in its orbit, it is closest to the sun, the oldest raging fire we know. Humans see the flying rock, from as close as humanly possible, streak across their sky. This riotous universe holds them in awe.

in 1803, the Great Fire of Bombay devastates hundreds of homes and buildings of this densely populated port city. When the flames die, the British begin to rebuild a Bombay in their own image, as those in power always do.

in 1921, Fascist Party workers in Italy clash with Italian communists. Later they destroy trade union centres and burn down the socialist newspaper *Avanti!* Ink and paper turn to ash. Hate and othering fill the air.

in 1933, the Reichstag burns down in a deadly blaze. Nazis blame the communists. A national emergency is declared. Soon after, the first labour camp opens.

in 2002, two train carriages light on fire outside a small town railway station in the Indian state of Gujarat, killing dozens of people. The head of the state, the chief minister, calls the burning an 'act of terror', code since 9/11 for something the Muslims must have done. A state of mourning is declared. Three weeks later, more than two thousand Muslims have been killed in response. One of the largest massacres in the history of independent India begins and ends in fire.

Prologue

On 27 February 2002

At 7 P.M., Amma has been missing for two hours. Papa paces the living room. He stops short of the dining table, turns around, and reflexively ducks under Dadi's precious crystal chandelier, missing its sharp spikes.

He walks out through the French windows onto the balcony and peers over the parapet, down eight floors. The street is lined with cars and scooters, and Papa's eyes search for the slightest movement between them, a bird scouring for a worm. She isn't there.

He bites out the words 'Careless. Lying. Always lying', and back he marches into the living room, ignoring my younger sister, Misba, and me. We sit, hands folded in our laps, by the telephone, waiting for it to ring. It peals soon enough, echoes burning through our apartment. Papa swoops on the receiver.

'Walekum-as-salaam! Kya? Haan curfew toh hoga. Allah sabka bhalaa kare.' And peace unto you. What? Oh no. Yes, a curfew is likely, then. Allah be kind.

If Papa is invoking Allah, it is safe to assume he is talking to Shah Sahab, our family priest, or pir.

Where is Amma?

The doorbell rings. Gulshan, our maid, rushes to open it; our eyes meet briefly. We share the same dread for Amma. We know what awaits inside. The bell isn't Amma. Hussain bhai, Jasmine Apartments' liftman, stands in the doorway telling Papa that the neighbours are all moving their cars off-street. The Holiday Inn across from Jasmine is offering to let us move vehicles inside its gates. Hussain bhai asks if Papa wants to move his new Hyundai Santro. Everyone in a one-mile radius around Jasmine has heard Papa boast about how it is the first car he's bought in twenty years with his hard-earned savings, his khoon paseene ki kamaai. Everyone in a one-mile radius also laughs at how six months later he still hasn't taken the plastic covering off the seats. Hussain bhai says someone might set fire to it if rioting starts.

Riot? What is going on? Where is Amma?

Papa and Dadi whisper to each other, which in and of itself is unusual. Something about a train on fire.

Where is Amma?

Papa grabs the car keys and leaves with Hussain bhai. Dadi finally notices us sitting by the phone and turns to us. 'Kahaan gayi hai tumhaari ma?' Where is your mother?

How would I know? I want to snap back, but that will only fuel her.

'Kuchh bolti bhi nahin hai. Aaney do. Aaj padegi usko Zaheer se.' She never informs us. Let her come back tonight. She's going to get it from Zaheer. *Or more like she will make sure Amma gets it.* Dadi walks away muttering.

I leave Misba sitting there and walk to the majoos—this ornately carved antique chest filled with more of Dadi's precious crystal ware and neatly arranged china. I hate her bloody majoos almost as much as I hate her when she speaks of Amma like that. Like vermin to be crushed under her chappals just because she's bored.

Past the majoos, between its sharp edges and the wall, is a tiny corner where Amma stacks all our namaz items: soft cotton dupattas, velvety jaanemaaz mats. That corner has a worn, comforting scent I've otherwise smelt only in old hole-in-the-wall libraries where Amma takes me some evenings, where I spend hours scavenging for Famous Fives and she for tattered Danielle Steel romances. This corner smells of Amma. I pick up a jaanemaaz and go into Dadi's room, where I've been sleeping with her on her large, low bed for the past two years, since her husband, our grandfather Dada, died. She hates the loneliness more than she hates me, I guess.

I wash my arms, my feet, rub water into my face and scalp. I lay down the jaanemaaz and step onto it, wrap the dupatta around my head, careful to cover every inch of my skin except my palms and fingers. Allah doesn't mind seeing my fingers, I'm told. But can They see and hear my heart under all this cloth?

Where is my mother, Allah?

I stand, head bowed, hands folded across my chest and start to pray. I can feel Dadi stop by the room, make a face and walk away.

The muezzin cries out from the mosque behind our building as if sensing my urgency to start namaz today.

'Allah hu-akbar Allah . . . hu-akbar . . .'

When I was younger, and Indians had only the state-run Doordarshan channel, which syndicated a handful of foreign shows, I used to watch Hindi-dubbed *Aladdin* with almost religious zeal. When Amma first taught me how to read namaz, I couldn't focus on the ritual, so while she chanted aloud in Arabic, a language I couldn't understand, I would distract myself pretending the jaanemaaz was a flying carpet. I'd sway back and forth on my heels, mimicking Amma's trance, but really in my head, I was steering, racing through the clouds, higher, lower, faster, away from any shadow that could catch me. Every time I passed by that musty corner near the majoos, I'd look at the jaanemaaz stack and smile to myself thinking here they were, these magical things, hiding in a dark corner of this darkness-filled apartment, my secret spaces of silence in a house full of noise and people always in each other's business. Amma also unwittingly fuelled this fantasy.

'Allah listens to the voices of innocent children before He listens to anyone else.' What other incentive does a child full of things to pray and plead for need, right?

Wave after wave of azaans blare from loudspeakers in all four directions; muezzins from six mosques chase one another. Papa jokes that, five times a day, the maulanas are participating in a talent competition, crying louder, hoarser, outshouting each other vying for our attention. Our neighbourhood, Khanpur, doesn't have fancy malls or restaurants, but we have something few others do: the burden of guilt if you don't answer six separate, belligerent calls to prayer.

Today my ears strain for another sound, though. Through all the holy cacophony: the sound of Amma ringing the doorbell.

While my lips softly recite each Arabic word with blind devotion, my ears are pricked for the sound of the lift. Living in a forty-year-old apartment building with a groaning elevator system has trained our ears with a strange gift: the ability to tell which floor the lift car stops at and whether the doors are opening or closing based on which of the two metal grill doors clanks into place first. The rusty pulley system is somewhere above our apartment, and now I hear it grating and squeaking as the lift car travels up the shaft from the ground floor. I lie facedown on my jaanemaaz, palms facing the ceiling, breathing in the smells of Amma and counting the floors as the lift passes each one—fourth, fifth, sixth, seventh—it hasn't stopped! Heart thumping, I quickly mutter, 'Sorry, Allah miyan,' jump off and fold the jaanemaaz, and run to the door, pulling it open before she can ring the bell, before the wrath of Dadi welcomes her in. Gulshan is in the kitchen passage peering through the unlit hallway, forehead creased.

There she is. On the threshold of the apartment, hands laden with grocery bags. My amma.

'Bhabhi!' Gulshan hisses with urgency and rushes to help her with the bag. 'Kidhar chale gaye the? Mummy aur bhai ne toh dimaag kha liya.' Where'd you disappear to? Your mother-in-law and husband chewed our brains out! She bursts into giggles as only Gulshan can in a moment of tension. I've learnt this from her—a heart full of fear and a mouth full of mirth—I catch myself doing it even today, giggling when I'm most scared.

Gulshan is the first domestic worker to stick it out in a series of many who vanish within months, sometimes weeks, of dealing with Dadi. Gulshan has worked in apartment C-8 Jasmine for five years, carrying groceries with Amma, checking our heads for lice, kneading endless balls of dough, washing all our clothes and utensils, being bullied by Dadi and my aunt Phupu. All thanks to her only friend and ally in the house: Amma. After all, they are treated pretty much on par in this home. Gulshan truly relishes it whenever she can whinge about Dadi.

Amma hurries into the kitchen and unloads her armfuls of plastic bags. She's speaking as quickly as her hands move. She went out at four saying she needed to pick up kadipatta-mirchi-dhania. Curry leaves, green chillies and coriander, which was code for 'I need a minute to get away and breathe'. She walked down the building stairs to the pavement, took the long way around the block rather than cut through the narrow alleys in between the buildings. She went to the small bazaar in the chowk where vendors stand all day, lorries overflowing with seasonal vegetables and fruits, covered in equal parts mud and flies. She bought her herbs and was headed back to Jasmine feeling somewhat restored when on the front steps she ran into Nasheman auntie, her morning walk companion from the seventh floor, who told her the same thing Dadi and Papa had been whispering about. A train was set on fire in some town called Godhra. There was talk of a curfew. Amma turned right around and went back to the market, this time for everything else she would need if the shops stayed shut all week—milk, bread, eggs, onions, potatoes, meat, fish. Only this time, she found herself among frenzied, frantic neighbours, longer lines, an entire community hurrying to get back home before dark.

We hear the elevator doors open and shut again in the hallway. Papa, who had gone down to look for her, is returning. He stomps back into the apartment.

'Where is she?'

The four of us in the kitchen freeze. I peek outside to watch him ask Dadi, who is at the dining table reading her namaz on a chair with her bad knees and all. Because she is supposed to be deep in prayerful contemplation, she can't speak, and surely cannot tattle, so she gestures towards the kitchen, her mouth still moving rapidly in Arabic.

Amma doesn't wait for the storm to find her. She rushes out to it instead. 'Zaheer, did you hear?'

At the sight of her, Papa seems to forget how furious he has been the past two hours.

'Yeah.' He slowly nods, distracted. 'The train. They're clamping down by seven thirty. How did you find out . . .' He trails off, walking into the living room. Amma follows him, eager to show him she brings more news, that her transgression of absence was worth it.

'And it wasn't some random passenger train.'

Papa sits down in his favourite armchair, the one directly pointed at the TV. He pauses while he fumbles with the remote, also still in its plastic cover, and turns on the evening news. She continues.

'I heard downstairs. The people were karsevaks. They were coming back from Ayodhya, it seems.' This doesn't sound good at all.

Amma looks at us where we are once again perched on the little cushion by the phone. She smiles at us quickly in a way only she can to reassure us, and turns back to Papa. 'It might be bad this time, no?'

He doesn't look at her as he carefully wipes the remote with the white sleeve of his spotless cotton kurta and gently blows any remaining dust off it. 'Probably.' He shrugs. 'I don't know. This is all very new. We should be ready in case it's a long curfew.'

Amma pulls out a dining table chair and sits next to him, gingerly touching his arm now that he doesn't seem ready to blow.

'Yes, yes. That's why I went back. I've got bread, eggs, milk, even mutton.'

He simply nods.

'Haan, good idea.' He switches from the English news, which doesn't seem to have caught up yet, to the local Gujarati one. The screen fills up with flames.

We gather around him to watch.

Ayodhya, the Nightmare

On the morning of 27 February 2002, a train on its way from Ayodhya, a small city in north-central India, to my home state of Gujarat in the west stopped at a small, dusty station called Godhra. Travellers disembarked for snacks and chai; vendors climbed on board to sell their wares. No one really knows what happened next, but as the train tooted its horn and departed the station, the emergency brake was pulled. Two of the train's carriages were on fire; their doors were locked from the inside. At least fifty-eight people died.

In Ayodhya, a Mughal-era mosque called the Babri Masjid had stood for five hundred years. At some point during the British Raj, an idea spread among radicalised Hindus that the mosque had been built over the bones of an old Hindu temple, perhaps even the very birthplace of Lord Ram. Over the decades, demands grew to 'return' the land to Hindus, even though its modern-day ownership lay with the Muslim Waqf Board, an administrative body that oversaw the care and maintenance of Indo-Islamic monuments. In 1992, a mob of more than a hundred thousand Hindu karsevaks stormed the ancient monument and tore it down. Religious violence broke across India in response. The right-wing Bharatiya Janata Party, which had led the call for the Ram temple to be built where the mosque stood, gained immense popularity after this moment. And each year after, groups of these karsevaks would travel to Ayodhya and protest at the demolition site. The hope was to pressure the Supreme Court, which was hearing a suit on the ownership of the property, to hand over the property to them. Ten years after the mosque's destruction, on 27 February 2002, one such group was returning to their homes in Gujarat on that train.

Theories abound: that a kerosene stove got knocked over; that a Muslim vendor on board got into an argument with the pilgrims; that there was a fight on the platform between a Muslim chai seller and the passengers. But on that day, local news agencies heavily controlled by the state rushed to call it an 'Islamic terrorist attack'. The state's chief minister, Narendra Modi, immediately declared it an 'act of terror'. The next day, raging Hindu mobs, comprising thousands of people, poured into Gujarat's streets, in cities, villages and towns, looting, raping and burning alive the state's Muslim citizens.

The massacre continued for three months.

Ayodhya, the Dream

Every two years Papa, a Gujarat state government employee, would get free tickets to take his family anywhere he wished within the country's vast and mind-boggling train system. Every two years, Papa would use these free tickets to take us to only one place: Ayodhya.

This Ayodhya was not the small, dusty town in north-central India that lay at the heart of the 'Hindu–Muslim problem'. Our Ayodhya was a home; a beautiful red-brick, three-storey home fragrant with jasmine blossoms and filter coffee. A home for which we sat in a train for thirty-six hours, crossed five states and travelled fifteen hundred kilometres south. A home that welcomed us with open arms and belonged to Papa's friends from his time in the United States as a student. Ila auntie and her brother had met Papa in California in 1975 when they all landed in the same graduate programme. Now their children, pets and extended families filled the red-brick home. And every two years this home would take us under its care. It became our most enduring memory of summer.

Sometimes Dadi and Dada would also tag along to this Ayodhya. Together, the Muslim Chowdharys and the Hindu Reddys would spend two months road-tripping across southern India in a convoy of cars, eating at roadside restaurants, staying with old friends along the way and bumbling about the jungles of the misty Nilgiri Hills looking for elephants, tigers and bison.

We would make stops in Mysore, Madras, Coorg and Chittoor, crisscrossing three southern states. Tamil, Telugu, Kannada, Tulu, Urdu and English would flow in and out of rolled-down windows into our ears and mingle in our mouths. Back in Ayodhya, the grown-ups would congregate each night around dinner and Scotch. Amma would stand in the kitchen orchestrating Ila auntie's domestic staff in a rendition of her biryani. Papa would be outside drinking himself senseless, but he'd remain in mostly good spirits, rubbing and comparing beer bellies with Rishi uncle, Ila auntie's brother. He became the closest thing our father had to a brother too. Papa, who was terrible with languages and generally hated everything South Indian because that's where his wife came from, would marvel at the sweetness of the staff's Telugu, calling it 'music to his ears'. Every two years for two whole months, Papa was among friends, people who loved and accepted him despite all his late-night raucousness.

Rishi uncle would arrive for dinner from a long day at his candy factory, bearing huge plastic bags of multicoloured treats for Misba and me. Sugary bars made of fresh South Indian mango pulp, hard-boiled sweets in flavours like guava and tamarind and banana and butter. At some point he and his wife would sweep us away to their apartment, a short car ride away in Bangalore. Their daughters and Misba and I would curl up on their couch and watch Julia Roberts's rom-coms and episodes of *Friends* (a treat for us, since Papa didn't allow cable TV in our house and Dadi wouldn't let us sit on her sofa). At their kitchen table, our mothers would hold cups of tea and each others' hands, swapping stories of their husbands and mothers-in-law, how nothing changed in the tapestries of their lives except the reminiscing over the wide-eyed young women they'd once been and the current sagging of their breasts.

In Ayodhya, we'd gather around a huge dinner table, eating and laughing for hours until Papa would say something caustic to Amma. The men, women and children would immediately coalesce around us, shielding Amma, ruffling our hair and smoothing our troubled cheeks. Someone would distract Papa and softly chastise him just enough so that that side of him would shamefully, quickly retreat.

At night, the older kids would spoil us with late-night ice cream drives and movies at the new malls that were sprouting up around 1990s Bangalore. On hotter days, we'd simply run around their garden with the dog or sit under the giant jackfruit tree in the yard, eating mangoes. I'd often slow down in front of the beautiful Ganesh idol in Ayodhya's hallway, take in its lines and curves, its every bronze detail, watch the ghee lamp at its base burn, lazy and luminous as our days.

The children would sit around their elders and speak and argue freely. Misba and I would listen in awe to these kids who knew so much, read so much, lived such rich lives. They were wealthy, no doubt. But in more than money. On these children had been bestowed indiscriminate acceptance from their elders and an almost miraculous courage that came with it. Misba and I would marvel at how easily they loved us. During those summers at Ayodhya, there was safety in numbers. Those who loved us and protected our mother outnumbered Papa. In a way, through these summers at Ayodhya we experienced for ourselves what keeps humans and their awkwardly built societies together, a society made of people as different as a Zaheer and a Rishi, a Rukhsana and an Ila. Misba and I quickly learnt that, when we were among them, they took turns keeping watch over us. And Amma and us girls poured out our food, our holidays, our stories, our politics, our dreams, our biases in wholly unfiltered ways. We felt encouraged to. Everyone gave of themselves generously, saw differences as something to learn from rather than to fear, and everyone protected the children. And we in turn let it shape us. We learnt to love the parts of one another we didn't quite understand: the language, the food, the distinctive beauties of our monotheistic and pluralistic faiths. But, most important, Misba and I learnt how daughters deserved to be spoken to and asked who they wanted to be. We learnt that our mother was loved, even admired, in this other world. It was as if for a brief while every two years, under this Ayodhya's magnanimous roof, we mattered. We were awake and we were alive.

Fire and Faith

In Hinduism, fire is a means by which physical life transforms into something more eternal, ethereal, rid of its material prison—the body. Mukti, they call it. *Freedom.*

In Islam, to have been touched by fire is to know Allah's wrath. Azaab, they call it. *Hellfire.*

The first time I played with fire, lit a matchstick I didn't quite know how to hold, I was ten. I set a Sufi saint's photo aflame on the dresser in Dadi's room. She had ordered me to place two smoking incense sticks in the marble holder in front of this picture as part of her daily ritual to cleanse her apartment of evil energies. Seeing no one around, and the matchbox unattended, I couldn't help myself. The next morning, there was just a small powdery grey mound of ash where the saint had stood. *It was an accident,* I swore to myself. But I didn't dare own up. I couldn't risk it. Our home believed in many things but not its daughters.

When Misba was three, she was touched by fire like the azaab it can be. Both her thighs were thoroughly scorched by a misdirected Diwali rocket that, instead of soaring towards the stars, plummeted down to where she was sitting in our cousin's veranda. It struck right between her knees, exploding, setting the child alight. Her lady parts were fortunately spared, but she developed a lifelong fear of any kind of flame afterwards. Seeing her burnt flesh hanging loose in chunks like that, the shock in her big, dark eyes, I felt confused about Allah for the first time. If Allah listened to young children first, how could They let this happen? Her screams had been loud enough for the whole neighbourhood to come rushing. Papa said sometimes he still heard them in his dreams. When Diwali rolled around each year and our neighbourhood erupted in a cacophony of fireworks, little Misba would crawl under our parents' bed, her chubby hands punching her ears, her eyes squeezed shut. She would remain there, curled in the dark underbelly of the bed, waiting for Diwali—the night of her nightmares—to end.

. . .

We watch the state-run Gujarati news together. Two train compartments of the Sabarmati Express set alight with sixty-odd persons on board. At least ten children, in the official figure. The news anchor, a woman with a beautiful aquiline nose, wearing bright red lipstick, struggles to remain poker-faced as she reads through the grisly details: doors locked, kerosene poured, coaches set on fire, people trapped inside screaming.

I can feel my whole family, all six of us, holding our breath. It is unusual for news to be this graphic and unfiltered, as if the news channel has gone straight from the shocked mouths of the field reporters to live telecast unedited. This is a new feeling for us. The only other time we saw something like this on Indian television was when the Twin Towers came crashing down in America and we watched it live from our little corner in real time, jaws dropping in sync with jaws in the streets of New York City.

Firefighters rush about on-screen, dousing the last flames while the chief minister and his team survey the charred interiors of the maroon coaches. This man, our chief minister, Narendra Modi, is a man none of us have heard much from before, nor do we care. In Gujarat, which party governs doesn't really matter when it comes to Muslims.

The news anchor repeatedly and emphatically points out that these passengers were karsevaks, *religious workers*, travelling back from the sacred city of Ayodhya on a 'holy cause'. They were helping campaign for building a temple to Lord Ram over the debris of a five-hundred-year-old mosque they had demolished a decade ago.

I'm too naïve then to understand why these words are being repeated. Cruelty is wrong. It's as simple as that, the way Amma explains it. No one deserves to die in this terrible, grisly way. How did the person who pulled the chain and stopped the train, or the hand that poured the kerosene, not see the children? Do they not know how much it hurts to burn?

The newscaster continues: 'The chief minister while visiting the town of Godhra declared this the worst terrorist attack on the state.'

Something about his words sends another chill around the room. When the Twin Towers were attacked, America kicked off a global 'war' against terror. We've seen their planes on our TV screens, bombing mountains, flattening homes and hospitals. The Americans have redefined how a strong, powerful nation deals with those who try to terrorise it. And in Gujarat, the average Gujarati is very much in awe of America. We want their malls, we want their clothes, we want their McDonald's and Pizza Huts and suitcases stuffed with everything a Walmart shopping cart can fit. Americans make war and decimating an enemy look cool.

Now here he is, on our screens, our guy Modi, basically calling the burning a pre-planned act of terror. It just happened. There has been no investigation. And tomorrow the bodies of the dead are to be driven in a parade across the state, in a decision sanctioned by the government. The dead will be brought to our big city hospital in Ahmedabad before being handed over to their kin. We're going under a bandh. *A people's curfew.* Shops, businesses, schools and offices must remain closed by the order of not the government but the party of the chief minister, the BJP. Usually this means anyone who dares to defy it will face the wrath of its volunteers and grassroots members, who call themselves funky names and acronyms like the Bajrang Dal or the Vishwa Hindu Parishad.

Papa turns to watch our faces for the first time all evening. He has a weird habit of smirking when things are about to go wrong. As if he knew they would. Or perhaps he's steeling himself with mirth.

Our city, Ahmedabad, has a long history of religious violence, dating back way before 9/11. Doesn't matter if the clash is over worker rights, caste rights or property; issues have a way of alchemising into a Hindu–Muslim fight here. Our peace is tentative. Our trust is fractured. Bikes are routinely set on fire here, TV sets smashed at the slightest provocation, like when India loses a cricket match to Pakistan. But this is no cricket match. And Papa's smirk looks tremulous at best.

The city outside our balcony has quietened. Frenzied groceries bought. Shops shuttered. Building gates locked down. Birds frozen in the giant neem and banyan trees that stand sentinel along our streets, holding their breath in their wings. I walk away from the family and out onto the balcony. 'Pre-planned act of terror', my chief minister's words, ring in my ears. A thousand invisible fingers from every direction are pointing towards our balcony, a million eyes turning to where the Muslims sit huddled in their homes all over the state.

It doesn't matter this evening that this land we all stand on is the land of Gandhi. Something has been eviscerated. Something has changed. A new land and a new people reborn in fire.

Burning Bridges

On any given day in Jasmine, if we stand on our toes and crane our necks past the balcony, we can see the borders of the slum where Gulshan lives. The slum stretches along the great river Sabarmati, and where it ends marks the borderland between Khanpur and the neighbouring Shahpur. Small pockets of working-class Hindus and Muslims cohabit in these borderlands. We often buy weekly vegetables from the street market there. In a single evening, these pockets transform into tinderboxes.

Gulshan has lost most of her teeth to chewing tobacco. She has a deep brown face with wrinkles lining every inch. I like to think the lines on her face come from smirking constantly behind Dadi's back. The hatred is mutual with those two: the servant–madam relationship just barely upends the mother-in-law–daughter-in-law hostility between Amma and Dadi. Gulshan has taught Amma to find humour in it. With sarcasm and twinkle-eyed mischief, she survives in this home eight storeys above her own, all day every day.

She is younger than Amma, but she's had an earlier start in domestication: married at fourteen, mother of two by nineteen, after which she got her tubes tied, unlike Amma, who waits to have two abortions before she says 'Enough'. Gulshan is clearly the smarter of the two women actively raising us in this household. She's also implacable. You should see her every year when head lice season rolls in. She finishes her evening cleaning, orders us to lie on our bellies on the cot in the laundry room, our heads of silky black hair lolling over the edge, and she squats on the tiles and starts to pull out little critters with ruthless efficiency. If we whine about her tugging too hard at a strand, she thwacks our heads and says, 'Phir ghumo sar mein joowaan leke.' She laughs at her own joke. *Run around with lice then. See if I care!* Dadi stands at a safe distance by the door watching. Gulshan holds up a wriggling mother louse between her fingers and shows her.

'Dekho, Mummy. Bachchon ka khoon pee-pee ke kitne mote ho gaye.' I giggle into the mattress. Without punctuation or context, Gulshan is saying more than one thing through her darkened teeth. *Look, Mother. So fat from sucking the blood of these poor children.*

But this evening as Gulshan watches news on the television with us, the fiery images leave her shaken. She looks at Amma and asks if she can leave early.

'Bhabhi main zaraa jaldi jaaoon aaj?'

Amma nods, replies, 'Haan haan,' and quickly pulls a few notes from her wallet, crushing them into Gulshan's hand. 'Tum bhi jaake samaan khareed lo,' she says, urging Gulshan to get her groceries.

As Gulshan leaves, Asha-ma, Dadi's spinster sister who lives farther north from us, calls. Dadi and Asha-ma speak in hushed croaks, wondering how bad it will possibly get this time. They have lived through the Partition, the textile workers' riots in the sixties, the anti–affirmative action rioting in the eighties, the violence after the Babri Mosque demolition in the nineties. Neither sister is easily perturbed. Their iron-clip curls hardly move out of place—whether the city erupts or their sons do.

But Dadi loves drama. She clutches the cordless phone now, hand cupped over the speaker, sounding alarmed and urgent. I hover around, unable to tell if they're discussing the train burning or the fact that the store down the street has run out of Godrej hair dye. Dadi would die without the latter.

After Asha-ma, Shah Sahab calls again, this time with even more dire and cryptic warnings to keep any friends in the police on standby. Papa hangs up and declares Shah Sahab is 'just like all these bloody maulvis as usual. Overdramatic.'

Phupu, my father's younger sister, calls next. An argument ensues between her, Dadi, and Papa. The cordless phone is a godsend for these family standoffs. One on the old telephone, another on the cordless and the third across the river are all shouting at one another, no one being heard. Papa predicts it will be safest for everyone to stay put. People moving around in the open will be targets. Dadi is worried about her daughter and granddaughter, alone in an apartment across the river. She insists they move back in temporarily. Phupu counters, as always, that she can handle it. Plus—they each shout at the other—this will be over in a day or two. At the most. It always is. Papa is the most optimistic.

'Arre kuchh nahin hoga. Sab natak hai,' he says, proclaiming like he often does with zero context that *nothing will happen. It's all an act.*

After his death, I will often wonder if that's how Papa thought of his life in its entire passive emptiness.

But for now, his staunch belief in the meaninglessness of our existence confounds my riotous sixteen-year-old mind. I want to believe everything has a purpose. I have a purpose.

I can't sleep that night. Yes, we have grown up seeing occasional rioting outside our windows over a stolen bike. We have heard swords and knives clash in the chowk behind our building over a game of gully cricket, but that was then, when enough Hindus and Muslims lived cheek by jowl here to fight it out. In the last few years, Ahmedabad has parted along the banks of the Sabarmati like the Red Sea. Most of 'them' live on the west, and 'we' live on the east. Call me as dramatic as Dadi, but through this divide of hate and confusion, I sense something terrible approaching.

I lie awake in the dead silence, glancing towards a door in Dadi's bedroom that leads out to the balcony. I wonder if we should bolt it. I close my eyes, chant my prayers under my breath, and lie there pretending to sleep. That's when I realise why I'm so unnerved. Dadi's thunderous snores usually rattle our bed. So does Papa's obesity-induced sleep apnea from across the hall. No sounds tonight.

All of us are pretending to sleep.

Gulshan comes to work early the next morning, eyes sunken holes of sleep deprivation. She has sneaked up Jasmine's front stairs in the tiny sliver of time when the cops on our street rotate out. On her way up, the liftman, Hussain bhai, told her that our ailing elderly neighbour from upstairs passed away in the night. She tells Dadi and Amma the news. Amma quickly prays the Arabic dua'a for a passing soul. Dadi struggles not to smirk. The deceased gentleman and she have history. He would shave on his balcony upstairs sometimes and afterwards fling the mug of soapy water out into the universe. It would usually land on Dadi's chiffon saris drying there, and once even landed on her well-coiffed hair.

The newspapers, like Gulshan, have made it past the cops too. Dadi and I usually battle over the main sheet. The loser is stuck with the city supplement. Dadi uses the 'elder' card and orders me to fetch her something or the other from the kitchen, knowing I won't refuse and risk Amma bearing the brunt of her taunt. By the time I fetch her water/spectacles/chai, I find her nose deep in the broadsheet. But I also have teenage athleticism on my side. Some mornings I grab my favourite section straight from the letter plate in the door and run into the bathroom before she can hobble to it on her weak knees. Today, though, she is up earlier than usual. Only her floral nightgown, her lace-trimmed petticoat and the tips of her curlers are visible around the edges of *The Times of India*. The front pages covering her body are smattered with bloody, graphic images. In broad daylight, the pictures of the train are no less disturbing, but it's the headlines that scream off the page:

> 'Two Muslims Stabbed in Anand and Baroda'
> 'Mob Sets Bus on Fire in Ahmedabad'

'Police Makes 53 Arrests'
'We Will Not Remain Silent Spectators, Says the VHP'

The day hasn't even begun. I don't argue with Dadi over the paper. Instead, I quietly pick up the supplement covered in Bollywood gossip and walk out to the balcony. I never get to reading it.

All around me the dying winter sky is streaked with thick columns of grey smoke. Later, as a grown-up, a dream will haunt me: tornadoes streak across the skyline of Ahmedabad—a city that has no history of tornadoes. My mind filled with images from the 1996 movie *Twister*, and an inner child whose body never fully released this fear will conflate the two. Spinning wildly, thunderous and all-consuming, these grey, dusty tornadoes will always head directly towards C-8 Jasmine. In the dream I will see only my fingernails grasping at the French windows' knobs, pulling with all my teenage bodily strength, protecting all whom I love within this catacomb, knowing I can't hold on much longer. I won't realise until the day I start to write this part of the story that the tornadoes that have chased me in my dreams, always putting me back in C-8 Jasmine, helpless and struggling, are these columns I see in front of me now.

I look to my east. The old city is drowned in haze. The new city to the west looks even more menacing. *Those could be buses. They always burn the buses*, I tell myself. *That's the worst they can do, right?*

The minute Papa wakes up, the TV is turned on. It stays on all day. We watch mobs—this new word sticks in our mouths, a word for a group of deranged, bloodthirsty humans, a word I will never again be able to hear without shuddering. On the news, it looks like this human horde is running over the city. The newscaster sitting in a studio in New Delhi looks solemn as he rattles off names of neighbourhoods he has never seen.

Neighbourhoods we live next door to. There are the usual suspects with the highest concentration of Muslims: Kalupur. Dariyapur. Juhapura. Sarkhej. Shah Alam. But the list keeps going; names I have never heard get etched into my brain. Naroda Patiya. Dani Limda. Twenty-three, forty-two, fifty, ninety . . . Dead. Killed. Burnt. The numbers climb all day. One day, when I'm twenty years away from this day, I will understand the numbers never stopped climbing. But here this morning, I still believe the state. My family has always worked for this state. How can I not? *There is a statewide curfew. The police are stopping maids and checking them. How are these figures even real?*

Around midday of this first day we hear the first sounds. Muffled booms. Like the clap of approaching thunder. Somewhere close. Maybe Shahpur, half a mile north. We freeze. Waiting. Another. Then another. Then the roar of jeeps rushing down the street. And a cracking noise. And another. And another. Police rifles firing. Then silence. Nobody in the house utters a word. I'm supposed to be loading clothes into the laundry cupboard. Instead, I bury my nose in my father's shirt collar. The smell of his baby talcum powder floods my senses as the shots ring.

We aren't sure how to react, so we look to the man of the house. Papa simply turns and disappears into the bathroom for a long shower. He comes out smelling of soap and doused in more talcum powder an hour later. He lays Dada's maroon and white jaanemaaz on the dinner table, slumps into the chair, palms extended on the mat, counts Allah's name on his fingers thirty-two times. Papa never prayed before Dada died. He does sometimes now, perhaps when his own silence threatens to run him over. The booms and cracks explode again. They go on for about an hour. Papa finishes praying and goes into Dadi's room to take his mid-morning nap. Around evening, Phupu calls. She and her daughter, who live across the river from us, are safe, but the building one street down from theirs has been attacked. Phupu says she'll wait for the curfew to lift for a few hours in the morning and hurry over with her daughter then. 'Only for a few days,' she insists.

There is no news from school. Only a ringing tone that suggests the school office is shut too. Will we have to go to school tomorrow, or will it remain indefinitely shut, like our street? Who knows. With homework and studying out of the question, Misba and I flip through news channels all day, scouring them for details. The local Gujarati news lady doesn't say much except to cite official government numbers, which seem lower than what the national channels are reporting. They also keep replaying the smug face of a local doctor who is the general secretary of the VHP. His name is Pravin Togadia and he seems to particularly relish saying things like 'Demolition of the Ram temple by Babar 450 years ago and destruction of the World Trade Center on September 11 last year are two faces of Islamic terrorism.' It seems like the state channel is trilling with voices like his. We switch to the more sensible national network, NDTV.

They finally have boots on the ground in Ahmedabad and other major cities of Gujarat. Their shocked, ghostly faces will become forever etched in my brain. One woman is trying to hold her voice steady as she describes what she has seen on the roads of our city: men, women, teenage boys, clutching tridents and swords, swarming in mobs of more than a hundred. All day they have surrounded entire neighbourhoods of Muslims. They've dragged people out of homes, slit through their bodies, covered them in gasoline and set them on fire. All while raising one slogan: 'Jai Shree Ram'. *Praise be to our Lord Ram.*

The camera cuts to them bellowing the words at the news crew. They're dancing with joy amid smoke, ash, burning flesh and smoking buildings. I lose my ability to breathe.

'Hey Ram' were the last words uttered by Mahatma Gandhi, his dying plea to a god he worshipped, Ram—the ideal Indian man, so ideal he became divine. Gandhi was assassinated because a madman named Godse and his Hindu supremacist organisation, the Rashtriya Swayamsevak Sangh—the ideological inspiration for the party that ruled our state—believed that Gandhi loved India's Muslims more than its Hindus. As if Gandhi were a parent choosing one sibling over another. They blamed him for giving away part of Akhand Bharat, an imaginary precolonial subcontinental nation, to the Muslims so they could form Pakistan. Now Gandhi's god was being invoked, the ideal Indian, as Indian Muslims were being murdered on their own streets.

My dada's last word was 'Allah'. As he'd lain on the balcony, dying in the home, the city, the country he chose and loved, his body sagged, his fingers still counting Allah's name thirty-two times.

Thank god Gandhi died when he did, I find myself thinking as I watch the news. *Thank god Dada died when he did.* Their deaths were cleaner, swifter than whatever this is. *Who are these people? What is this madness? Who have we become in a matter of a day?* But none of this happens in a day, does it?

That night, Papa stands on the balcony, his eyes thin slits like an eagle studying the bridges over the Sabarmati.

'Do you think they can come over Nehru Bridge while we're sleeping?' I ask him. Papa looks surprised. Perhaps he didn't realise I was close by, or he doesn't expect me to address him so directly. I'm certainly never the one asking questions. He doesn't hurry to respond. Instead, he leans over the balcony and spits. As if something is stuck on his tongue. Then he turns to me and says, 'Nahin, nahin, police are there. And we can see everything from here. This place is like a bloody fort. Nothing will happen,' he insists again. I turn away from him, eyes searching the pitch-black riverbed. I'm looking for signs of movement. Or a more comforting father. Anything. I see nothing.

We live in this eastern Muslim side of Sultan Ahmad Shah's city, with the expanse of the river and the bridges between this side and that. And living on the east has been a lot of things but it has never been scary. This is my home, however unsettled it has always been on the inside. I've never thought of it as the place I might die in before I've had a chance to live. There must be a life beyond this fort that I feel so trapped inside. It can't end this way before it's even begun. A meaningless life ended by meaningless death. The silence around me is of a city that has warred with itself all day and is now pretending to sleep.

I am sick of pretending.

I want to stay up, keep watch, turn on every light in every home so no one can sneak up on us in the dark. Images from the day's news are searing through my brain. It's over—this act we've maintained all our lives of being one country, children of the same, equally doting parents. I wish I could burn these bloody bridges. Cut the cord. I wish these parents would divorce. I wish we didn't have to sit helpless in our own homes waiting for the mob to find us. After what I've seen on the TV all day, I don't believe there is law, or rules, or that anyone will hear or come if we scream. I want to burn the bridges, stop the smoke spirals from crossing the river. Let those who come to burn us know that I am awake. I will not be killed in my sleep. I refuse to die in my bed mumbling, 'Nothing will happen.'

Fire

At the outset it is important to underline the fact that the events in Ahmedabad do not fit into any conceivable definition of a communal riot. All evidence suggests that what happened there was a completely one-sided and targeted carnage of innocent Muslims, something much closer to a pogrom or an ethnic cleansing.

Moreover, the selective violence that was perpetrated was done with remarkable precision, suggesting meticulous planning and collation of information over a protracted period, rather than the spontaneous mob frenzy characteristic of a communal riot. It also clearly indicates collusion and not merely indulgence of the state machinery and the ruling political establishment. The condemnable Godhra massacre was of course the trigger in this case. But the point is that it could have been anything else, any provocative act on the part of any Muslim individual or group, possibly even of a lesser magnitude, would have led to similar consequences. The ground for this communal genocide was cleared in Gujarat much prior to the Godhra massacre. It is noteworthy that the attacks on the Muslims in Ahmedabad and the rest of Gujarat started a day after the Godhra tragedy, further indicating that this was no merely spontaneous reaction, but one connected to the Vishwa Hindu Parishad Gujarat Bandh call on 28th February.

Prasenjit Bose, Dr Kamal Mitra Chenoy, Vijoo Krishnan and Vishnu Nagar, 'Ethnic Cleansing in Ahmedabad: A Preliminary Report,' SAHMAT, 10–11 March 2002

On 10 March, more than a week after the train's burning, a human rights collective comprising activists, writers and academics, called SAHMAT, arrives in Ahmedabad. These observers are shocked at what they observe. They release this immediate preliminary report to document what they see and hear on the ground.

A bandh is a powerful political tool: a party or organisation forces/requests/commands society to come to a standstill, asking citizens to voluntarily cease all life and business so the powers that be are forced to listen. It is meant as a form of civil strike. But in the hands of a mob, a bandh becomes a call to strike *at* someone whose hands have been forcibly tied behind his back. It is a call for a mob to devour him whom the powers that be do not like.

The Man Who Saved Sparrows

Ahsan Jafri, a former member of Parliament, lives in a small, gated community called Gulbarg just thirteen miles north of us. I will never meet him. One day I will have only tattered photos and scattered stories to piece him back together with. I will sit with these and weep and realise why I feel like I've known him. In these pictures and stories, I recognise wisdom like my grandfather's, faith in Allah's justice like my amma's, a penchant for white kurta pajamas like Papa's.

In a picture of Gulbarg before it is burnt, his spotless ivory house will stand out among seventies-style mini duplexes. A large pink bougainvillea will loom over the low garden wall, a canopy threatening to shower delicate paper-like petals at the slightest breeze. The bougainvillea will grow with a sort of wild generosity.

I will call him Ahsan sahab from here on, as my elders have taught me to.

Ahsan sahab's son will remember how his father's study was lined with wooden bookcases bent under the weight of legal volumes in red-gold trim. That the Indian Constitution was his father's passion and profession for over forty years. That his study was on the first floor of his two-storey house. And its door always remained ajar for anyone in need of counsel. That Ahsan sahab and his wife didn't open their doors *only* to humans in need.

On dusty summer afternoons in Ahmedabad, just before the cool southwestern monsoons arrived, Ahsan sahab's grandson Tauseef will remember his nana picking up a roll of tape and a pair of scissors and meticulously cutting little strips of tape and sticking them over the fan switches of his study, barring anyone from turning them on. One summer, this grandson—born and raised in the United States and sweating in the oppressive Ahmedabad heat—will remember watching his grandfather's jovial face, shining with sweat, as he smiled and pointed to the gaps above the bookcases. In the absence of the whirring fan, he will remember hearing the excited chitter of the common Indian house sparrow. We call it a 'chakli'. Each year, for a few months, several chakli clans took over the crevices of his grandfather's roof, this boy will remember. They built their nests, birthed their young and flew across the ceiling, twittering in their aerial village.

Somewhere in those shelves in the study, Ahsan sahab's son Tanvir will remember a smaller book tucked away, a volume of famous speeches, among them Martin Luther King Jr's 1965 address in which King claimed: 'The arc of the moral universe is long, but it bends toward justice.' A few shelves down his son will remember always finding a copy of Ahsan sahab's own poetry collection: *Qandeel*. Arabic for 'candle'.

In the Gujarati language, that epiglottal *q* becomes a simpler, flatter *k*, and the kandeel becomes a lantern kite. At the end of Uttarayan, our annual kite-flying festival, as nightfall descends on the city, colourful paper lanterns are flown into the dark skies, stars sent up on a string. As a child I would stand in the window late and breathe gently in and out as the twinkling kites flew up, up and away. There was freedom in their burning.

In both etymologies—qandeel and kandeel—the burning happens within. This obstinacy of who we are is set on fire, and from it light springs and warmth spreads. The ultimate jihad. The fight to become one's finest self, an individual dedicated to community.

Gulbarg was Ahsan sahab's experiment in building community, a neighbourhood for working- and middle-class Ahmedabadis of all faiths who still wanted to live together. It's where Ahsan sahab's politics and altruism best thrived. His own home was the embodiment of this. In 1969, when the textile workers' riots had turned into a Hindu–Muslim riot, the family had fled out the back door with just the clothes on their backs, Ahsan sahab carrying his four-year-old daughter in his arms as he ran along the railway tracks and hoisted his children and wife onto a slow-moving coal train. The family had slept on coal mounds all night and the next day made their way to a refugee camp where the children, homeless in their own city, hungrily joined in the long line for food packets.

A year later, when the government handed out compensation to riot victims, Ahsan sahab and his family returned to Gulbarg. His wife took in the charred ruins of their home, slumping to the ground in tears that somewhere in there were the burnt remains of the only photograph of her wedding. Ahsan sahab stood beside her and made his family a promise:

> Girti hui divaar ka saaya na bataao,
> phir se nayi divaar uthaao toh bane baat.
> *Don't point at the shadow of a fallen wall.*
> *Let's see you build one. Yet again.*

Scaffolding rose out of the earth. Trees bloomed anew. Slowly, as Ahsan sahab revived his legal practice, he joined the Congress Party—the same one that fought for India's independence and established its first government. He knew his dream was radical and would need political protection. Stories of the grit and courage of this newly elected, educated and devoted Muslim representative drew other Muslim families out of the old sultan's city and into the promise of Gulbarg. Ahsan sahab's daughter remembers growing up in this oasis her father built. How on cold winter evenings, she, her brothers and their neighbours' kids would build a fire with paper and twigs in the yard and sit around telling stories until their mothers called them home for dinner. In a simple tenement house across from theirs a woman lived with her husband and sons. Ahsan sahab's children called her Chachi, auntie. Ahsan sahab's daughter remembers how Chachi, who didn't own very much, had a metal trunk whose insides she had decorated with photos of Bollywood superstar Amitabh Bachchan that she had cut out of newspapers and magazines. She even had his photos lovingly straightened and preserved in between her saris. Gulbarg protected its humans and birds and this—an illiterate woman's secret altar to her hero, a man who made a career out of playing the angry young man, champion of the working class, a tragic hero crippled by everything wrong with this new India.

Outside Gulbarg's walls, temples sprouted, slums pressed in. More families like Chachi's coagulated around Ahsan sahab. Each year Gulbarg's residents added metal bars to their doors and windows as small skirmishes, robberies or clashes grew outside. The walls of Gulbarg rose higher each year until, in 2002, they were fifteen feet tall. Inside, every time Ahsan sahab's daughter found a picture of Bachchan in a newspaper or magazine, she cut it out and ran across to give it to Chachi.

One day I will find out that this man who saved sparrows was not an anomaly. In the years after 2002, whenever 28 February rolls around, I will find myself thinking of Ahsan sahab. One such February day I will pick up the Quran and find this within.

> I have come to you, with a Sign from your Lord, in that I make for you out of clay, as it were, the figure of a bird, and breathe into it, and it becomes a bird by Allah's leave. (Quran 3:49)

These words by Isa Ibn Maryam, or as you might better know him, Jesus, will shake me. These stories and more I will collect in vain, trying to avoid writing what happens next.

The morning of 28 February, as I watch the columns of smoke from thirteen miles away, mobs clad in saffron, armed with tridents, swords, knives and cans of petrol, approach and surround Gulbarg.

All morning Ahsan sahab's neighbours and Muslims from the slum outside their gates pour into his living room. This has become their general riot protocol. Ahsan sahab starts making calls to local cops. Within a couple of hours, a small team of the State Reserve Police Force are posted outside Gulbarg.

Rupa is one of his neighbours who understands this protocol. She isn't Muslim but Parsi. And like a lot of the Parsis in the city, given their history of exodus and assimilation, families like hers navigate the tensions of days like these with learnt ease. At 9 A.M., the first Molotov cocktail flies over Gulbarg's walls. It arcs in through Rupa's kitchen window and sets her home on fire. She grabs her young son and daughter, rushes to join the throng already packing themselves into Ahsan sahab's home. Around ten thirty, the city's police commissioner personally visits Jafri. He assures the terrified families and children that police reinforcements are coming. Outside, police guards push back an angry, growing mob from the gates.

In the hours that follow, no reinforcements show up. Rupa and others gather on the second floor of Ahsan sahab's house as he starts to make more frantic calls, going down his phone book: the director general of police, the commissioner of police, the mayor, the state's leader of opposition, other top government officials. The neighbours finally beg him to call the chief minister. Call Modi.

Outside, a bunch of usual suspects from the neighbouring slums, street gangs run by VHP, are yelling slogans and throwing handmade bombs against the walls. Rupa later tells a journalist, 'We even asked Jafri sahab to call the goons if he could and convince them to spare our lives.' But at the time neither Rupa nor Ahsan sahab realise that these gangs are not operating as hired assassins today. They have been turned into killing machines; their own deep-seated hate, after years of feeling outcast, forgotten, downtrodden, has been shaped, directed and ignited into a fireball. And this has been done by the very people Ahsan sahab now frantically tries to call. Rupa stands close by, huddled with her children in his room, overhearing as Ahsan sahab finally calls Narendra Modi himself.

She hears him answer the phone and cuss, saying he is surprised Jafri hasn't been killed already.

Years later, Modi will tell the investigating state commission looking into his collusion in the massacre that he heard about what happened at Gulbarg only later that night. The commission, in a shocking revelation, will admit that all proof of the phone call ever happening is 'missing or has been destroyed'.

Ahsan sahab hangs up and turns to the hundreds of innocent, cowering neighbours in his home to tell them the news: no help is coming. Then the phone rings again. The room quiets. Ahsan sahab's twelve-year-old granddaughter is on the line. He was supposed to drive to see her this morning. She lives six hours away in the neighbouring city of Surat. Her dada had made a promise that he would come watch her dance at her school programme today. 'Have you not left?' the little girl asks. Ahsan sahab hates to break promises. 'Not yet,' he says, and then hangs up.

Growing up in the Ahmedabad that existed before this day has bequeathed me a strange privilege. I can pick up a Bible just as easily as I do the Quran or Bhagavad Gita. They all feel mine. When I will start to write this next moment, my body will feel heavy, my fingers will lose feeling, my mouth will dry. So I will stop typing and reach for these words instead, from the Infancy Gospel of Thomas:

> When the boy Jesus was five years old, he was playing at the ford of a rushing stream. And he gathered the disturbed water into pools and made them pure and excellent, commanding them by the character of his word alone and not by means of a deed. Then, taking soft clay from the mud, he formed twelve sparrows. It was

> the Sabbath when he did these things, and many children were with him. And a certain Jew, seeing the boy Jesus with the other children doing these things, went to his father Joseph and falsely accused the boy Jesus, saying that on the Sabbath he made clay, which is not lawful, and fashioned twelve sparrows. And Joseph came and rebuked him, saying, 'Why are you doing these things on the Sabbath?' But Jesus, clapping his hands, commanded the birds with a shout in front of everyone and said, 'Go, take flight, and remember me, living ones.' And the sparrows, taking flight, went away squawking.

As Ahsan sahab waits inside, cylinders of natural gas used in the average Indian kitchen are being piled into trunks of cars to be delivered to the growing mob outside. Someone pulls out pipes from a nearby bakery. Someone else grabs torched pieces of cloth, attaches them to the pipes. Together this nameless mob of someones hurls these cylinder 'bombs'—wicks burning bright—at Gulbarg. By midday, the wall finally crumbles. The mob throws itself inside the grounds.

'At this point, Ahsan Jafri decided to step out and talk to the rioters to save us,' Rupa will later tell a journalist. The mob waits, bloodthirsty; a sacrifice is due. Ahsan sahab opens his front door and with hands folded yells, 'Please take me, but spare those inside.'

The attackers jump on him and drag him out. Madan Chawal, a man in the mob, will also speak of this later to another journalist, unaware he is being interviewed as part of a sting operation.

'He [Ahsan sahab] was pulled by his hand . . . Five or six people held him, then someone struck him with a sword . . . chopped off his hand, then his legs . . . chopped out all his organs.'

Not realising he is indicting himself, Madan will gleefully continue.

'After cutting him to pieces, they put him on the wood they'd piled and set it on fire . . . burnt him alive.'

. . .

On 28 February, Rupa watches Ahsan sahab's murder from inside his home and knows it is over. Every house in Gulbarg is burning. Smoke fills this one too. They can't breathe. Rupa decides to follow the neighbours who are scattering and fleeing for their lives now. She drags her son and daughter along.

'The three of us were running, holding each other's hands. There were a lot of people lying unconscious on the ground. I tripped over somebody and fell. My daughter let go of her brother's hand and turned back to help me up.'

Rupa and her daughter run up the stairs to the terrace, where they see a policeman on another terrace. There's hope for a quick second.

'He threw a stone at me.' Bottles of acid, burnt tyres, balls of flames rain down on them; the screams of their neighbours fill the air. 'A little girl was lying unconscious. I wanted to help her but couldn't because my hands and feet were burnt.'

There, lying crouched with her daughter on the terrace, Rupa realises her son isn't with her.

Oceans away in the United States, Ahsan sahab's daughter sits glued to the news. She lives in Delaware with her family. Her brother calls to tell her he can't reach their parents. She wonders about Chachi.

The mob ransacking and annihilating Gulbarg finds Anwar, Chachi's husband. They behead him. Her youngest son, Akhtar, and his wife will later be found in pieces in Ahsan sahab's backyard, where they tried to hide. Chachi's senile mother-in-law will be found burnt to death in her bed. Chachi will be found several days later, alive. She will be severely burnt and numb with shock.

A year later, when Ahsan sahab's daughter will finally summon the strength to step foot inside a charred Gulbarg, she will find Chachi. Together they will walk through the barren husks of their former homes, now filled only with the last shrieks of their loved ones. Together they will stand where their families dissipated into ash, bone and memory. The women will stare at the lone neem tree that has somehow survived the inferno, green and abundant still, a silent witness to the full lives now extinguished.

Ahsan sahab's and Rupa's ten-year-old son's bodies will never be found.

The casualties reported officially are understatements. According to those involved in relief and rehabilitation work the number of people killed in Ahmedabad alone would be nearly 1000. As against the total of around 700 including victims of Godhra, which the government has cited as the total figures of casualties for the whole of Gujarat, they say the number would be around 2000 if not more. Since the violence has spread to remote villages, access to which has been denied by the government, any estimation of the number of casualties by non-governmental sources has been rendered difficult. An overwhelming majority of those who have been killed are Muslims, including women and children . . . Some eyewitness accounts of those who had fled from nearby villages and taken refuge in the relief camps, suggest large-scale massacres of Muslims continuing in the countryside. Entire families have been exterminated in villages with nobody left to lodge complaints or claim the dead bodies.

'Ethnic Cleansing in Ahmedabad:
A Preliminary Report', SAHMAT,
10–11 March 2002

How do you *count* your dead when the dying happens on the run? How do you *account for* them when there is only so much you can pick up? Only so much you can carry?

Daughters of Fire

Bano was nineteen in 1999 when her family arranged for her to marry a cattle trader a decade older than her. Her groom's family lived in Randhikpur, a village about two hundred kilometres from Ahmedabad. I was thirteen at the time she was being married off, her name meaning nothing to my mouth. I was busy discovering my body's ability to crush on a man much older than me, as I ogled a green-eyed, handsome Bollywood actor making his debut. Marriage was on my mind too, but only in that I started locking the bedroom door when I showered. I took out Amma's beautiful dupattas from her cupboard, twirled them around my head, dancing, and pretended I was getting married to Hrithik Roshan.

Meanwhile, in Randhikpur, Yakub and Bano fell in love. Their daughter Saleha was born a year later. Then two years later, in 2002, to her family's delight, Bano announced she was pregnant again. It was in her fourth month pregnant that the mob found her.

On the twenty-eighth of February, as the killing begins in Randhikpur, Bano and Yakub's home is set on fire. The whole family, all fourteen members, escape into the nearby fields. A kind Hindu neighbour then hides them for a while, but soon, with news of a mob approaching, they are asked to leave again. They eventually sneak into a nearby abandoned mosque. Bano's cousin Shamim is also nine months pregnant and goes into labour.

A midwife is found to quickly help deliver Shamim's baby. As the mother and baby rest, the family huddle close in the middle of the night. It is decided Yakub will leave the next day to search for a new refuge. Bano doesn't sleep all night. Early in the morning, she bids Yakub goodbye. A few hours later, a mob descends on the mosque looking for them.

'Aa rahya Musalman. Emne maaro, kaato,' people arriving in vehicles with sticks and swords are screaming. *Here are the Muslims. Kill them, cut them.*

Bano grabs little Saleha, Shamim clutches her newborn to her chest, and with the rest of the family, the mothers run through the dense woods beyond their village, hoping to reach a Muslim settlement that will take them in. When they reach the highway, they flag down a passing truck. The driver agrees to drive them to Ahmedabad, where they are sure to find refuge. The mothers herd their families into the back of the truck, believing, as all mothers do, that their prayers are being heard.

A few hours later, the truck carrying them shudders to a halt, and loud, angry men are heard outside demanding the hatch be opened. Bano is so terrified that her body starts to convulse and wakes up little Saleha. The mother rocks her wailing child hard against her chest but fails to quiet her screams. Within seconds the mob wrenches open the shutter and clambers into the back of the truck. They tear Saleha from her mother's arms. As Bano screams, horrified, one man picks up a rock and smashes Saleha's head in.

Over the next few minutes, twelve of those men take turns raping pregnant Bano. Nearby she hears the bloodcurdling screams of Shamim, who is being forced to watch as the men butcher her newborn. The mob murders all fourteen members of Bano's family in the back of the truck, raping eight of the women in the process.

Bano loses consciousness, and the men dump her on the roadside, assuming she is dead. Bano will carry this void of memory with her for the rest of her life. She will say this to a bench of judges. She will recount it hundreds of times over the next fifteen years to lawyers, journalists and activists. The darkness her mind and body succumb to will be hers to carry. For now, the men abandon her limp body and move on.

When she comes back to light, Bano's first realisation is that she is bruised and scratched all over. And that she is naked. Everything hurts. Her heart is a dull, dark hole. Her next realisation is that, all around, her family lie murdered. She sees the other mother who ran with her, Shamim, dead too. Then she finds her baby.

'I looked at Saleha one last time, found a piece of clothing to cover myself, and walked into a nearby forest,' Bano will later say in her testimony. Bano spends the next twenty-four hours alone in the woods—naked, terrified, too shocked to mourn how her life turned to blood and ash in two days.

In the morning, some remember an Adivasi woman finding and clothing Bilkis, which would make sense. Our forests have known the first indignity of greed, hate and rape. Others say the police finally arrived, found and clothed her. Somewhere in between these versions, a case was loosely filed. These moments after—minutes, hours, days in which one is left with nothing more to lose—become an abandoned field, littered with irrelevant minutiae, details to argue over so we never have to grapple with the true darkness of what was done to just this one family looking to escape hate.

'I wasn't in the truck with my family that day,' Yakub will later say in regretful testimony. The young father, having left the mosque to find them a place of safety, came back to find his family gone. He then ran to their burnt home but couldn't find his wife or daughter.

'I read about the truck incident through a newspaper report. They revealed that the lone survivor, a woman named Bilkis, was living in a relief camp.'

Bilkis Yakub Rasool is her full name. The case of *Bilkis Yakub Rasool v. The Union of India* will become writ on our conscience in the next twenty years. Inside our homes, written in our newspapers, we will know her as Bilkis Bano. In the years that follow this day, this name will haunt every step of Narendra Modi's ascent to power, sometimes a whisper, other times a roar.

Yakub rushes to the camp. There he spots her sitting in a corner. A ghost of the Bano he loved. A nineteen-year-old mother with one baby in her womb, and another's ghost in her arms. She's sitting there tearless and silent, in the wreckage of lost children, amputated men and raped women.

Yakub does not ask her any questions. He simply hugs her limp figure and starts to wail. Over the years, he will hear her testify hundreds of times. But the couple—who now have five children—will never talk to each other about what happened to their family in 2002.

'I don't know what I'd say if she ever discussed her ordeal with me,' Yakub will tell a journalist.

Their children, four girls and a boy, will also learn better than to broach the topic.

'I think they know what happened with their mother,' Yakub will say, 'they used to ask questions when they were little. But as they grew up, our two oldest daughters took care of their inquiries, never letting them reach us. It's like they're trying to protect us.'

Even though Bano registered a police complaint in those very first days of the violence, the case is dismissed after three weeks, the police citing a lack of evidence. We will later find out that the police took out specific names of the accused from her statement. These were men Bano recognised from her own village community. We will also find out that doctors deliberately omitted crucial pieces of evidence, and the fourteen bodies of her family members were decapitated and buried in unmarked graves before any real identification could happen.

Although illiterate and penniless, Bano will continue in her fight for justice.

'When you lose everything, you gain the courage to fight,' she will say. 'I knew it was going to be a long road, but I had to tread it for Saleha.'

Her eyes will always dim into nothingness when she says her daughter's name.

. . .

Two years after the attack, Bano's eleven attackers, including two with formal connections to Modi's BJP, will be arrested. In May 2004, Central Bureau of Investigation will submit a report. They will ask for the case to be moved outside Gujarat to ensure a free and fair trial. Their investigation will find the state complicit in the cover-up. Six police officers will be accused of tampering with evidence.

In 2008, a special court will convict thirteen of the twenty men accused of the carnage: eleven will be sentenced for life for the carnage inflicted on Bano and her family. A police officer will be convicted of tampering with evidence; one accused will die during the trial. Fifteen years from the day, the Bombay High Court will uphold these sentences. Bano will be offered monetary compensation: Rs 5,00,000 will be the arbitrary reparation offered for her loss by Modi's government. Bano will turn it down.

She will go to the Supreme Court and fight on for two more years. In 2017, the Indian Supreme Court will finally speak on her compensation, calling it inadequate. The chief justice will say, 'Money is the best healer. What else can we do for her?' and order the Gujarat government to pay her ten times the original amount. In their decision they will note that after waiting fifteen long years for justice, Bano must receive that money within two weeks. The court will also direct the state to give her a home and a job. Bano and her children will move to twenty homes in these seventeen years because of the harassment they face. They will never be offered witness protection.

When I hear the story of the night Bano spent in the forest, I will think often about Bano's body, carrying not only the scars of the violence done to her but also that deeper hollow within where once her Saleha lived. I will think of her hands, which carry the imprint of the way Saleha's head curved, how soft her hair felt. I will think of her fingers, which remember the last wisp of her daughter's dress being ripped from her arms. I will think of her nose, which holds Saleha's baby smell, and her ears, which will never stop hearing that last yelp for life. I will think of this and brush it away when I hold my child.

Mothers who hold their dead children in their arms, they grow to carry a weight of hollowness constantly with them. They may force themselves to mould new smiles, new dreams, new children around that hollowness. I will learn this when I learn of my mother's loss and the price she paid to have me.

On 1 March, when Bano climbed into the back of that truck, she didn't yet know the sex of the second baby inside her—another little girl. She didn't know that this little girl would live, and grow up haunted by her older sister's ghost and the silence of her mother. Bano's daughter will watch her empty eyes and vow to grow up and be a lawyer. Her mother's grief will shape how she sees her place in this world. I sense she will always carry her mother's void too—she will never fill it, but she will spend her life trying.

In these first ten days of the pogrom, Bilkis Bano's name means nothing to me. It becomes common every morning over breakfast, over every cup of evening chai, for Amma, Papa, Dadi, Phupu, her daughter Apa, Misba and I to count and recount atrocities, bodies, numbers in clipped tones before moving on to something 'less depressing', something easier to live with. *Are we all turning into numbers?* I ask myself. When this curfew outside my window ends, and it must, and I see my school friends again, will they see me as the Zara before this week? Or as simply one of those many we're still counting? Will I see them the same way? *Why haven't any of them called?*

The *accounting for* will come later.

Someday I will grow out of these questions. And instead I will start to carry a similar void inside of me when someone mentions 2002. For the next twenty years, I will hungrily read every word in the paper, on the internet, in books that mention Bilkis Bano. Every time I read her name, see those eyes in a picture, my womb will contract with sharp, unreasonable pain, my arms and legs will lose feeling. Every time I hear of the eleven men from the truck who walk free in 2022 on remission approved by Prime Minister Modi's Home Ministry, my head will hurt as if being struck by a rock. My body will hear a thousand little knives bristling just past my ear, readying to feed us to the fire.

❖ ❖ ❖

> Residents of Naroda Patiya identified Vipin (owner of an Auto Agency), Jai Bhagwan of Gangotri Society, Mukesh alias Gudda, Naresh and Chotta, all local level BJP/VHP workers, as having murdered and raped before their eyes.
>
> 'Ethnic Cleansing in Ahmedabad:
> A Preliminary Report', SAHMAT,
> 10–11 March 2002

In India, a name is a powerful thing. It explains not merely what one can call you but really what one may internally label you as: your last name often shows your caste. Your first usually gives away your religion. The presence of a pet name means you had a childhood of knowing love. People choose to name their children after many things in India—the natural world, yes, the ocean, the earth, the wind—but also attributes: courage, tenderness, greatness, intelligence, pride, dignity, sacredness, benevolence.

Then there are the names we give those we want to demean: the garbage cleaner, the scavenger, the butcher, the tanner. These are also caste-based slurs. They break down grown men and women who can see no road, no light or escape ahead of them from this lifelong oppression. And if we truly want to break a child, we attack their body: the cross-eyed, the baldy, the shorty, the limp.

The grotesque is what fascinates us most. The grotesque allows us to choose. The grotesque is a box where we put everything that we don't wish for ourselves but that we gawk at shamelessly when it afflicts another. The grotesque is a label we pin on the other so we may enjoy moral or physical superiority, the freedom to judge, to feel better off. That somehow, we were lucky to have escaped this rotten luck.

Names that come from our need to desecrate another's being often stick like the sweat that comes from standing too close to the flames. Names that needn't become our second skin. But they do.

Alias

Farzana, like Bilkis Bano, was also a mere teenager when she fell in love in the late nineties. It was the peak of Bollywood romances: love was conquering all. The chivalrous London-returned hero on our big screens was refusing to elope with the heroine and instead lingering till the family wholeheartedly and joyously gave her hand in marriage, till this hero won them all over. Because, in our movies, family is everything.

But this isn't Farzana's story. Or her family's. At least not of the one she was born in. This story is about the man she made the mistake of falling in love with: Suresh.

Farzana was the Muslim daughter of a daily wage–earning family who lived in a northern Ahmedabad neighbourhood called Naroda, close to the city's police headquarters. Her parents were migrant labourers, like the rest of their neighbours from nearby Karnataka and Maharashtra, who had moved to Ahmedabad hoping for a better life for their daughter. They had, after all, given her the Arabic name for a girl who is intelligent or wise. Farzana ran away with a man more than a decade older than her as soon as she struck puberty. The man was struck too. With childhood polio. He was known in the neighbourhood by an alias: Suresh Langdo, Suresh *the Limp*.

Ahmedabad in 1995 was not yet a place of genocide, only of casual intolerance. When my parents attended one of Papa's office events, his Hindu colleagues and their wives would simply huddle together chatting while my parents stood around awkwardly holding paper plates of dhokla. Once when I wore a green T-shirt, a little Jain boy, not more than five years old, called me a Pakistani for wearing their flag colour. In the winters, when we girls from the old city wore shalwars under our convent school uniforms to keep the biting wind out, our Hindu classmates would snigger at us in hallways, trying out the slur 'mossi' on their fresh, young tongues.

'Mossi', short for 'Muslims'. Also for 'bloodsucking mosquitoes'. So you can imagine when fifteen-year-old Farzana ran away with an almost-thirty-year-old, limping Suresh what a scandal that caused. Like most women who crossed this line between the two religions, Farzana too was cast out by her family and neighbourhood. And to be an outcaste, an ostracisation modelling the English 'outcast', meaning *to be thrown out,* is an important idea around here.

Suresh comes from the Chhara caste. For more than 150 years, the Chhara people have borne the invisible mark of the British Raj's legislative cruelties. In 1871, the British declared the Chharas, along with 150 other tribal, forest-dwelling and nomadic communities, 'Criminal Tribes'. These were basically members of castes lower than the hierarchy the British understood or cared to negotiate with, like the Brahmins, Kshatriyas, Vaishyas and others: these were the *outcastes* of the Hindu varna system. According to the Criminal Tribes Act of 1871, any children born in these tribes were automatically 'presumed to be born criminals'. The British claimed this was a step towards their social reformation, these 'troubled groups who tended to vandalise, steal and murder', because they were just so inclined by birth. In passing this act they succeeded in codifying caste and tribe into our law. The sorting, separating and labelling of South Asia into a million tiny, taxonomic boxes of discontent and ill will against 'the other' was the perfect antidote to any future imagination of mass revolt. There would never be another 1857 Sepoy Mutiny. Indians would never rise together to fight again. The Raj, though, was simply re-engineering and legalising the invisible, often permanent social boundaries between people that were a result of our greatest sin as a society: our caste system. Communities like the Chharas were rounded up and registered by the census, restricted in movement; children were separated from their parents and held in 'correctional facilities' between the ages of eight and fourteen. Many adults were confined in prison labour camps.

In 1952, the British law was repealed. The imprisoned from these criminalised communities were finally released, five years after India's independence. But in the absence of the Raj, we became our own oppressors, though slightly smarter at renaming things. The Habitual Offenders Act was passed, a law that operated under a similar principle but with a new alias.

Most young Chhara boys in the nineties, including Suresh, grew up seeing their people move in and out of the Indian jail system. The constant stigma over decades drove many of their community into extreme poverty, unemployment and petty crime. Often Chhara children were expelled or would drop out voluntarily from school because teachers would accuse them of stealing. Suresh's father berated him when he started beating up other teenage boys, stealing their things, drinking. Once he molested a young girl from the neighbourhood. A Muslim vendor who had seen this young boy grow into a man intervened. Suresh and his friends looted and vandalised the vendor's cart instead. Suresh's father, a drunk himself, finally cast him out. By the time Farzana and Suresh had their second child in 2000, Suresh wore the label of 'criminal' as a badge of honour. It seemed to help him feel more complete. This was how he provided for his family. Perhaps it made him more whole, more man. Farzana also basked in the power that gave her, often proudly threatening neighbours, letting them know that her husband was a goon.

Babu Bajrangi, a slightly built, upper-caste henchman, is Suresh's contractor, in a sense. He wields tremendous power and influence in these streets of broken boys. Like Suresh, Bajrangi is driven by a need to assert his masculinity. A longtime worker for the VHP, Bajrangi's pet peeve is seeing Hindu girls crossing the line to marry Muslim boys.

'Nine hundred and fifty-seven—that's how many Hindu girls I have saved. On average, one girl married to a Muslim produces five children. So, in effect, I have killed five thousand Muslims before they were born,' Bajrangi boasts to an undercover journalist on camera. Bajrangi recruits Chhara men like Suresh to complete these 'rescue missions,' abducting and forcefully 'returning' Hindu women to their parents.

On the morning of 28 February 2002, mobs begin to besiege Ahsan Jafri's Gulbarg Society, which is only three miles from where Farzana's family lives in Naroda Patiya. At 10 A.M. when Bajrangi's co–party workers try to enter Naroda Patiya, the residents fight them back valiantly with stones and knives and manage to drive them away. Bajrangi observes this from a distance, waiting for Dr Maya Kodnani to arrive. Kodnani, whom a trial court will one day call the 'kingpin' of the massacre, is an obstetrician and the local representative for the Naroda neighbourhood. After her contributions on this day, she will go on to get re-elected with an even greater majority and become the minister for the Women and Child Development Department in the Gujarat government.

Bajrangi and Kodnani decide that the only way to overcome Naroda's Muslims is to bring the Chhara men in for the next attack. They've grown up here and know the neighbourhood intimately. Kodnani sets out in her little Maruti 800 with ammunition and arms to drive around and encourage rioters to join in and kill 'as many as they can'. Around 10.30 A.M., Suresh gathers his Chhara gang members and sets out again, leaving Farzana and his young son and daughter at home. This time Bajrangi gets down where the action is. Along with Suresh and his men, Bajrangi leads the mob to force their way into Muslim houses, using the gas cylinders in the kitchens to incinerate the occupants of each home. They clear the entrance of the narrow lane into Naroda for a diesel tanker.

The tanker is rammed into a small mosque at the entrance called the Noorani Masjid. This is done repeatedly, until the fuel explodes and the old brick prayer house comes crumbling down. Naroda's families barricade themselves inside their homes against the assault. But by lunchtime, every door has been broken through, men pulled out and killed, women raped by multiple men and then hacked and burnt, children thrown into the fires around them. Kauser Bano, a pregnant young woman, is raped, the foetus cut out of her belly and burnt as she screams. Then the mother is burnt too. As with Bilkis, we will hear Kausar's nameless story repeatedly in the coming weeks. The details will vary only slightly each time, but the effect will be the same. We will know it's over. This mob will stop at nothing. This is a mob of blind and broken men for whom every woman is a triumph, her body a battleground, her womb a pile of kindling to be lit and danced around.

Members of SAHMAT's fact-finding mission visiting Naroda Patiya a few days later will see photographic evidence of the burnt bodies of a mother and a foetus lying on her belly 'as if torn from it and left on the gash'.

Meanwhile, as the carnage in her parents' street continues, Farzana and her five-year-old daughter and two-year-old son cower in their home. Outside, Suresh seems to have forgotten they even exist. All he will remember later, while speaking to the same undercover journalist on camera, is how he pinned the Muslim scrap dealer's young daughter Naseemo, raped her and then 'pulped her, made her into a pickle'.

When the journalist asks him why he did it, he will simply say:

> Bhookhe ghuse to koi na koi to phal khayega, na.
> *When the hungry finally break in, they will grab the fruit, no?*

Aise bhi, phal ko kuchal ke phek denge.
In any case, the fruits are going to get crushed, discarded . . .
Look, I'm not telling lies . . .
Mata is before me.

He will gesture to an image of a female Hindu goddess on the wall.

Look, my wife is sitting here but let me say . . . the fruit was there, so it had to be eaten.

For Suresh, this day, and his role in it, has been 130 years in the making. I will not understand what that means until the day I understand how caste works.

Bajrangi's men continue killing for more than ten hours. Shouts and bloody screams fill the air as a group of twenty or thirty people are corralled into a pit with a slope on one side and an unscalable wall on the other, doused with kerosene and set alight. Through all this, in broad daylight in one of the biggest cities of twenty-first-century independent India, no help arrives.

'We hacked, we burnt, did a lot of that,' Bajrangi will later brag to an undercover reporter. 'We believe in setting them on fire because these bastards say they don't want to be cremated, they're afraid of it . . . They shouldn't be allowed to breed. Whoever they are, even if they're women or children, there's nothing to be done with them . . . Burn the bastards.'

He will also offer a few solutions to the undercover journalist for the 'Muslim problem': 'Delhi should issue orders to kill—higher caste people and the rich won't do it, but slum dwellers and the poor will. They should be told that they can take whatever they want of the Muslims—land, wealth, houses, everything—but they should do it in three days.'

This, he opines, will ensure that Muslims are wiped out across

India. He will add other suggestions: that Muslims should be allowed only one marriage and one child by law and that it would also be a good idea to deny them the right to vote.

Later that night, as the flames continue to cast an eerie orange glow on the neighbourhood, trucks, trailers and jeeps will arrive. Bodies, limbs, burnt bits will be piled into these vehicles and driven away to be disposed of, to keep the death count low. Bajrangi will later claim he telephoned the minister of state and told him how many Muslims he had killed and that, as a loyal servant, it was now up to the party to protect him.

'Their [Muslims'] dharmjunoon [religious fervour] is very high . . . In comparison, ours is low,' he will lament to the journalist.

Bajrangi could not be more wrong. All through this day, Farzana has sat silently at home, cooking and waiting for her husband, as people she grew up among were annihilated. Suresh returns later that night, smelling of blood and burning flesh. She cooks him a simple vegetarian meal of lentils and rice.

A decade from this day, she will be heard still defending Suresh in court: 'He couldn't have raped or brutalised women because he was married to me, a Muslim.'

This could have been Farzana's story. But it won't be. Her name will always exist only in the shadow of Suresh's. Suresh will serve some time, then get out on parole or medical reasons, like Bajrangi and Kodnani and all the other murderers and rapists from that day. When he comes home in 2015 on his most recent parole, he will go looking for Farzana and rape her too. This cannot be Farzana's story because broken men like Suresh won't let it be—men who were told what they were, men shown the extent of who they could be, men primed to exact revenge for a lifetime of humiliation from an unsuspecting other, and so that is who they became.

The Morning After

On the first of March, an uneasy quiet seems to have settled over the city. I look out through the balcony's tightly bolted doors at a world blanketed in smoke. No bird sings, no dog yelps. Only the occasional eerie siren of a police jeep wails beneath us. The newspapers have yet again somehow made it to our doors, their pages brimming with gore.

'Common Man Will Be Hit', a front-page headline in *The Hindu* screams amid pictures of carnage and death. I read the actual article, only to realise it's talking about a budget proposal to increase the price of cooking-gas cylinders again. *This common man, Mr Finance Minister, would you by any chance happen to know his religion?* I want to ask. Because yesterday one common man needed it only to cook rotis, while another used his to burn a neighbour.

Gulshan arrives around nine, again sneaking past the police downstairs. She's so clever, always finding a way to slink through the alleys between Jasmine and the other two apartment buildings flanking us. She's also loyal to Amma, whom she can't leave alone with the mob in her own home a single day.

'Bhabhi, woh unke-ich gas cylinder se unko-ich jalaa raile hain,' Gulshan tells Amma through moist, wide eyes, still shaken by the fact that the gas cylinder she helps make our meals over each afternoon is now a weapon of mass death and destruction. Misba, Gulshan and I sit on our apartment's mosaic grey-and-green tiles in a tight circle around Amma. When it gets stormy in our house, we tend to circle around Amma as if she's a raft. She always knows how to put her body between Papa's or Phupu's or Dadi's thunder and us.

It seems like Gulshan and the other maids are a quicker news network right now than the newspapers. Their homes are the front lines; their sisters, brothers, cousins, parents, living in similar slums across the city, have died in less than twenty-four hours since the burning of that train. Stories from neighbourhoods that stood isolated in a sea of Hindu colonies—Naroda Patiya, Vatva, Gomtipur—are pouring in through them.

Apa and Phupu have arrived and have stories of their own to tell of haunted streets, smoke everywhere, Phupu cutting through it all at full speed in her Hyundai Santro to make the quick five-minute drive as soon as curfew across the bridges eased. It is weirdly starting to feel like the 'good old times' now that Phupu and Apa have moved in for god knows how long. Lunch is a debate stage again.

Papa and Dadi talk about Ahsan Jafri in hushed tones between morsels that we are all struggling to swallow. Dadi remembers how Jafri would lead cycle rallies through Relief Road and the crowds would part to let this workers' messiah through, hundreds of cycles and young people following him. Mill workers, unemployed youth hungry for opportunity, they would cover the distance from their ghettos to the chief minister's office in a satellite town outside Ahmedabad, in the burning heat, on two wheels. The rallies would block off several roads, causing traffic diversions, and people like Papa who never had to ride a bike anywhere except for leisure would crib about it. But there would also be some grudging admiration that 'at least someone is standing up to these chaps!'

At lunch Papa is quiet now. He isn't insisting anymore that arre kuchh nahin hoga. Phupu is waiting for her mother to say some classist rubbish again so she can pounce on her, something about how only the skullcap/bushy-beard kind are in trouble. Not people like us. But Dadi is mumbling in shock too. If they can do this to Jafri, they won't spare anyone now.

Men like Ahsan sahab and Dada—educated Muslims with public-service occupations—had spent their lives thinking themselves immutable parts of India's social fabric. They'd braved this choice they'd made of remaining in India over leaving for Pakistan, choosing to live as a minority and fight for their dignity and a secular nation. Yet here we were.

Ahsan sahab's wife, Zakia, is found by a neighbour several days after the massacre, alive. She survived because when this rage-blind mob came, she was dressed in a sari as always, and had the wherewithal to pretend to be Hindu. When I hear this, I think of the women in my home.

Phupu, Dadi and Amma so proudly, lovingly tie their saris: Dadi her floral chiffons, Phupu her starched block-printed cottons, Amma her gold-bordered kanjeevarams. Indian Muslim women who choose to dress this way. Yet now they must lose their dignity, pretend to be something they are not, if they want to survive. I shudder with a sudden thought. Gulshan will not survive if the mob ever finds her. She can't tie a sari or couldn't pretend to be anyone but herself even if only to save her life.

The long history of riots had already altered the geography of Ahmedabad on communal lines with the majority of the Muslims being ghettoized in certain areas. This time several such Muslim dominated areas, mostly working-class localities were targeted, some for the first time, by huge mobs numbering 5,000 to 15,000.

'Ethnic Cleansing in Ahmedabad:
A Preliminary Report', SAHMAT,
10–11 March 2002

In sixteenth-century Venice, city officials decided to confine their Jewish population—many of them refugees from the hundreds of wars and civil conflicts plaguing Europe—within an old copper foundry on the outskirts of the city. They did this because their majority-Christian citizenry viewed the Jews with growing suspicion because of the Catholic church's propaganda that Jews were 'impure' and 'polluting the serenity of Venice'. But they also needed the community. Contrary to what the church claimed, Venice was a city brimming with poverty and inequity. And Jewish bankers and moneylenders kept their economy rolling by microfinancing small traders and borrowers. So instead of completely expelling them, as England had done in 1290, the Venetians built two gates to retrofit this foundry complex. Each evening the gates were locked, and in the morning they were opened. For almost two centuries, any Jews found outside the gates at night were punished. This was where the word *ghetto* entered the English language.

In the beginning of the twentieth century, when Jewish immigrants started to arrive in America, they brought this word with them. The habit of living separate from a whole now needed no legal bill or law. Jews and other minorities that followed enacted innate ways to self-segregate, to live in concentrated neighbourhoods that both deprived and nourished them. To become aware of your minority status brings with it this understanding of the *ghetto*. It is a place that constantly saves you, even as every day it threatens to kill you on the inside.

The Making of Our Ghetto

When I was little, I'd stand on my tiptoes on our balcony and watch cars, cows and buses pass over the three bridges visible in the distance from my lofty eighth-floor perch in Jasmine Apartments.

These three bridges were all concrete monstrosities stained and disfigured by decades of monsoon deluges and bone-cracking summers, patterned by many generations of paan-chewing and paan-spitting Gujaratis in fountains of deep maroon expectoration. In other words, sort of regular ugly in the way of all seventies-style brutalist construction.

Named after men of our history—Nehru, Ellis and Sardar Patel—these bridges connected the old walled city of Ahmedabad to the new one across the river. None of them bore the name of Ahmad Shah, the first Muslim king of the Gujarat sultanate, who built the old city walls in 1411 C.E. along the east embankment of the lazy, winding Sabarmati. To understand these bridges and walls of my childhood you must first know the city itself.

When we were little, Dada would entertain us with Ahmedabad's history, often embellished with little folksy details—like how Ahmad Shah's hunting caravan was riding along the riverbank once and witnessed something bewildering: a wild desert hare, startled by the hunting party, giving chase to the sultan's dogs. Ahmad Shah, as the story goes, saw this as a sign of the Sabarmati's innately powerful waters. The meek here had truly inherited the earth.

Dada would emphasise that, when the sultan built this capital, he encased it in a fort called Bhadra, named after the ancient Rajput citadel the sultans had captured and held for two generations.

Man may have defeated man, but not the Hindu goddess Bhadra, whose name remained on the fort. The old king had worshipped her, and even as he lost his throne, Bhadra's legend had been carried and preserved by the Muslims who took the throne.

Bhadra housed the royal palaces, the Nagina Baugh (the Garden of Gems), the royal Ahmad Shah Mosque, the Maidan Shah (the King's Market), fourteen towers, eight gates and two large open areas for gatherings. Ahmad Shah and his descendants' fort had not four or five or ten but twenty-five doors carved into its length. The darwazas welcomed traders, migrants, settlers, humans and beasts.

We lived near one of the smaller darwazas closest to the river's edge—Khanpur Darwaza. Each of the darwazas had giant brass studs and handles, beautiful floral motifs carved into timber. If you walked through them and weren't being hustled by a rickshaw or farsaan peddler, you could stop and tilt your head up and take in the breathtaking awesomeness and beauty of these doors. If you kept the Sabarmati to your west and walked north from Khanpur Darwaza past ancient temples, mosques, churches and unnamed shrines of Sufi saints, over railway crossings, past cemeteries, across the dry riverbed and up the west bank, soon the city's din would drop behind you and you would have arrived in the solace-filled grounds of Gandhi's Sabarmati Ashram.

I often wondered what it would be like to set out on this route, but of course I never did. Everything considered necessary to my life by Papa was in and around Khanpur Darwaza. We lived in Jasmine Apartments, two blocks south of the door, went to elementary school two blocks north, bought our supplies from the grocer a few feet from the darwaza, candy from the tuckshop under our building. Our tailor worked in the basement of the neighbouring building, Firdaus; the vegetable and meat bazaar bustled in the square behind. For the first sixteen years of my life, this edge of Ahmad Shah's wall was my whole world.

The bigger of our two balconies ran east to west. I would watch from this big balcony as the sun rose over the old city—small, crammed-in homes, dargahs, a dilapidated theatre or two and a winding street that burrowed farther into its heart. I'd watch the same sun set across Sabarmati's sandy bed, which felt just beyond my reach, the width of three cricket pitches. In the evenings we would stand on our balcony and choose to watch any of the multiple cricket matches being played across the length and breadth of the dry riverbed.

When the monsoon would arrive, and the dam farther north would release excess water, for a few weeks the Sabarmati would be a river again. We would make sure to take all our family photographs against its backdrop in those few weeks.

When Misba was barely a toddler, we'd wake up to the peach-tinged sky, plod out to the balcony and stand on our tiptoes. I would point out to her buffaloes plodding down the street past the parked cars and scooters. They'd swagger onto the riverbank like they owned it. Misba and I would watch them roll in the mud until it was time for them to saunter back to their sheds around noon. Then the donkeys would arrive—braying the place down, their feet tied together in a measured trot. Somewhere in between the two, Misba would toss her milk bottle, or Dada's glasses rolled up in the day's newspaper, or all our clothespins, over the edge of the balcony. And Amma would have to go down to the street and hunt for the lost items while Dadi spied on her from above.

If you never visited Ahmedabad, this would all sound faintly pastoral. But like most small towns in nineties India, brimming with the aspirations of lives we'd newly discovered on cable TV, it was anything but. Slums and apartments crammed into the gaps of Ahmad Shah's crumbling old city, while across the river a new city mushroomed and sprawled, including the world's 'first all-vegetarian McDonald's'.

When we graduated from elementary school, Papa had no choice but to expand our horizons and send us over the bridge to the middle and high school built on the western bank. Long ago, when Dadi was a young girl who studied here, the campus was only one small building surrounded by dense old-growth banyan trees. But slowly, as a new Ahmedabad grew around it, Mount Carmel and the young women who went there were swept up in the burgeoning cafés, restaurants and mall around it.

Each morning, our little gang from the east—the Muslim side—would ride an autorickshaw bursting with grey pinafore uniforms and our plastic water bottles and canteens. I felt a confusing mix of pride and guilt walking through the lofty gates of Mount Carmel. Dadi would often boast how she had learnt to play tennis on these grounds in the 1930s. Old teachers still remembered Phupu as the brilliant young girl who had won accolades and corridor arguments in the sixties. These women, like the buffaloes that swam in the Sabarmati, could claim ownership and belonging in these halls. They had Gujarat in their blood; Ahmedabad on both sides of the river was theirs. But Misba and I were daughters of the outsider, the daughter-in-law: a dead military man's daughter, dark in complexion, a woman who couldn't speak Gujarati, who came from the South with its funny languages and customs, and, most important, a girl who brought no dowry, and because she didn't come from the class and caste circles they were used to, no dowry would ever come.

As her daughters we belonged where she stood, in a tiny kitchen with its jammed window and pigeons shitting outside in the old city. And so coming across Nehru Bridge each morning, dressed to learn and raring to escape, felt like a tiny act of treason.

Most children in our classrooms were from wealthier Hindu families settled on the new side and seemed to care very little for what went on in Ahmad Shah's city across the river.

Phupu, our older, divorced aunt, was a single mother and respected economics professor at the city's big Jesuit college. In the mid-nineties, she bought herself a flat on the new side and moved out of Jasmine with her daughter, whom I called Apa, *elder sister*. There was something so thrilling for us in watching Phupu make it.

This too was possible. It was also scary because sometimes she would scoff at the rest of the Chowdharys for not leaving Khanpur and moving out of what was quickly becoming a ghetto. But for Dada, Dadi and Papa, Khanpur Darwaza was home. They were part of its history just like it was a part of theirs. The fighting each evening would start there. A taunt about not moving forwards. And the evening would somehow always end at Amma, the minority they could all gang up and blame their misfortunes on.

The Chowdharys had been stuck in Jasmine since long before Amma and Papa's marriage. In the seventies, when Dada was still in government service, his friends and he had chosen to build homes in Khanpur in the ways that people today build ghettos almost with an urgency to commune with like-minded dreamers. These were post-Partition men hoping that their secular and cosmopolitan spirit would rub off on these muddy banks. Dada's buddy, Pant uncle (a former police chief of the state), and he (a retired sales tax commissioner) had ultimately helped Jasmine's developer complete the project after construction stalled for seven years in a slowly corrupting city. They raised funds, found vendors, convinced friends to buy flats too. Parsi small business owners built small bungalows near Shah Wajiuddin's dargah; a Khoja (Aga Khan) family built a terraced townhouse across from Jasmine. The Goan Catholic Ferros moved in on the fourth floor, the Bengali travelling salesman uncle moved into the street-level flat. And for two decades after, Jasmine became their haven, one they'd built themselves. To our right, Firdaus Apartments rose to equal height. And to our left, Usha Kiran Apartments. These too filled with families of every state, faith, language and caste of India. Secularism and pluralism weren't distant constitutional values here; they constituted the very names on the Jasmine nameboard by the elevators.

When Papa would head to the second floor to his school friend Porus uncle for Sunday beers, I would tag along and keep Porus's octogenarian mother company with my eight-year-old chatter. On

Sundays, Dadi would take me along for an afternoon gossip session with the Maharashtrian Mrs Pant. Both women kept beautiful homes, brimming like museums of the dead with curios antique, shiny and pointy. I'd walk around Mrs Pant's kitchen, peep into the big vat of steaming poha, or sneak out to play hallway cricket with our Baha'i neighbour Mrs Misaqi's grandson.

In the late eighties, the triptych of Khanpur I saw from this balcony started to come apart and reconfigure. Blue tarps began to creep along the riverbanks as the poorer Muslim textile workers and craftsmen started to huddle closer to Khanpur after an upper-caste agitation against increased benefits for oppressed-caste people turned violent and morphed into anti-Muslim rioting. Slowly, the temporary huts turned into pucca houses with corrugated doors and flowery plastic curtains. Suddenly there was no shortage of domestic labour. Dadi was going through maids and cleaning ladies for a few months with frenzy. That's how she ended up with the neighbourhood rap as 'that lady whom no maid will work for beyond two weeks'.

The mosque attached to Shah Wajiuddin's shrine spored and mushroomed into six to fulfil the needs of a growing Muslim population downstairs. Then, after the 1992 demolition of Babri Mosque in faraway Ayodhya, our building floors started to transform too.

Dawoodi Bohras—members of a Shi'ite denomination that has lived in Gujarat since at least 1067 C.E.—who owned most of the plumbing and hardware stores in the old city, began to buy out the Parsis, Hindus and Christians. Some of them would tell us their grand priest, the Syedna, had decreed that Ahmedabad's Bohra community should live on this side of the river no matter how much it cost to buy out the apartments. He had a premonition or something, they claimed. People like our friend Tasneem's parents on the second floor had made a killing with their grocery store business in Dubai. So now Tasneem rode in the school autorickshaw with us to Mount Carmel down the street, and on weekends her grandmother sneaked me out from under Papa's nose to eat pani puri on the street behind the mosque.

With the high prices they were offered, our old neighbours moved away to modern new developments across the river where there were 'more of their kind'. Gujarati Hindus in the west categorically started to refuse to sell apartments to Muslims or anyone mistaken for Muslim because they had an Arabic-sounding name. Everyone could sense change in the air. It didn't matter if you were one of the impoverished Bengali or Bihari migrant Muslims in the slums, the wealthier, enterprising Bohras or whatever drinking-smoking-cussing kind of mishmash in-between Muslims we were. We'd all be met with derision across the river.

Papa would gloat about how our apartment's market value was rising as more and more Muslims from the new city got kicked out and looked for homes on 'our side'. In all my brand-new teenage courage to counter him, I would make wide, innocent eyes and ask, 'Oh, so we might sell this Jasmine home, and then we go where?' I knew my father. There was no label he wore more proudly than that of being his father's son. And this was the home his father had built. The only thing bequeathed to him, besides a sputtering old Fiat. He would look at me angrily in those moments and sputter too.

Not every non-Muslim left. Porus uncle, the Ferros, the Misaqis, the Pants, they stayed. And perhaps that is why theirs are the names I remember.

When Dada was alive, he and I would stand on the balcony some evenings, the cool river breeze on our cheeks, and watch the sun sink behind the burgeoning new skyline. The lights would come on and twinkle in the river water; neon signs would tease from the roofs of tall new apartments, multiplex theatres, restaurants and malls.

Then we'd look down our street at what were now 'our people':

the men, women and children living under blue tarps, many of whom worked as watchmen and maids in the ageing buildings and bungalows of Khanpur. The Dawoodi Bohra families milling about in their sparkling white-and-gold-trimmed prayer caps, their colourful veils, helping their elders and children into cars and auto-rickshaws to evening prayers. The azaans would blare from all six mosques. Dada would lift his palms to the sky and say thanks.

Some evenings Amma would stand on the balcony with me, her elbows resting on the parapet, her eyes fixed on the other side of Nehru Bridge. Papa didn't allow her to go for morning walks beyond the bridge, needing to be able to see her always. The sun would glint then in her honey-brown eyes, turning them into pools of fire. I would sense inside my mother a deep hollow. Amma didn't care for either side of the river. Some days the sadness inside was a deep abyss and none of these were her people. I would watch my mother standing on the edge of Ahmad Shah's wall dreaming of setting off on foot to be with 'her people'—her mother and brothers who had migrated to America. People she could see only when her husband and mother-in-law allowed it. People she hadn't seen for five years when the looting and burning started.

If she could just walk across the riverbed, towards the sun, on and on, she'd reach the edge of this state, then push on to the borders of this country. Over this continent, and another, and across oceans she'd walk, to get away from this place where she was told over and over that she didn't belong. And that she was worth nothing. That her womb, which had yielded only daughters, was worth nothing. On those evenings I wished Amma would just look down to her waist where I stood—tiny and yet carrying the ghosts of her dreams in my arms, feeling her unsettled heart like my own, wishing I could build her a bridge, a way out of the ghetto.

The graffiti left behind by the rioters on the charred walls of the completely burnt madrasa at Sundaramnagar boasted of the police support:

Yeh andar ki baat hai
Police hamaarey saath hai.
This is inside information;
the police is with us.

Jaan se maar denge
Bajrang Dal zindabad
Narendra Modi zindabad.
We will kill.
Long live the Bajrang Dal.
Long live Narendra Modi.

'Ethnic Cleansing in Ahmedabad: A Preliminary Report', SAHMAT, 10–11 March 2002

Threads

Darning

India weaves as much cloth as it reaps food. Ahmedabad is no different. The city has a centuries-old legacy of beauty woven into cloth. As Amma's daughter, I have spent many sweaty afternoons in the cloth markets of Dhalgarwad and Teen Darwaza, sifting through reams of hand block–printed cottons and brilliant floral muslins. From the dozens of little nighties with their inverted dome necklines the tailor under the building made to the simple polka-dotted frocks Amma would sew us on her rickety but reliable Singer machine, this cloth woven by Ahmedabad's mostly Muslim weaving and milling communities literally had our backs in a home where Papa never budgeted for his children's clothing.

Today Ahmedabad is the site of arguably India's finest design school, specifically in textile research. NID—National Institute of Design, where in 2018 two graduate students are studying the historical weaves of India. Rashi and Arjunvir pick a rather mundane household linen—khes—from the North Indian states of Punjab and Haryana, where they come from. That's part of the assignment: to pick something from their own lineages. Khes can be fashioned into anything from dish towels to blankets to scarves. In archival literature, Rashi and Arjunvir read about a particularly intricate variant called majnu khes. But during their fieldwork, nobody in the region seems to have any memory of majnu khes; not the weavers or shopkeepers who weave or sell this humble fabric nor the people in the villages who wrap it around their necks on winter mornings.

Disappointed and nearing their project deadline, Rashi and Arjunvir are discussing this lost thread when Arjunvir's mother overhears them. She disappears into her room and comes back with a scarf, holding it close to her heart. 'This was your grandfather's,' she says, 'and he never let anybody use it,' adding that it was perhaps 'older than the Partition'. The scarf is woven in majnu khes.

Rashi and Arjunvir submit their project. But their investigation into khes has only just begun. Over the next two years they start a conversation with two textile researchers like themselves across the Radcliffe Line in Pakistan—Noorjehan and Zeb. Not only have these Pakistani researchers heard of majnu khes, but they have photos, stories, samples of it! These stories and fragments of fabric are from the western part of the once-whole Punjab. The western side, now in Pakistan, is the only side of Punjab where this weave is practised. As all four young people dig deeper, they realise Arjunvir's grandfather was one of many Punjabis who, simply by migrating from one end of Punjab to the other, ended up in a new nation and lost so much of their heritage. What they carried on their bodies, and in their trunks, in these little fragments, snatches of thread, were hopes of remaining tied in some invisible way to home. Dada's story also came to me in snatches like this. And they brought hope. From the ashes of 2002 and of my family's slow demise, I found fragments of belonging and memory, an assertion of who we were and how we had always belonged.

The Runaway

When we were growing up, Dada never spoke much to us about his home before this one. All I vaguely knew was that our last name was a landowning title from Punjab. Dadi's strong sense of belonging to Gujarat consumed the daily life and workings of our home—her children mostly spoke to her in Gujarati, sugar was heaped into every dal she cooked, the furniture we lived entombed among and were forbidden from touching came from her ancestral village. Her roots pervaded every inch of our lives so much that in some ways Dada's last name was the only scrap of his heritage bequeathed to us. Once, when I caught him at his table writing a letter in Urdu to god knows who, he looked at me with a faraway sense of pride and said, 'You know, beta, you actually come from Gurdaspur.' I remember feeling amused and thinking, *I only come from C-8 Jasmine.* It's hard to be able to imagine belonging anywhere when you don't know what it feels like to belong in your own home.

When I started to write my dada's story, that's all I had to hold on to. The fact that we came from Gurdaspur, somewhere in Punjab. And a handful of tiny little clues I can remember through the uncaring lens of those early teen years: how Dada would visit every dargah in town on Thursdays and pour rose petals on each saint's shrine. How he would sometimes hold Dadi and gently waltz. How he sat at the dining table some mornings, filling yellow-and-black letter sheets with ink, packing every line of space with his calligraphic Urdu handwriting, sending off stories to some stranger, stories he refused to tell us. So in 2018, when I started to write his story, when I had only these little details, I started by looking for him in poetry, the one thing I remembered would make his eyes twinkle. I found Baba Fariduddin Ganjshakar, a twelfth-century Sufi poet from Punjab.

'Galli sikkar dur ghar, naal piyaare ninh,' he wrote. *My promise to her is a long, muddy lane.* 'Challaan te bhijje kambli, rahaan taa tutte ninh.' *If I walk through it, I soil my cloak. If I don't, I break my word.* Dada's story, I soon discovered, was a story of a man trying to keep his cloak unsoiled while trying to keep his word.

If the land we call Punjab were a cloak, its threads would be the five rivers that weave through it: the Jhelum, Chenab, Ravi, Beas and Sutlej. They originate from different glaciers in the great Himalayas but all end in the Indus, that mighty shared artery of the subcontinent. All five make irrigation possible. But they also fracture and divide this land into who has power and legacy, who owns land and who will never belong.

The Ravi forms a natural border between India and Pakistan for a few hundred miles before she makes her choice and veers west into modern Pakistan. Without a passport or visa, she merges with the Indus and empties into the Arabian Sea. Her brother, the Beas, is in no hurry. In Punjab, he merges into the Sutlej and irrigates hundreds of thousands of acres of mustard and corn, pushes against hydroelectric dams and village waterwheels, fills up canals and cattle water tubs, and helps sustain millions of Indians across the northern and central plains. The lush green district of Gurdaspur, where Dada says we come from, is nestled between these two gushing sibling rivers. It is Punjab's northernmost district, the edge beyond which the valleys of Kashmir begin.

In the 1930s, a young farmer named Ghulam Mohammad dies in Gurdaspur, leaving his widow, Khatija, the caretaker in his stead of hundreds of acres of rich, alluvial land. Her three children—two sons, Anwar and Ashraf, and daughter, Bilqis—are too young to register what has changed with their father's death. But later they recall flashes of their stout, short mother angrily waving her sickle in the fields at bandits and greedy relatives alike, defending the blood right of her children. In Punjab, where land is the difference between affluence and serfdom, being a young widow with land is, as Dada's brother Ashraf once described it, 'like being a lottery ticket dropped in the street'. Everyone from distant cousins to the village hakim tries their luck to convince her either to remarry and bring her land in dowry to them or to sign it away to one of the men for better safekeeping.

One night the village wakes up to the smell that no farmer ever wants to smell. Burning crops. Khatija has set fire to her own field, a year's worth of toil going up in ash. *'I'll burn the world,'* she yells in Punjabi, standing there silhouetted by the flames. *'I'll never hand over my children's legacy.'* In Punjab it doesn't matter if you are Hindu, Muslim or Sikh. It matters only that you are willing to lay down your life for your land.

Anwar—Khatija's eldest son—my dada, is sixteen years old when he decides to run away from this land. As the older son, he would have inherited it, along with its wounds. A young Anwar wants nothing to do with wounds. He wants poetry and cricket. He knows how this land came to be. How they came to be 'Chowdharys'. *Landowners.* His father, a humble teacher, had simply been gifted land by a happy nawab, a *lord.* This land, tilled by the labour of another, was unearned.

'Haraam ka paisa kabhi nahin tikta,' I remember Dada always saying to us, and after him Papa. *Prosperity that is unearned doesn't last.* I don't know if these stories of his childhood are where he made up this mantra. All I know is, one morning, sixteen-year-old Anwar wakes up in pre-Partition Gurdaspur. And he runs away.

In 1940s London, demands for India's independence are reverberating. So are voices arguing that Hindus and Muslims cannot remain a single nation. Cyril Radcliffe, a British administrator who has never travelled east of Paris, is chosen to draw lines across a map, to carve two nations out of nothing. In 1941, the British conducted a census. Based on it, wheels are set into motion to separate the Hindu-majority regions from the Muslim ones. Separating the everyday lived realities of these two groups, though, interspersed over more than a thousand years of coexistence, is like trying to make two cloths out of one. Threads of blood and belonging must tear.

News of this possible partition reaches Bombay, where Anwar, now nineteen, has been living in a Muslim home for orphaned boys. Hearing of clashes and violence in Punjab, he writes a letter to his mother. He is safe and well, he writes, and studying under the tutelage of a Dr Rahman, a kind Muslim intellectual who helped him get into college and often invites him for tea and discussion on politics, literature and economics. He is going to be an afsar, *a civil servant*, someday, he proudly writes.

A few weeks later, Khatija arrives in Bombay with her daughter, Bilqis, and, following the return address, ends up at Dr Rahman's door. They want Anwar to return with them. The land she has guarded for her children is being ripped apart in Gurdaspur. Come August, Radcliffe's imaginary line will leave them standing in the wrong country. This is the right country, Anwar quietly insists, scared even as an adult to look his mother in the eye. They are promising more land in the new country, Khatija offers. I don't need more, Anwar insists, looking at Dr Rahman and the people he has surrounded himself with—men and women who'd rather die fighting than let the British rule or divide them any longer, people who write and sing songs of freedom in lilting Urdu, people who teach Hindus, Muslims, Christians, Parsis and Sikhs alike in their classrooms. Khatija has two younger children left to raise. Her firstborn's idealism cannot feed them. She holds Anwar in tears, thanks Dr Rahman for raising her son, and leaves with young Bilqis, who can't seem to tear her eyes away from her brother, her hero.

. . .

By the 1950s, Anwar is the landless Chowdhary Sahab, a handsome public servant posted to the small cloth-milling town of Ahmedabad in the state of Gujarat. He is a far cry from the impoverished farmer's son. His broad forehead, dimpled chin and twinkling eyes have Ahmedabad's finest young ladies vying for his attention, but one evening, at the Ahmedabad Gymkhana, as couples waltz to an army string orchestra, he has eyes only for Hawwa, the precocious youngest daughter of a retired British-era magistrate. Named literally for the ultimate temptress—'Hawwa' is the Arabic name for Eve. Pale-skinned, petite and draped in French chiffon and pearls, she has him enraptured. Anwar takes a single red rose and approaches Hawwa to ask her for a dance. A few months later Anwar writes to his mother and siblings in Pakistan of his decision to marry Hawwa and settle down in Ahmedabad, where her family are well established. It is a quiet little town; he is rising in rank and respect in the sales tax office. Khatija replies with her blessings but also a hint of mother-in-law snark: 'What sort of obnoxious name is Hawwa? Call her Nahid.' This is typical of North Indian families—Punjabi, Sindhi, Haryanvi, where women are consumed whole by their in-laws. Not only are they expected to take their husband's last name, but often they are stripped of their first names too, names with which they were raised, first loved and held. These are taken. Like land, these women are never asked before lines are redrawn across their being.

Hawwa, who is also madly in love with this dashing man with his mysterious past, agrees to be renamed Nahid—honourable and elevated in Arabic, the planet Venus in Persian, some even say an ancient word for a perfectly round-breasted woman!

Hawwa becomes Nahid on the whim of a mother, a stranger across the border whom she is unlikely to ever see, given the animosity between the two young nations, but knowing full well what she is getting in return: a man with no home and belonging, a man who will be hopelessly devoted to her family and her.

Nahid is wrong. In 1965, a few years after their last child is born, by which time Anwar and Nahid are fully ensconced in Ahmedabad's social fabric, its parties and growing affluent circles, a letter arrives from Pakistan. In it the ageing Khatija begs her son. 'Even Lord Ram returned from his exile after fourteen years. I haven't seen you in twenty-one,' she pleads. She has seen her grandchildren through grainy black-and-white photos stuffed into envelopes too small to contain their full, vibrant lives in India. Khatija's second son, Ashraf, now oversees the lands in Pakistani Punjab. Her daughter, Bilqis, is married. A brood of nephews and nieces grow in the village who have only heard of their 'gentleman uncle' in India.

Meanwhile Anwar is up for the ultimate promotion: sales tax commissioner. He has a beautiful two-storey home in the middle of a rapidly urbanising city. His neighbours are Parsis, Hindus and Muslims from the local community; he has a beautiful wife who turns heads and throws great dinners, children whom he stays up with all night when they have exams. Being a government officer in the sixties opens doors to the homes of royalty and bureaucrats, professors and police chiefs. It is a spot on the ultimate ladder in modern India's slowly congealing hierarchies.

When the letter arrives, Anwar breaks down. And then breaks into his savings to buy his family tickets to Pakistan. Nahid is less enthusiastic. She must present herself and her family to these 'village bumpkins' whom she has never seen. But her worries are put aside as soon as they land in Okara, the small agricultural town across the border where Anwar's people settled. As the eldest daughter-in-law, she and her children are swamped with the sort of overload of affection only Punjabis seem capable of. Later, Papa, the eldest child, remembers faint snatches of this trip. How his dadi, Khatija, would pull him, a big-boned boy, into her little lap and feed him from her plate rotis soaked in country ghee and sugar. How his father and uncle would take off each morning to stroll through the corn and mustard fields. How his mother brought her spinster sister Asha-ma along for moral support and then left her to nanny the kids while she napped through the hours when the women were meant to cook and clean.

After a nearly month-long trip, the Chowdharys return home fattened on makki ki roti, home-churned butter, clean pastoral air and their relatives' abundant affection. The Radcliffe line that tore apart Anwar's family seems to blur now that these two parts of his being have met and formed bonds of blood.

But in Ahmedabad, whispers of his trip to Pakistan congeal into vicious rumours about divided loyalties. In 1971, war breaks out between India and Pakistan and Bangladesh is born to the east. In the west, in Gujarat, Anwar is denied the promotion he has been waiting for. Despite being seniormost and dedicating his life's service to the government, till the day he retires Anwar Chowdhary will remain only the assistant sales tax commissioner. He challenges the decision in court, but only half-heartedly. It takes years and comes to nothing. Soon, as retirement looms—a time to age gracefully in one's fading bureaucratic glory—the lawsuit becomes a place Anwar hides each morning. He wakes up, dresses in his work shirts and chequered lungis, sits at the dining table and studies his case papers. Nahid keeps an eye out to see if it is case papers or if he's writing another lovesick letter to the people who, according to her, cost them their place on the ladder.

For Nahid, the family's sepia fondness for their Pakistan trip has now discoloured with resentment. She fills her children's heads with stories of how Khatija is conspiring to get her grandsons in Pakistan married to her granddaughters in India to seal the land's ownership within the family. 'Bloody illiterates,' she mutters loud enough to be heard over her husband's file rustling. Nahid and Anwar are not the sort of couple to fight publicly, but the language of broken promises, unkept words, hurt sentiments, has started to poison their home and filter into their children's mouths.

It's not like all love is lost. Nahid still saves the rose from their first dance, pressed within the pages of her barely used Quran. She still lays out his ironed shirt and handkerchief every morning for him. She hums 'Paan Khaaye Saiyaan Humaaro' on Sundays to herself when she pulls her curlers out. But she mocks him cruelly too. Anwar has a soft spot for orphans, runaways, young people trying to make a life outside of their given circumstances. Each person he helps she gives a disparaging name: the limp, the one with the bad teeth, the bald one. Their marriage ages like everything around them: with a stubbornness to hold on to the good old times and under constant suspicion of divided loyalties.

Yet, among all this unseen cruelty there is a softness that remains in Anwar. It is the softness that comes from believing that what he chose was good, was true. Despite the fight he puts up on the outside and within his marriage, the only word he holds on to is shukar. *Gratitude.*

'Allah ne bohot diya. Jitna shukar karo kum hai.' Giving thanks, believing that he had plenty, that is the miraculous old man who remains in my memory. As I grew up in a changing Ahmedabad, it got harder to reconcile his gratitude with the cruelty of the state.

When he ran away from home at sixteen, this young boy and his nation were both tasting a new freedom for the first time in six generations. When a new world like this is born, perhaps it is hard then to rage too much. Sometimes people cower even lower in freedom than they did under oppression, believing that this relief, this breath of fresh air, is all they deserve, all they need, that itna hi kaafi hai. *This much is enough.* Dada was the opposite of everything his birthplace and birth order set him up to be.

Owning a tract of land was not his idea of belonging. When he passed suddenly at seventy-seven, an aunt kept muttering in shock,

'He was a Sufi. He was a wali.' *A saint? A friend of god?* Misba and I smirked at the hyperbole.

It would take me decades to see this truth, to see the flawed, broken saint that was my grandfather, Anwar Chowdhary. The truth would come through another Sufi by the name of Wali Gujarati. *The Saint of Gujarat.*

Gujarat ke firaaq se hai khaar-khaar dil, betaab hai seenay mann-e-aatish bahaar dil
Marham nahin hai iske zakhm ka jahaan mein, shamshir e hijr se jo hua hai figaar dil

My thorny heart longs for Gujarat, restless, frantic, aflame in spring
No balm can heal it, my heart shredded, bleeds on a blade
That has severed us.

—Wali Gujarati (1667–1707)

A Wali

A wali in Islamic thought is someone considered 'a friend of god'. Wali Gujarati, *Wali of Gujarat,* dates back so far in our shared histories we don't know for sure what his given name was, or his real birthplace. He is remembered only by this place where he died—Gujarat. Today Wali Gujarati is also known as the father of the Urdu ghazal, that delicate poetic style emanating from South Asia that gently keens for lovers, that aches to belong. Like Dada, Wali too wandered far from his home in central India, and like Dada, he too died in Ahmedabad. In 1707, he was buried here. For centuries aspiring poets and romantics travelled to Ahmedabad to bow their heads at his shrine. Like Dada, Wali Gujarati was a measure of the softness that remained in us. And it is Dada who brought us to Wali's dargah, his *shrine,* which stood less than five miles from our apartment.

My dada didn't come across as the most devout Muslim, at least on the surface. He didn't wear a skullcap or pray at the mosque or even wear the white kurta pajama Bollywood so stereotypes us in.

In fact, for as long as we could remember, Dada had worn checkered, soft cotton lungis, a lot like the khes ones his father and mother perhaps wore. He couldn't find those in North India, so he would make Amma promise to bring him back lungis every summer when we went down south to visit Papa's friends the Reddys at their home *Ayodhya*. The South produces the softest cotton lungis, and in Madras, where Amma is from, you get them in a chequered pattern called Madras checks. Americans wear these often in summer shirts that they mistakenly call plaid.

Each morning Dada would walk out to the balcony after his namaz in his Madras-chequered lungi, smile up to the sky, and chant 'subhanallah, subhanallah' a hundred times. After a breakfast of tea, toast and eggs fried over easy, some of which he would let Misba climb into his lap and slurp with him, he would shower, dab on Premium eau de cologne and sit down at the dining table, files towering in front of him. He would carefully write correspondence and petitions to local city organisations and sponsors as part as his post-retirement voluntary role as president of the Waqf Committee, the Ahmedabad chapter of the nation-wide Islamic organisation that oversees the maintenance of Indo-Islamic monuments, properties and community welfare in the city, especially orphanages and schools for underprivileged children.

I would peer over his shoulder, always fascinated by the act of writing itself. I'd watch the ink from his fountain pen transform into gentle, beautiful cursive. Then he would take off for his afternoon walk and return just as the family were settling in for a siesta.

The fragrance of Dada's eau de cologne would linger all the way from the bedroom to the lift. While I remember his smell most vividly, Misba remembers his sounds. How after he'd return and hang his pants up in his bedroom and change into his lungi, she would race to his hung-up trousers and feel the pockets for the familiar crackling of candy wrappers: Hajmola, the boiled spicy-sweet candy she loved, smuggled past Papa, who didn't believe in bringing candy for his children. Dada's little treat for his littlest granddaughter.

On Thursdays and on the eves of Ramzan and Bakri Eid, Dada would take Misba and me to visit Ahmedabad's saints, his oldest friends. We drove to mosques, dargahs and cemeteries in his sputtering teal Fiat, then parked and jumped into an auto-rickshaw when the lanes got too narrow. He showed us how to offer rose petals and incense, made us sit still and listen to the fatihas being read out, the qawwalis being sung. I realised that if I sat completely quiet, I could hear a multitude of people's softly whispered prayers. Their stories. I'd watch devotees, their hands raised, heads bowed, tears streaming as they thanked or beseeched the saint for everything from good exam results to a cure for a loved one's illness.

I remember feeling self-conscious in my oversize T-shirt and jeans and the hurriedly wrapped shawl that would keep slipping off my head. Amma always had my hair cut boyishly short, and uneven bangs and slipping scarves made it all quite confusing for onlookers in these more devout neighbourhoods.

But we were the 'president's granddaughters', and in some of these neighbourhoods, Dada may as well have been the president of India. He held hands and hugged people wherever he went, and he would take our tiny hands and walk us through musty hallways, his secretary, this other old man, noting down quickly as Dada called out directives—fix a broken plaque here, a missing lightbulb there, cracks in the boundary wall or trash to be cleared from near an abandoned grave. Dada would stand and stare longest at forgotten graves. Then he would start to clear the weeds and brush away and instruct the secretary to plant trees around them.

One Ramzan Eve, he took us up the minaret of the Jama Masjid, where Ahmad Shah I used to pray his namaz. The tiny prayer room tucked away inside was the sultan's humble namaz space, where 'even kings are brought to their knees in front of Allah', Dada said. He knelt despite his arthritic knees and showed us the indentations in the marble where Ahmad Shah Badshah had knelt and prostrated himself in prayer for decades. Later he took us to see the Jhulta Minara or Shaking Minarets and told us how the British tore one minaret down to solve the mystery of their 'tandem motion'. Dada, Misba and I would stand in the late-afternoon sun under the imposing ceiling of the Siddi Saiyyad Mosque as the rays streamed through the finely filigreed stone and cast floral shadows on our faces. Sometimes Dada would take us to see Wali.

The shrine was a humble little structure, no bigger than a freight elevator, dark and dingy inside but filled with the smell of roses. On Sundays, when we piled into Dada's Fiat and drove to visit Dadi's family in the north of the city, our car would join a sea of traffic that would curve around the shrine. As our town grew into a massive urban centre and vehicles on the street doubled, Wali's shrine became a little ancient roundabout where people rushing mindlessly all day had to pause and yield. Rickshaws, cycles, cars, scooters blared horns around this poet frozen in stone. Everyone in the Fiat would do a quick salaam, a *hello* to our friendly neighbourhood saint. I would see others around us, regardless of religion, doing the same. I wouldn't. Instead, I would crane my neck to keep the tiny dargah in sight as we moved past, wondering if all our incessant honking was waking up the dead. Whenever Dada took us to visit Wali, he told us how the municipal corporation had been trying for years to dig up and move the shrine to widen the road.

On the night of 28 February 2002, five miles from us, a mob wielding axes and hammers reaches Wali's tomb and starts to slam into the stone. Two hours later, a road construction crew sweeps away the dirt and debris that remain. They scramble to pour dark and glistening tar. A bulldozer rolls. No one will ever circle the poet now. It is as if Wali were never here. Years later, a food seller on the street will notice young poets, lost and looking for Wali. They will leave rose petals on the divider that runs across the road.

Dada had been dead for two years by the time this happened to his old friend. He died in the summer of 2000. His mother, Khatija, was long dead too. But hearing the news of his passing, his younger brother Ashraf and nephew Tanveer boarded a train from Pakistan, crossed the border, then took a bus and another train across fifteen hundred kilometres to be at Dada's funeral.

Tanveer uncle would wake up earliest in the household to pray his Fajr namaz. So would I. Waking before the rest of the family was allowing me a few minutes to grieve my grandfather in the way no one allowed fourteen-year-old girls to cry anymore. I was shocked to see the burly forty-year-old Tanveer uncle choke back tears as his head touched the mat. I learnt then that grown men are more in need of crying than any of us.

After namaz, he and I stood on the balcony in silence. I smiled, watching him take in our concrete neighbourhood, smoky skies and cable lines crisscrossing the dry riverbed. He was probably wondering how Dada could have given up his lush home in Punjab for this wasteland.

As a second azaan rose from the east, I looked down the street in its direction. There at the end of our lane lay another one of Dada's favourite saints: Shah Wajiuddin. His dargah stood just past the banyan trees where the parrots flocked. I found myself wondering how Dada would feel about my new decision to not go to dargahs anymore. I'm not sure why I chose to say this to Tanveer uncle. The man was a stranger to me. Perhaps because he had my dada's eyes.

'Meri friend Amal kehti hai buth ke saamne sar jhukaana haraam hai, aur dargah ek tarah se buth hai.' My friend Amal, who was half Yemeni and full of precocious piety, had recently chided me about my family's love for dargahs. She said it was un-Islamic to bow to idols or shrines and we Muslims from the subcontinent were fools for becoming half Hindus. Dargahs were us Indians making saints out of mere mortals.

Tanveer uncle smiled softly. My throat caught. There was that twinkle in his eyes, the same as Dada.

'Aapko pataa hai bete, aapke dada ki ek behen thi, Bilqis?' Yes, I had heard of Dada's darling sister, Bilqis.

'Bohot hi young age mein unki faut ho gayi. Woh peero mein bada maanti thi. Ek dargah ke baahar baithi thi jab ek truck road se utar gayi aur unka accident ho gaya.' I had heard that too. How she died young, sitting by the roadside outside a saint's shrine in Pakistan when a truck skidded off the road and slammed into her.

His brown, Dada-like eyes pooled with tears.

'Kabhi-kabhi na beta, dilaase ki baat hoti hai. Bilqis apne bade bhai ko bohot yaad kia karti thi. Unke liye mannatein maangti. Shayad Dada bhi apno ki yaad mein dargah-peero ke paas jaate the.' His words cut through me. Sometimes it is about seeking solace. Bilqis missed her brother. And she went to shrines making vows to each saint just so she could see him, talk to him. Perhaps Dada was answering her prayers in these shrines across the border.

Dadi came out of her room just then, scowled at Tanveer uncle and headed into the kitchen. Tanveer uncle kissed my forehead and walked away to start his most futile daily exercise: to chat with his Indian aunt and get her to like him. A man who understood so much, he couldn't quite fathom why she rankled at the sight of his father or him.

I stared at the trees. *Perhaps I needn't bow my head*, I thought. *Maybe I could just sit on the steps and smell the flowers and listen to the sounds of prayer*. The cool morning breeze wafted up my arms just then, leaving a trail of goosebumps. My nostrils flared to take in big streams of river air. Then I froze. The breeze didn't just smell of night sand. It smelled distinctly of incense. And roses. And a hint of eau de cologne.

The next morning Tanveer uncle and I stood on the balcony again. I told him how the breeze smelt. It was strange how I wasn't afraid to tell this man anything. He smiled at me like he saw our shared blood in my eyes.

Years later, Misba will confide in me that some days, when she feels alone, away from home, missing Dada terribly, she smells it too. What is faith if not memory emanating from the dark shrines of our being, our own bodies, and finding us in moments when we most need it?

Years later, I will find a plaque at the Shah Wajiuddin dargah placed there by some unknown poet, perhaps a ghazal writer like Wali.

'Jisne jhukaai aapki dehleez par jabeen, arzee se pehle, uski dua'a qubool hai,' it will read. *Whoever comes to your door, head bowed in faith, her prayer will be answered before her plea is made.*

Tanveer uncle will die soon after Dada, from a heart attack. But not before he gives us the gift of knowing we always have a home with them. He instructs his firstborn to remain in touch with us and to always be there for us, even if merely in spirit. In writing Dada's story, I will finally make the effort to find Khatija's great-grandchildren on the other side of the border. I will ask my cousin whom I've never met what he remembers of these fraying threads. He will remember receiving the letters I watched Dada write.

> Unhone ek baar likha tha ki beta jis tarah hamein Islam mein sikhaaya jata hai ki jis khuda aur paigambar ko ham dekh sun nahin sakte, unhein phir bhi itna maante hain, us tarah, mera dil bhar jaata hai, ki aap sab ne bhi mujhe kabhi na dekha na suna, phir bhi mujh mein maante ho.
>
> Dear son—
> Our faith teaches us to believe in a God and a Prophet we have never seen nor whose voices we shall ever hear, my heart flows over to think that despite never seeing me nor hearing my voice, you believe I exist.

That word again. *Faith.*

I will ask my Pakistani cousin if he remembers which dargah Bilqis died at.

'Of course!' he will say. 'It's the most famous dargah in our entire district. Baba Farid Ganjshakar's dargah. Bilqis, your dada, the whole family, were all ardent believers in him.'

All I will do as I hear these words is stare at my screen, where a cursor blinks next to Baba Fariduddin's poem, lines I chose randomly to begin my excavations of Dada's past. A story come back to complete itself, a thread re-entwined.

Tightly Wound

We are three granddaughters living entwined and entangled lives in one apartment, and each of us has a name carefully and lovingly picked by Amma from her fondness for Pakistani soap characters. But each of us also has a series of labels we must live with, aliases designed and bestowed on us by the rest of our family. How else would they tell us apart? There are some for Misba, some for me. And then there are many for Apa, my phupu's daughter.

Phupu, my father's younger sister, walked out of her marriage and moved in with us when Amma was eight months pregnant with me. In her arms Phupu held a scrawny, colicky little baby girl who immediately attached herself to Amma. If Misba and I were daughters of an unhappy marriage, she was marked at birth as the child of divorce. And for the ten years Apa and Phupu lived crammed with us in C-8 Jasmine after that, this little girl lived with the shadow of her mother's 'failure' looming over her diminutive frame.

Amma, who sat Apa on one knee and me on the other and fed us our lunch every day from the same plate, became as much her respite as she was mine. She was an oasis, and Apa and I, like tiny, weary travellers in this emotionally barren wasteland of our family, found sisterhood and comradeship in her shade. For the first three years of my life, till Misba was born, this angry little child was my only idea of a sister and so, despite her having a beautiful name of her own, to me she was and remains Apa, the respectful Urdu moniker for *older sister*.

Because she was her mother's daughter, and her mother a beloved and much-celebrated professor of economics at the city's biggest Jesuit college, Apa was expected to accomplish great things too. She was always most likely to have her nose deep in a textbook and know the answer to everything. She was also marked for having inherited her mother's fiery temper. She flew into arguments with the elders, calling them by their first names when she got particularly mad; she'd yell at the maids, imitating Dadi's tone to perfection; and she could cite and reference the date, time, and place each time something unfair in her imagination had occurred.

'She'll make a great lawyer,' relatives would say, 'but god help whoever marries her.'

I, on the other hand, was labelled by the same aunts and uncles as having the best husband-finding prospects. By 2002, when I'd barely turned sixteen, I was checking every box one finds in those obnoxious newspaper matrimonial ads: 'Fair-skinned. Soft-spoken. Convent-educated. English-speaking.' Check. Check. Check. These were obviously important qualities for a woman primed and trained to live in another's shadow for the rest of her life. I'd already had good practice living in Apa's.

Misba, meanwhile, could shake her hips like Bollywood queen Madhuri Dixit, and was legendary for once having eaten a whole supersize Cadbury Dairy Milk bar as a toddler. Misba also had Amma's darker complexion, and if Apa and I hung around Amma for solace and respite, Misba hid in the crevices of Amma's soft body and emerged only when she heard the crinkling sounds of candy wrappers. She had no interest in school. Not even enough to find a husband. And so in a strange way she was spared the pressure of doing well in school, because who even knew what to do with a little girl who only loved dance and roasted almond chocolate? Over the years, the dismissiveness congealed into Misba being called 'almost the boy'. She sat and ate and scowled as she pleased. She had nothing to prove. That was left to the older two.

. . .

At school Apa was a year ahead of me, and it was the consensus now that everything Apa did, I would do only second best. In 2001, Apa had taken her board. The pressure is so high on these exams that it isn't uncommon for suicide-prevention ads to run across TV and radio stations in early March, when they're typically taken.

Apa exiled herself all year to her room; Phupu got her all the extra tutoring she wanted, and homeopathy for her stress levels. Apa tested herself with hundreds of mock papers, memorised every available theorem with that elephantine memory of hers, paced up and down our hallway loudly rattling off historical dates and events. When the results came, she scored 84.16 per cent. Not scale-breaking, but more than enough to set her on that track to take her mother's faculty job someday. Enough for our middle-class aspirations. It was such a big deal in the family that our rich aunt and cousins in Bombay gave her a diamond-and-pearl necklace. Now, in 2002, it was my turn.

As January rolled around, I should have felt like a boxer being primed for the ring, and yet all I wanted was to hide under a blanket and wake up on the other side of spring, exams done and Apa holding up my shameful average B+ transcript for the world to see. *Just get it over with*, I was praying. I didn't have any aspirations for diamonds and pearls. I just wanted to score well enough so Papa wouldn't blame Amma for how dumb I possibly was.

At the beginning of tenth grade, I asked Amma to convince him to spend a little bit and let me at least have a tutor for maths. I was terrified of trigonometry. Almost everyone in my grade had private tutors for every subject. Some even for easy, high-scoring electives like Sanskrit.

. . .

Mana, who went to school with me and lived on the fourth floor in Jasmine Apartments, was tutored by an elderly Parsi gentleman five days a week. Amma and I went down to her apartment one afternoon and watched their tutoring session. It was like watching a silent movie where the conflict is polynomials and quadratic equations. Afterwards, Amma negotiated the tutor down to the minimum he'd be willing to accept. They reached an agreement: twice a week, only maths, six hundred rupees a month. Papa refused to pay it. So Amma put out an ad for herself as an English-speaking tutor. She found four young Muslim women who were moving in a year to the United States with their engineer husbands. For twelve hundred rupees a month, she tutored them in spoken, functional English so they could kick-start their American dreams. Shop at Walmart. Take the Greyhound. That sort of thing. This was why those matrimonial ads in India asked for English-speaking, convent-educated, tall, slim, soft-spoken girls. They could earn the pittance they might need to supplement their own needs when their husbands refused.

Amma taught these women in the tiny laundry room in C-8, which doubled as my bedroom. When she got called away to the kitchen by Dadi, I would sneak into her chair and slip the girls all the answers.

My own maths tutoring started a few weeks afterwards in 2001. Khodadad sir was the surliest man I'd ever met. His hair was dyed jet-black. Eyebrows too. And he still managed to look consistently unkempt. He'd speak very little, drink copious amounts of chai and try not to look too disappointed in me no matter how many proofs I got wrong. He even made trigonometry comprehensible. Mana and I each studied with him individually, at our own dinner tables, an hour and four building storeys apart, but we never compared notes. Come to think of it, Mana and I never studied together, despite being building besties. It was the same rat race as Apa and me. We'd known each other since kindergarten, and yet something about being girls, Muslims, all stuck in the same ghettoised neighbourhood, aching to break free, had pitted us against one another.

We were vying for the same college seats, the same jobs, and finally, the same tiny pool of educated, well-earning Muslim boys.

26 February 2002 was my last lesson with Khodadad sir. He looked at me proudly and announced, 'That's it. Portions complete. Now you just practise, practise, practise.'

He probably said the same to Mana. And to the half dozen other tenth-graders he was prepping. But this was the first time someone had plainly said to me that I could actually do it. That whatever happened now, I wouldn't fail.

On 2 March, when I wake up in the morning, two days since the fires started, I can't remember Khodadad sir's words. Or that feeling.

Early in the morning, I grab the newspaper, hoping for news about the exams. *What will happen now?* We were supposed to be in our exam halls today, cramming sentences into ruled sheets, furiously battling one another for our dreams. Instead, mobs are roaming our streets, scouring them of circumcised, bearded and veiled humans.

The phone rings around midday. 'Zara! It's for you,' Amma yells. As I near the majoos, where the phone is, she raises an eyebrow and adds, 'It's Mana.' I grab it gladly.

'Hi,' Mana's soft, shy voice comes through the receiver, 'do you want to come downstairs and study with me?' I marvel at how she sounds so deliberate. So steady.

I quickly pull on a bra under my T-shirt, wrap a dupatta around my growing chest and fly down the apartment staircase, hugging my textbook.

. . .

In her apartment, Mana sits on the sofa, an intricate old wooden bench with a faded mirror embedded in the middle and a worn-out mat to cushion our bony butts. Their apartment has less natural light than ours, but it still always feels warm. Like you're being hugged. In her palms, Mana's history textbook lies open. I sit on the mosaic tiles across from her. It is still cool this early in the year in Gujarat, but after the sleep deprivation of the past two nights, I don't care. We stare at the printed pages in our laps. We've never done this before—studying together—certainly not with our minds on fire like this.

'Maybe we can quiz each other on timelines?' I offer.

'Yeah, sure,' Mana says, squinting at the blinding, hazy morning outside her small, crumbling balcony.

While C-8 upstairs faces the river, the bridges, the Holiday Inn, their flat faces the bazaars in the back, the tiny alleys, mosques and more slums all within inches of one another. Past the low terraces of old houses, the city stretches to a faint concrete skyline. Mana walks towards her balcony but stops at its threshold, hugging the glass door. The first time Mana and I met, on our first day of kindergarten, she was hugging her mother's leg like this: scared Mana, strong Mana, trying-to-be-older-than-her-years Mana. The skyline she's watching now is a blur of grey smoke. The city continues to burn before her eyes, fresh plumes rising and feeding the frenzy.

I look at the heavy book pressing its shape into my calves. Czars, monarchies, declarations of independence, holocausts, liberté, egalité, fraternité, Nazis, cold wars, refugees, camps, death. The book contains everything Gujarat's Education Board deems important about the world beyond our borders. Later, when Modi is solidly established as Gujarat's longest-governing leader, these books will change to include Hindu sages and saints and their 'history'. Documented facts will start to matter less.

But for now, Mana and I sit trapped within Jasmine, watching the fires grow closer. History is happening to us. And no one seems to care.

We turn on the TV and stare blankly at the news. I keep stealing glances at Mana—the quiet woman she's growing into. She's sitting at the dining table, shoulders hunched. Mana needs these exams to happen as much as I do. She is the eldest of three girls. Their father died when Mana was four. Their mother, Shilu auntie, struggled to raise them even as her own health has declined. The girls, like us, go to the best convent school in the city. But unlike my family, Shilu auntie is the champion her girls most need. Over the years, Misba and I have watched enviously as she's scrounged together pennies to take the girls on vacations to explore a new city or state of India each year. They have albums full of holidays in mountains, by lakes, in big cities, in front of historical monuments, each vacation paid for by their mother, in each photo the girls grinning wide. I'm envious of how they always have beautiful new clothes for Eid, how Shilu auntie sits with them each evening poring over homework, how she buys them lipsticks in the brightest red and chortles with them at their favourite cartoons on their nice big TV. We lie about homework, hide our calendars full of remarks from complaining teachers, and run down here any opportunity we get so we can watch cable TV with them.

Shilu auntie and the three girls are making their own destiny in a way Amma, Misba and I simply can't. This home is built on the promise that the girls will succeed. Ours is built on the hope that the girls will remain seen, not heard.

'Khodadad sir called to wish me good luck,' Mana says over the voice of the news anchor.

It bothers me that I haven't got a call from Khodadad sir. The only person who calls me every few minutes is Apa, sounding more gleeful than worried about the stasis and confusion around when the boards will be held, or *if* they will be held at all. Now that she's moved back to C-8, she hunts me down while I'm down here too to torture me.

I put my book away and stand by the window, watching the smoke outside. I hear the news lady reading off a teleprompter somewhere far away in Bombay or Delhi, telling me of the horror this smoke is hiding.

> 'Car surrounded by a mob on the highway . . . people made to strip down. Men chopped alive . . . women dragged into the fields . . .'
>
> 'Only Muslim family living in a building of Hindus . . . neighbours are the mob . . . poured kerosene and set them alight.'
>
> 'Reports suggest there are lists going around of businesses and homes owned by Muslims.'
>
> 'The Pantaloons store, whose owner is a Muslim, was looted and then burnt down. People were seen driving away with cars full of goods.'

Who were these people? What made them become like this? Part of me knows the answer. This has been a long-simmering fire.

I can't sit still any longer. Plus, it's not like I can hide here forever. I will have to go upstairs and face Apa at some point. If things look as bad as the news says, she will live at C-8 long enough for us to die together.

As I put on my slippers by the door, readying to leave, Mana walks up to me. She's always been so stoic. But she's softly crying now. When she starts, I can't stop myself. It's kindergarten all over again.

'Let's try again tomorrow.' I manage to mumble.

She nods and stands, fingers threaded around the metal grille of her home, holding it always open for me. I leave thinking, *At least here, I'll always be safe, if such a thing as safety remains.* I get into the elevator and let it carry me upstairs, my textbook forgotten on her tiled floor.

When They Come for Us

That first night of March, the moon doesn't come out.

Somewhere across the river, an armed mob starts to make its way.

We are on their list. But they know of the slums underneath. And that the darkness can work in their favour to catch us in our sleep. We don't know any of this as we sleep in our beds, eight storeys above the slums.

Suddenly my eyes crack open, disturbed dreams coursing through my vision as I start to adjust to the bedroom's black air.

'Naara-e-takbeer . . .' Someone is screaming a rallying cry far away.

'Allah hu-akbar!' a crowd is roaring back. The crowd is below our building.

We jump out of our beds, feeling in our bones the rumbling mass of bodies below. The mob on the riverbed yells more belligerently, 'Maaro, kaato!' *Kill them, chop them!*

The voices of 'our people' lift in reply, 'Allah hu-akbar!'

The Hindu mob's stealth has been of no use. Molotov cocktails rise out of the Muslim slums, their soft cotton rags dipped in petrol, ripping, flaming, streaking across the dark riverbed, telling the bloodthirsty mob: 'We are ready. God is great.'

The next morning, I will hear from Hussain bhai and Gulshan and whispers in the hallways how the slums started to prepare the minute the news of the train burning broke. Shift after shift of hot-blooded, underfed, impoverished Muslim bodies preparing crude ammunition, digging a moat in the riverbed, men, women, the sick, the elderly and underfed children, they had chosen to go down fighting.

Then I will understand the circles under Gulshan's eyes. These people whom I am staring down at, who have fought poverty and persecution elsewhere, travelled miles to come to this river and make it their home, who sweep our floors and wash our clothes and plait our hair and kill our lice; they know they will be killed first by this raging, mutilating machine that is sweeping through our streets. Their bodies are fighting for their own survival, and for their children's, and in the bargain saving us too. They have lived cheek by jowl with this hate for years before it has risen now to hit all of us. They've been denied home, land, a classroom, water, dignity. They're fighting like they have nothing to lose anymore.

My whole family stands like deer on the balcony, watching the conflagration, whimpering prayers in the dark. We have so many prayers for everything: birth, death, cleansing ourselves, travel, cooking, entering or leaving a home. But in this moment my brain can't process any of the hundreds of incantations I've spent a childhood memorising.

We're told that on the Day of Judgement the chant 'La-ilaha-illilah Muhammad-ur-rasool-illah' will be our pass to eternal Heaven. We must let the records show that when we died, we believed in Allah and his Messenger.

But right here, when it feels like our Night of Judgement has arrived, I can't remember what my dying words as a good Muslim should be. I'm convinced there is no heaven. I am frozen, watching figures rushing across the shadow-ripped riverbed, and all I can mouth is a strange combination of 'Amma . . . Allah . . . Amma . . . Allah.' *My mother, my god, my mother, my god.*

Thirteen months before this day, another kind of hell had struck these very streets. An earthquake 7.9 on the Richter scale had brought Ahmedabad and Gujarat to their knees, killing more than fifty thousand Gujaratis of all castes, colours and faiths. Our Hindu friends across the river had taken us into their bungalow, where we lived for a whole month as structural engineers poked and prodded Jasmine's foundations to make sure it was safe for residents to return. We had fled with the clothes on our backs on a night just like this. A week after we started sheltering with them, an aftershock had struck, sending us all scampering outside in the cold spring night in only our pajamas and kurtas and braless nighties. Facing imminent death then as we are now, Amma had started to chant. 'La-illaha-illilah Muhammad-ur-rasool-illah.' The Hindu lady whose house we were living in, spooked and trembling, grabbed me tight and started saying the chant too. When the earth finally stilled, we slunk back to the house and stayed up the rest of the night in their living room playing charades. At one point, Amma suddenly looked at this auntie and snidely asked: 'Bina ben, did you start saying the Shahadah with me earlier? I guess now you are a Muslim!'

Embarrassed, this auntie turned into a human tomato and laughed it off.

'Haan, haan, sab mantra ek hi toh hain. Sab Bhagwan ek hain.'

All our chants are for the same god.

These friends sleep soundly in their beds tonight. They will not find out till the morning if we die tonight. I don't know how to call anyone who lives across this strip of land from me a friend anymore.

As I watch the shadows fight, two voices are wrestling in my head: one wants 'our people', the slum-dwelling, Molotov cocktail–building saviours to destroy these dark, invisible others, this mob who so refuses to see our humanity that it has come sneaking and slithering in the dark to laugh at the terror in our eyes.

This mob sees us only as pests, to be stamped out, chopped up, raped, set fire to, annihilated.

I can feel Amma grabbing the soft patchwork blanket I sleep with, to cover my body. I didn't realise I was shivering.

I want this mob to die the death it seeks to give me.

Place of Origin

'You will never speak like that. Where you grow up doesn't have to be who you become.'

It is difficult to remember Amma's words or believe them whenever the screaming happens. Especially since the third kid in the house, Apa, has been calling Dadi a 'bitch' since she learnt to speak. It's almost comical when it isn't completely horrifying.

After Dada's death, we have started to yell and cuss more openly, like some last membrane of civility among us has died with him. Papa and Phupu yell words like 'bitch' and 'bastard' with spiteful ease after the drinks start. Dadi's favourite is 'suvar', the menacing and less cute word for a pig. Amma tries to gently chide Apa for using 'bad words', and Apa usually sulks and withdraws from her for a few days afterwards, joining her mother and Dadi in mocking us. Truth is, she cares too much what Amma thinks of her. Because later, she often bursts into the bedroom, pushes Misba and me out of the way, and flings herself into Amma's arms, crying her beautiful eyes out, insisting she doesn't want to be this way but she can't help it. Amma always hugs her and strokes her curls in silence.

Apa will never change by much. But cussing and loud noises terrify me even today. They make me feel like I'm picking at a knot above my skill level to untangle. Then I feel the knot in the back of my neck. Then in my back. I touch them sometimes, these knots, and feel two thoughts spring from them, as they did that night on the balcony—one is a potent mix of fear and anger, wanting the person who scares me to die, wishing to transfer my pain to someone who deserves it, in my churlish mind.

The other voice is Amma's, calmly chanting in my ears for as long as it takes my breathing to return to normal, for the knot to release.

Where you come from does not have to be who you become.

Pulling Strings

In 1978, a low-budget slasher film called *Halloween* was released in the United States and quickly became the highest-grossing independent film of the year. It spawned a franchise of twelve more films and launched the career of Jamie Lee Curtis. *Halloween* and its seven sequels were produced by a lesser-known Hollywood producer, an immigrant from Aleppo, Syria: Moustapha Akkad.

Akkad's career would come to be defined by two genres of cinema: horror and religion. While he continued to produce the slasher films, he also invested all his earnings into producing and directing stories he hoped would bridge the gap between his home in the West and the rich history, origins and tenets of his roots, Islam—that faith so vilified by the same Hollywood. In 1976, he made *The Message*, and in 1980, The *Lion of the Desert*. The latter, based on true historical events, tells the story of a Libyan tribal leader Omar Mukhtar, who defeated Mussolini's army just as Fascism reared its ugly head in Europe.

The film, funded in part by Gaddafi's government, fared poorly in Hollywood but today is considered one of the most accurate historical representations of the region told in the language of the true American epic. Yet, it is his earlier film, *The Message*—which tells the story of the birth of Islam and the life of our Prophet Muhammad—that became a VHS sensation across Africa and Asia, in countries with sizeable Muslim populations and ancient ties to their lands.

Two weeks into our genocide, I watch *The Message* for the first time in my life. And it becomes clear to me, by the end of three excruciating hours, that Akkad's Islam is the one I want the world to see and know.

Now that schools remain shut and all tests and exams indefinitely postponed, there isn't much to do. We ride up and down in the lift all day between our home on the eighth floor and the fourth floor, where Mana and her sisters live and, down the hall from them, our Yemeni friend Amal.

Like all childhood cliques nurtured in apartment complexes, our group has weathered its share of politics. We've swung from tying friendship bracelets and making 'best friends forever' vows to resentful shouting matches over birthday party invitations and school-rickshaw drama. We are all Muslim, we have that in common, but when you live in a monotheistic ghetto, the sameness starts to wither, dry and flake into smaller subcategories. In the absence of an 'other' to collectively hate on, you turn inwards, creating your own childish caste system, rating the piety of those within your community, comparing family rituals for authenticity, whose grandmother twirls prayer beads faster, who still calls it the Indian dialectical 'Ramzan' instead of the purer Arabic 'Ramadan', whose family still visits dargahs, whose women show more skin, and whose hair never catches the sun under a hijab.

And yet a psychotic mob out to annihilate all Muslims probably sees us only as one large, swarming ocean of green. An indistinguishable pile of Pakistan sympathisers. Even if the only time we genuinely care about Pakistan is when we whisper among ourselves, 'Tch-tch, they really have better tailors than us. So graceful their shalwars look! And ours? They sag like grocery bags.'

The fanatical horde out to kill us have spent so little time interacting with us that they don't see that, like them, we are busy obsessing over our immediate neighbours rather than those across our nation's border: nosing about their marriages, colonising their parking spaces, comparing and coveting one another's children's exam results. No, they don't see any of us as one of them. And having grown up segregated in Khanpur from non-Muslim children, our clique of six little Muslim girls has often turned on one another.

While our parents congenially wish one another salaam in the lift, and each Ramadan our mothers send us bearing heavy iftar plates full of delicious food to one another's homes, we girls have spent days and years comparing our backgrounds, looking for religious, cultural and moral superiority. Amal's father died when we were in elementary school. He was a Yemeni businessman and her mother a Gujarati Muslim from an old royal lineage in the state. So of course she has the natural-born claim to the top of our group's order. Her accent while reciting Arabic prayers sounds impressively like those folk we watch during hajj season on Makkah TV praying around the Ka'aba. Her three sisters and she all wear the hijab—their delicate faces framed by the shiny black cloth, their lithe forms gliding the building hallways, floor-length abayas swishing about their heeled designer boots. The Yemeni side of her family are all educated in England; her brothers, each one a handsome devil, have beards proportional in length to their ages.

From the very beginning, we were little bite-size projects for Amal, who spent much of our childhood trying to civilise us into the 'authentic' Arab way of Islam from our blended and confused Indian ways. She graded and rated and categorised us: Mana and her sisters lost points for using make-up. But bonus points for being a single mother's daughters. Losing a father in our society makes you an orphan, and orphans have the highest place of regard and honour in Islam. Our Prophet was an orphan too.

Misba and I were down a whole bunch of points for being the daughters of a 'man who drinks' and nieces of a woman who rode a scooter and kept her short, cropped hair uncovered for the world to mock.

I tried to make up for my family's deficiencies by showing potential for improvement. I so badly wanted to be a better Muslim, to be accepted by this lovely foreign family, that I prayed three of the five daily namaz with Amal and her sisters, mimicking their slightly different ways from how Amma has taught me. I stopped going to dargahs or participating in fatiha rituals for the various saints and legends passed down in our family. Amal considered these haraam; they were a sin according to the Book, she said. As a child I loved the storytelling aspect of fatihas, and of course the incredible food. But skipping them freed up my time to listen to this eighteen-year-old's sermons on more 'authentic' ways of Islamic prayer.

Six months before our own lives implode and crash around us, I was in Amal's apartment on 11 September 2001.

Daaya bhai, our janitor, came to Amal's flat looking for us. (I realised only many years later how Daaya bhai—a member of an 'untouchable' Hindu caste, lived a life of such entwined love with this Muslim neighbourhood, whose children he kept a close eye on, whose two Muslim watchmen he called brothers and chewed tobacco with, and whose charpoy bed he lay on through nights when it was too late to go back to his house in the slums below.)

'Papa jaldi upar bula re hain,' Daaya bhai said.

Your father has asked you to hurry home.

We rushed upstairs in the lift with him, worried that Papa had started drinking earlier than usual and was probably looking for his daughters, who had dared stay out past sunset. Misba and I entered the apartment ready to apologise, but instead we found Papa, Dadi and Amma all glued to the family's shiny new colour TV.

They were tuned in to BBC World News, a channel we'd recently started watching when Papa finally got us a cable connection and our horizons broadened beyond the state-run Doordarshan. A clipped British voice was speaking furiously over a scene of New York City, where two tall grey towers stood, one of them with thick black smoke billowing out of its top. We slumped on the floor by our father's feet and watched as a second plane entered the frame, coming out of nowhere and crashing into the second tower. The little 'Live' sign blinked, incredulous, next to the BBC logo. Our living room filled with gasps. Papa shouted 'Allah!' in shock.

This was 2001. In Ahmedabad we already lived under a constant shadow of Hindu suspicion. Our city had slowly splintered along two sides of a river, the Hindu side willing to leave us behind as it rushed westward into the new millennium. Simply being Muslim and navigating daily lives with the many labels—Pakistani, anti-national, miyas, mossis—was exhausting. As news started to pour in over the next few days of Arab and Muslim involvement in this 'act of terror', I remember studying Amma's eyes, trying to get a sense of how she was feeling, a compass I still used to direct my own emotions.

For years, the United States had been this distant promise, a possible refuge where Amma's brothers and mother lived; a place they would someday call us away to, from the daily terror of Papa, this home and the city outside. As the towers fell, we watched that gate to America shut in our faces.

Overnight Amal's stock in the group fell too. No amount of her explanations about white supremacy, settler colonialism or oil greed in the Middle East was enough to justify the death and mayhem, especially in this grotesque, terrifying manner we'd collectively witnessed.

'Your war is not our war,' I harshly snapped at her one day as she tried to lecture me on the mess that was Palestine. I didn't understand Palestine at fifteen, and I didn't care. All I cared was that, thanks to a bunch of bearded lunatics, there was no getting away from this hellhole of C-8 for Amma and us.

In the spring of 2002, we sit in Amal's home again, this time sharing horror stories of the pogrom, little grisly details from the day's news, when Daaya bhai comes to call us.

'Your mother is calling you for lunch,' he says quite sullenly.

We're all sullen nowadays. Nights spent sleepless, waiting for something to come screaming out of the shadows, can have that effect.

Misba and I dither around awhile longer. Amal's mother is telling us about her nephew who has been volunteering at a camp for riot refugees a few blocks from Khanpur. Hundreds of scarred, broken Muslims from within our own city and from villages around are pouring into this camp each day, their homes burnt, their families separated or killed, skin and bone hanging away from souls; lost children, raped girls, maimed men, people too numb to speak the horrors they've seen.

'Strap a bomb on me. I want to blow them up,' a small boy was heard saying. Amal has been trying to explain to me for more than a year that terrorists aren't born, they are made. I've seen it in a bunch of Bollywood movies about Kashmir and the Babri violence. Sure, fine. But part of me has always stubbornly held on to this belief that you have a choice. It's what Amma insists. Now I can't find the words to argue. How much pain does it take for a five-year-old to say something like that? This cycle of hate will never end, I realise. There is no way out. We're not going to make it.

As we sit around their dining table, Amal and I holding hands, tears in our eyes, loud noises erupt from the street below. By now we know that sound quite well: *the mob*.

We rush to Amal's kitchen window, but a giant banyan tree blocks our view.

'We'll be able to see better from upstairs,' I quickly say, running out the door. We've learnt, after last year's earthquake, that in times like these you don't take the lift. Your feet are your only true agency. We take the stairs two at a time. As I run, I realise Mana, her sisters and Amal are all following me. I keep an eye out to make sure Misba isn't lagging. My worst nightmare since the earthquake has been leaving her behind.

Our group has spoken about nothing but the massacre for weeks, a morbid fascination only children under trauma can have for death. We have even roughly calculated how long it will take for the mob to reach each of our apartments. Eight floors would take ten minutes to Misba and me. Four floors would mean half that much for the other girls. We have talked about where we might run to. One of us has said what everyone has thought. We'd rather throw ourselves off the roof of Jasmine than be caught alive to torture. Amal has, with angry desperation, reminded us that suicide is a sin too, according to the Book.

I ring the doorbell to C-8, and Gulshan opens the door, a panicked look on her face. We rush past her and squeeze into the tiny laundry room, where I usually sleep when Dadi's snoring becomes unbearable. This room has an east-facing balcony and lets you look over the trees, farther down the street. Though the balcony door is tightly locked now under curfew rules, it is also mostly glass, so we stand on our tiptoes, press our noses to it and look down the block. There is fighting going on past the trees. We hear the clang of swords, shrieks, slogans rising to the eighth floor.

'Jai Shree Ram!' *Long Live Ram!*

'Maaro saalo ko. Kaato!' *Kill the fuckers. Cut them!*

When you see death come for you with such vitality, something strange happens. Your body and mind go numb in preparation, as if bracing so that when the pain hits, you won't really feel it. I can sense my limbs losing feeling, my brain starting to consider rape as just a thing that can happen to my body. Death is just a change in state. One day you're a body, next a memory, a smell, eau de cologne and incense on a passing morning breeze. I haven't told the girls that I have been practising every night since the violence began—lying in bed, teaching myself to allow my mind to float out upward and look away from my body, believing that if I can detach well enough, I may not feel anything. I may not even remember it.

Papa, who is glued to the balcony doors in the living room, suddenly seems to notice his daughters are back home. He comes running into the laundry room to find six scared young women swarmed at the glass doors. He hovers tall over our heads to see what we're able to see. A police siren blares in the distance, approaching.

Is that help or more hell?

We can hear a cop on a loudspeaker now: 'Badha pot-pota na ghar jaao.' *Everybody return to your own homes!*

As if this weren't a murderous mob but bystanders gathered on the streets to watch a movie being shot. When the crowd won't disperse, we finally hear a rifle fire. Then another shot. The slogans and yelling move farther east. Painfully slowly. Away from us.

I turn around just before Papa packs his own panic away. He knows he's been seen. He puts an arm around me and presses my cheek into his chest, my breath still uneven, heart still racing. I can hear his strong, big, racing heart too. My nose fills with his talcum, mixed now with sweat and fear. Then he looks at the others.

'Don't be scared, bachcha log. Allah hai.' *God is there.*

We settle in the living room, sitting on the edges of the sofas as if ready to take off if the mob returns. I find myself thinking about the roof.

Papa is shuffling around in his bedroom. He comes out holding a VHS tape. He keeps all the tapes in his closet, even though the VCR itself is hooked up to the TV. The tapes sit in the most dust-free environment in all of C-8, on the middle shelf right next to his booze, his gold watch and a picture of a saint he used to pray to as a boy but whom he stopped believing in long ago.

He switches on the TV, carefully folding its cloth cover and draping it over the sofa arm. Next to this, the first TV he has ever bought, lies the VCR Amma's brothers have sent us from America. The brothers and mother aren't welcome in our house, but their gifts are. Occasionally, Papa and I open up the VCR and clean out its magnetic head, before he covers it and packs it away again for 'special occasions'. Those days I end up smiling to myself, thinking

I'll grow up and maybe become an engineer, some kind of manly career my father will respect, since he so desperately wants me to be the son he doesn't have. Now he carefully pushes the VHS into the slot, slouches back in his armchair, and grips the remote.

'Here. This will help,' he says, nodding at the screen.

The Message by Moustapha Akkad starts to play. Wind blows gently over Arabian dunes. Three horseback riders gallop across, then split in three directions, carrying the Messenger's words to the edges of the world.

The credits start to roll and Amma sits up straight on her floor cushion, clapping as Anthony Quinn's name appears. Quinn plays Hamza, the Prophet's uncle who becomes his protector later. In that late afternoon with my friends, with the world ending outside our window, the film carries us along like wind.

Mecca at the start of Muhammad's journey looks a lot like the India I know. Many flocks of humans, their bustling markets, lives intertwined despite tribal boundaries of colour, class and religion. Many gods. Even more slaves.

The actors all stare straight into the camera when they address Muhammad. He is the fourth wall. As Muslim children we need no explanation why. Some Muslims believe Muhammad must not be depicted on-screen, so instead Akkad simply shows us the world through his eyes. I am lost temporarily in wonderment. Cinema is usually mocking and parodying my faith. But here, through Akkad's lens, it is depicting it with such dignity: no bodily presence, no wisp of clothing, no shadow, no voice. And yet the world of this movie is filled with Muhammad's presence. Religion, like cinema, is its own suspension of disbelief, I guess.

In one scene, Muhammad's ragtag early followers sit huddled in a tiny room, waiting for word from their Prophet. A man arrives, hiding in the evening's shadows, bearing the Prophet's teachings. I know these lines because they are in every Quran in our home.

When the sun has been extinguished,
when stars fall,
when mountains move,
when pregnant camels are left untended,
when all creation is gathered,
and when the seas overflow,
when souls are reunited,
when the female infant buried alive asks for what crime she was killed,
when the books are opened,
and the sky is stripped bare,
when Hell is set ablaze and Heaven rolls closer,
every soul will know what it did and what it brings.

(Surah At-Takwir, 81:1–14)

Amaar, a young listener from this group, then returns home to find his parents sick with worry for his safety. Like now, that time in Mecca is a dangerous one for a person to be Muslim.

Amaar tells his mother what he learnt that evening: Muhammad has decreed that they 'stop the burial of newborn girls'. Amaar's father shrugs. That is the custom, he says. He was lucky his wife gave him only sons. But Amaar's mother stands frozen.

She tells her husband how Amaar would not be here, nor would she, if her father, having already buried two daughters alive, hadn't broken down, refusing to kill her, his third female child. She recounts how, as her father was burying his second daughter, the baby, smiling, took hold of his finger. He told his wife afterwards that it was a whole minute before the 'tender little grip released and he dared take away his hand'.

'When I was born, my father ran out of the house screaming that he couldn't do it again, that he could never do it again,' Amaar's mother tells him. 'The gods that let such things be are no gods.'

'You know, Sumaya, Amaar's mother, she was one of the first women to embrace Islam,' Amal proudly chimes, her eyes shining.

Six girls in C-8's living room sit glued to that TV for three hours. Six girls whose very girlhood has become a threat to their being slowly find hope in a movie from the seventies, which is telling them to believe that, even if there is no justice outside their windows, there will come a day when the sun will be overthrown, the stars will fall, the universe will turn in on itself, and on that day, a god we've never seen nor touched nor heard, but whom we know in our disparate Muslim ways, our childish, squabbling ways, will finally bring every lost girl home. And souls will have to answer. And justice will be done.

Bad Cops

My favourite thing to do besides finding dark, quiet corners to hide in around our apartment is watching television. But when you're living under curfew with six other people in a thousand square feet for weeks on end with nothing but the news blaring—in Indian English, then Gujarati, then Hindi, then British English, then Gujarati, then Hindi, then American English, then . . . you get the drift—the sound of death quickly trains you, Pavlov-dog-like, to run to the farthest corner of the house and find a space where perhaps it won't reach your ears. It still will. The numbers won't go away. The numb shock in the voices won't die down even if the voices themselves become fainter. The aura of death carries into your sleep as it does into your wakefulness. Desperately sleep-deprived by the fourth week in lockdown, I've slowly started to sleepwalk through the days and find myself becoming most awake as the sun goes down. Sentry-like I want to stand guard on our balcony till the sun comes up again. But they won't let me. Instead, we finish dinner on that cool March evening, and as Amma goes into the kitchen to clear up, I start to put down mattresses for Misba and me in the living room. If we are lucky and everyone retires early, we might even get to watch something besides the news on the living room TV.

In neighbourhoods like ours, police have shoot-at-sight orders. It is as if our last refuge has been taken away; the two balconies were the only outward-facing spaces in our fortress-like apartment complex. Now, choked indoors with Dadi, Papa, Amma, Phupu and Apa, we are desperate for a whiff of fresh air. I crawl over the mattress on my belly and nudge the French window open a slim crack. The ageing wood is swollen after years of termite attacks and treatments and creaks noisily. I look around to see if anyone heard. Wedging my fingers through, I open it a little more. The cool breeze, perhaps sensing my tiny rebellion, slips between the gaps and reaches for us. Misba and I lie smiling, taking in big gasps. The breeze reminds us of Dada. A soothing respite in the heat of our childhood, a breeze that died down too soon.

'What are you doing?' Dadi barks behind us. I quickly pull the door shut.

'It opened on its own with the breeze. I was closing it,' I mutter, not looking at her. I have started this thing in the past year or so, not looking at her as I speak. It irritates her to bits, and I love it. Another tiny rebellion.

I am not alone in wanting to keep watch. Most of the men in our building have made a routine of spending the nights watching from Jasmine's terrace, nine storeys above the street. Our buildings have turned into towers, and these are our keepers. We know this because each night we hear them all bidding their families goodnight and the lift making its groaning journeys up and down past our floor.

We leave our mattresses briefly to kiss Amma goodnight. As children we would kiss both parents, but over the years, something has shifted. There are nights Papa envelops us in a crushing bear hug and kisses both our cheeks with his evening beard. Sometimes when we were younger, he would even tickle us till we cried. Other nights he simply grunts and places a limp arm around us as if we were too far out to reach and he has very little strength. And then some nights he is a whole shaking mountain, one we know not to touch or get too close to, or we'll be buried beneath its debris. So we usually say goodnight from a distance now and measure his response. If his head turns immediately, twinkling eyes and all, we rush in and place a quick kiss on his cheek. But most nights we only hover, as close as we can bear to get to the smell of whisky on his breath. We respectfully say, 'Shabbakhair, Papa.' *Be well on this night.*

Tonight, though, he isn't drunk. And every minute alive these days feels precious. We kiss both our parents and linger till Papa gruffly says, 'Chalo, get into bed now.'

Misba and I slip under the thin cotton quilts. Worn and old, the kambal knows the shapes of our bodies. It smells of mothballs and comfort, of refuge. The linen closet used to be another one of my favourite hiding spots in the apartment, till I grew too tall to crawl into its shelf. I've spent hours like that, the door open a sliver so I could breathe, sitting on a stack of uneven old mattresses, humming songs to myself.

We lie in bed now, Misba and I, listening to each other breathe, the sounds of the apartment slowing to stillness. The rhythm of the lift—up, then down, then up, then down—helps us sleep. Around 11.30 P.M. the doorbell suddenly peals.

We wake and see down the hall Papa's burly silhouette in the door frame. Hussain bhai, our watchman, stands outside.

'Zaheer bhai woh aapko bulaa rahe hain.' *Someone is asking for Papa?*

I try to catch snatches of the conversation, even as Dadi and Amma block my path to the front door. The lift gates jangle open in the hallway and Allah Rakha bhai, the second night watchman, comes hurrying.

'Arre bohot boom paad rahe hain policewale. Zaheer bhai, jaraa neeche aaviney madi lo,' he says in his muddy half-Gujarati, half-Urdu. *The police are downstairs, shouting? At this hour?* All of us are wide awake now.

'Tum upar ho toh neeche darwaaze pe kaun hai?' Papa spits in frustration. Both watchmen have abandoned their posts at our heavy-duty metal gates on the ground floor to come get him. The gates always remain locked in chains and multiple padlocks now. Allah Rakha bhai, realising his stupidity, turns to go back down, beseeching Papa to come down too.

'Achha, achha, main jaataoon. Please tamey aao.'

It's almost funny that our watchman is scared to be alone at the gate. But it's a valid fear. What if the cops decide to shoot through the gate? We've heard enough stories by now of cops aiding the mob, cops encouraging the mob, cops *bringing* the mob.

All we understand from the snippets of the men talking is that two policemen are standing outside the gates right now, rattling and shaking it, demanding we open and let them in.

'They're saying someone threw a stone at them from our terrace,' Amma tells us in a whisper. *Who would dare do that right now? Why would we give them an excuse to storm us, to force their way into our homes?* Yes, there are a few young boys among the men up on the terraces who, perhaps, in a moment of jawaani ka josh, as Papa calls it, *youthful passion*, might relish a chance to hit back at a policewala right now. We have all seen and heard of enough cop-led brutality by this point. They have turned on us. Like we don't deserve their protection because of what someone somewhere else did. We are all saale Pakistani, miyabhai, second-class scum for them, hiding and cowering in our homes, not from a faceless mob but from these uniformed men sworn to protect us. They have failed us, their people on one side of the river. Come to think of it, is it that improbable one of us threw a brick down at them?

Hussain bhai is still trying his best to convince Papa to come down with him and reason with the cops.

'Agar andar ghuss gaye, toh phir kuchh bol nahin sakte, bhai,' he warns. *If they enter the building forcibly, no one can say what they might do.* I remember standing there in that moment, imagining them coming through our gates. Behind them, emerging from the shadows of the night, a gleaming mob. Swords, petrol cans, knives, men bursting through our door, burning Dadi's sofa, smashing our new TV that Papa finally caved in and bought a year ago. A mob rising like water, from the ground up, floor by floor, till they've bathed each storey in blood like in Gulbarg and a thousand other neighbourhoods. A mob reaching us, the only family still living on the deserted eighth floor, our neighbours now in Dubai and Israel and America and Bhutan. Too far away to save us. The mob cutting Papa in two before he's had a chance to say 'Kya kar rahe ho, bhai?' *What are you doing, brother?* The mob burning past Dadi as she tries to save her crystal laughing buddhas, burning past Amma as she tries saving her crying daughters. Then the mob seeing us. Two young girls. More young girls cowering under beds all over the building, the fear in our eyes and the pleasure in the eyes of the men who find us.

As these horrors play out in my mind, Papa argues with Hussain bhai over why he should go down and not any of the other elected officials of Jasmine's cooperative housing society. Papa was just named secretary or treasurer or something after many years of building politics between him plus some of the older residents and the newer Bohra residents who he felt were trying to push them out. He hated that Jasmine was becoming an investment property for Gujarati Muslims who were raising their kids in safety far away in the Middle East or Mumbai, while still owning a piece of Gujarat. Papa wanted people to tend to the things they claimed to belong to. The irony of it wasn't lost on me. A father who could so easily overlook his kids could also be a stickler for duty elsewhere. But he had sworn to never leave his parents and, by extension, Jasmine. So he was its secretary or treasurer or whatever. And I joked in my own head sometimes that soon Jasmine would be a husk of its present self, with only the Chowdharys haunting its every floor. We'd all die together here, come earthquake or pogrom.

'Why isn't he going?' I ask, pushing into Amma's side, promising myself I am not going to die here in Jasmine this night. I am so mad at Papa. Ashamed. Here I am, making mental lists of what we can use from our kitchen if the mob gets in: red chilli powder, knives (though most are too blunt), the slim sword concealed inside Dada's antique walking stick that hangs from the wall! And here is my mountain of a father, hunched over Hussain bhai, heels dug into the tiles, refusing to budge and go meet these cops. Finally he comes back inside, picks up the phone and dials the one person he knows to be braver than him: Mrs Pant.

Eighty-year-old Pant auntie is the widow of the late inspector general of the Gujarat Police, Parshuram Pant. She is Dadi's best friend and worst enemy. She has stood against Papa in building elections but also sent up boxes full of delicious Maharashtrian sweets when he has won.

With her sleeveless blouse, her neatly starched and pinned sari, her tall, straight figure barely stooped by age and her hair cut boyishly short—not very different from how mine has been for most of my childhood—I've often wanted to grow old like her. Roaring brave, and so certain of herself.

Even though rudely awakened in the middle of the night by Papa's call, she quickly springs to action, ordering Papa to meet her on the seventh floor. Papa is always a little scared of her. He quickly changes out of his grey rubber slippers and rushes downstairs in his pajamas. We hear them take the lift all the way down to the gate, which the cops, now impatient, are banging with their batons so loudly we hear them all the way up on the eighth floor.

We are frozen, listening. Amma is in the kitchen doorway, as if going through her own mental list of what she can use from her kitchen if it comes down to it. Dadi is sitting on a dining table chair where a jaanemaaz is now laid open at all times in case she wants to pray. She sits facing away from it, though, as if undecided what she wants her last prayer to be. I stand by the phone, taking in the details of our little black-and-gold phone book. Whom will I call if all I have time for is one call? My mother's family in faraway America? My grandfather's people in Pakistan? My childhood friend four storeys below us? Shah Sahab, our family pir, so he can prepare to pray for our souls?

I go through a mental list of my friends from school. Is there anyone I trust to get out of the comfort of their bed in this moment and do something? In that moment, the river between us and the rest of the world may as well be a whole continent. A space too wide to overcome, mired by a choice made quite consciously by my friends' parents and their parents and their parents: we are simply not worth it.

The sound of the lift leaving the ground floor clatters through the weight of silence. As it draws closer, we listen carefully.

Is that the mob? Or Papa? We know the voice of the mob now. We heard it rise from the riverbed just last week. Those wave-like shouts, not very different from how a cricket stadium erupts when India beats Pakistan. Except that our riverbed was shouting for our blood.

There is no sound except the cranked pulleys pressing closer into each other as the old engine whirs in a room directly above us. The lift stops on the seventh floor. We hear faint voices. The metal doors clang again, and the lift arrives on our floor. Amma runs to get the door. Papa enters but doesn't look us in the eyes.

He goes straight to the locked French windows, unlocks one side gingerly, and then, like a three-hundred-pound ballerina, steps tiptoed onto the balcony and peers over its edge.

I step into his shadow and look at the tar road below, ghoulish in the orange night lamps.

Below our apartment a jeep carrying the two policemen is driving down the Khanpur main road towards the end of the street, where trees block our view. The engine is killed there.

'They're probably deciding what to do next. This plan toh failed,' my father says.

We hear the jeep start up again. Our ears strain as we follow the sound of it heading towards Nehru Bridge, then over and across the river. Only then Papa snorts out a half sigh.

'What did they want?' Dadi asks aggressively, as Papa comes back inside and carefully locks the balcony doors again. He stands hunched over in the hall and recounts.

When Pant auntie and he reached downstairs, one of the cops was banging his baton on the door while another was speaking into a walkie.

'They both looked shocked to see this old woman limping up in her nightie,' Papa says with a half laugh. The cop who was banging on the gate demanded they open it so they could go up to the terrace and check for miscreants.

'First tell me: what is your designation, young man?' Pant auntie asked them, Papa says, mimicking her. She looked for his badge and saw he wasn't wearing one. The officer shot back, 'Tereko usse kya?' *It's none of your business.* Our language of law might be English, but to humiliate each other, we stick to our own ones.

Pant auntie coolly delivered a line she had repeated for more than half her life.

'I am the late inspector general's wife. Pant Sahab ka naam suna hai?' *Have you heard Pant sahab's name?*

The officers looked momentarily shaken, then the one who'd been on the phone replied nastily, 'Woh sab nahin pata. Miyaa ho? Ke Hindu?' *We don't know or care. Are you Muslim? Or Hindu?* That's all they wanted to know about the widowed police general's wife.

I want to laugh imagining the withering look Pant auntie must have given the cop. She can make your insides shrivel with shame. Nobody dared talk to her like that in our building. Even Papa was careful to use only 'aap' with her if he ever lapsed into Urdu instead of the crisp British English she insisted on speaking. Maharashtrians like the Pants, Gujaratis, Bengalis, Punjabis, Parsis, divided by language but united by their place in the upper echelons of society in an otherwise crumbling world, had all lived in Jasmine, holding on to their biases while loving one another's cuisines and clothes, hating anyone who broke rank and left to move across the river. Now this policewala with one swift question had broken through the edifice.

'Main Hindu hoon,' Pant auntie told him proudly but with an unmistakeable tremor, one that we hear in Papa's baritone now as he repeats this to us.

'Toh phir idhar kya kar rahi hai?' the cop spat at her, incredulous to have found a Hindu living among us. A traitor. I can almost imagine Pant auntie transforming from wispy old lady to fire-breathing dragon in that moment, raging and decimating the man who, with one callous swipe, reduced decades of her family's service to the state and this neighbourhood to something so primal. But Papa says she held on to her temper, admirably, asking instead to see a search warrant. They obviously didn't have one. She told them to come back when they did.

Papa seems quite stunned himself. 'One of them even had a rifle.'

Nothing could have stopped them, he keeps chanting. 'If they had got in, nothing could have stopped them!'

Except that a frail eighty-year-old in her nightgown had. We all chuckle nervously.

'See! Your papa is not stupid, beta,' he adds, looking at me, as if sensing I'm already thinking the words in my head. 'If I had gone alone, they would have finished me.'

I can't see in that moment that, for all his laziness, Papa's brain runs as sharp and shrewd as any average Gujarati's—Hindu or Muslim. All I see in front of me is a man who refuses each night to put his body between the mob and us. He never goes to the terrace to keep watch with the other dads. Only later, long after he has passed, will I look back at this moment and realise that my father is a more pragmatic sort of hero, the kind who wants to live to tell the tale.

Papa and Amma retreat to their bedroom. Dadi sits down to hum prayers at the table and the house falls back into darkness, heavy with the realisation that something fundamental has shifted in these few weeks. Who we were before 27 February as a neighbourhood, city or country—the many layers of where we work, whom we know, whom we are friends with, and who count us as their friends—none of this matters anymore. Now we are numbers and names on a list, vermin to be cleaned out of our fortresses and homes and holes under the bridges or up in the sky. Today Pant auntie stood between 'us' and 'them'. But she won't always be there.

Her husband died in 2000, within a few months of Dada. The widows of the two men will outlive them by at least a decade each, holding staunchly on to this old world they shared with their husbands. Then they will die within a few years of each other. Both their apartments will lie locked with all their precious furniture and linens and saris and crystals for a while, till their daughters divide up, keep and sell what they like. With these two women, the Khanpur neighbourhood their husbands tried to build will slowly fade away from memory too. I will not be around when either dies. Nor will I know what to feel when I hear it, except to think, *Wow, those bones really lasted.* Amma and I will joke about how maybe each of them would have loved to be buried with her favourite armchair or gold necklaces and bracelets, or saris and hair curlers. Or Dadi with her majoos.

Narendra Modi will become a sort of political legend in Gujarat by the end of 2002, then a national one, and finally one day in 2014, the man who presided over this nightmare will become prime minister to a nation both their husbands served. Towards the end of their lives, both women will even read of his national aspirations and praise him. Such is the grip and allure of strongmen. His shadow—which took this rich tapestry of their complex lives and flattened it all into Hindu or Muslim, saffron or green, this side of the river or that—will loom larger than the memory of the decent men they loved and lost.

Misba and I lie back down on the mattresses in the living room, holding hands, fingers intertwined. In our dreams, we hear distant screams, our eyes searching for dark corners where we can hide. Our fingers unravel and reach through the air for invisible knives; our hearts grow in anger and in courage to wield them if need be.

Camo

The next morning, I stand and watch from Dadi's window as an olive-green truck enters Khanpur. Followed by another identical one. Then another. The convoy winds its way through our street. I hug the grille on the window in hope. The army is here.

How long they will stay we don't know. I watch the trucks pass, soldiers sitting stuffed in rows in the back, wielding rifles, dressed in uniform, tired from their long journeys, airlifted and rushed from their various outposts across the country to this state where Indians have turned on Indians.

Dadi appears behind me, having changed into her nightie for bed and peeping over my shoulder to see what I am looking at. She's always hoping to catch us looking at a Firdaus boy and tell Papa.

'Police toh un log ka hi saath degi. Lekin army se kuchh hope kar sakte hain,' she says.

The army, Dadi and I agree, surely wouldn't take sides. We've given up on the police.

Sixteen years from this day, retired lieutenant general Zameer Uddin Shah will write a book called *The Sarkari Mussalman*. In it, he will describe in lucid detail how and when the army was finally brought in.

On the evening of 28 February, he was called by the chief of the army to rally as many troops as he could and travel to Ahmedabad. The armed forces were being called on to bring the violence under control. It would take the troops two days by road to get to the city. The chief asked the Indian Air Force to bring them to the base in

Ahmedabad sooner. By that very night, forty flights dropped off eighteen companies of soldiers under General Shah's command in our city. As General Shah's flight hovered over the city, he saw fires raging across its horizon.

He had been told there would be ground transport, magistrates, police guides, maps and cellphones waiting for them on arrival. When they landed, his local colleague informed him that providing these was the purview of the state government. The general asked to speak to a state official. The man in charge, he was told, was travelling abroad on an official visit. The general tried another official. He was unreachable. He then took his vehicle, a police guide, and a map and set out for Chief Minister Modi's bungalow half an hour outside of Ahmedabad. On the way he saw mobs surrounding homes and buildings filled with Muslims. He saw policemen firing into the windows of these homes rather than at the bloodthirsty mobs. It was 2 A.M. on 1 March when he reached Modi's home. The national defence minister, George Fernandes, was there dining with him. He welcomed the general, thanking him for bringing in the troops. The general insisted they needed transport, maps and guides to hit the ground running. The minister assured him those would be provided. General Shah then pulled out a tourist map of the city and asked them to plot the 'troubled' areas for him.

He went back to the airfield and waited till the middle of the next morning with his men. There was still no ground transport in sight. The defence minister arrived. Made a short speech. Then left. The army didn't deploy till 2 March.

In his memoir, General Shah will note how curfews were imposed everywhere but enforced only in Muslim neighbourhoods, how unruly mobs were roaming around unrestrained, how homes of Muslim police officers and judges were attacked within government-provided gated communities and no help came, how national guard members affiliated with the VHP and RSS were on the streets but looked away from their duty, allowing this mass annihilation of Muslim communities, how a mass migration of Muslim citizens away from their homes, towns and villages and into refugee camps was under way.

In many places, General Shah's troops retrieved burnt and mutilated bodies from wells and gave them a decent burial. In Godhra, he advised railway officers to move the burnt train coach out of public view but was ignored. He asked the defence minister to immediately change the police order and bring in a chief from outside the state. The defence minister agreed but never followed through. Nobody ever said no, General Shah will remember. But no one followed through.

The police 'melted away', he noticed, when faced by the Hindutva mob. And the national guard soldiers wore the same camouflage as the army but did nothing, even when posted right outside neighbourhoods on fire; this reduced any shock or relief perpetrators or victims could have felt when the real army arrived. They were reduced to holding signs that said 'Army' to show they were different, that they would be true to their oath when no one else was.

'Disgraceful and demeaning,' General Shah will call it.

I don't know any of this at sixteen, when I stand in the window watching the green trucks wind through my street and the grey smoke columns scatter into the evening sky. All I know is that my amma is a proud army daughter. My nana, her father who died when she was thirteen, whom I never knew, was a retired major with a roaring laugh. She says she gets her wide grin from him. She was born in the mountains, raised in the plains, watched her father die by the ocean, because that's the life of an army daughter. Because his postings tossed the family around the country's wide and varied landscapes, living alongside captains and generals and orderlies and wives and children of all castes and creeds, Amma and her brothers didn't think of themselves as belonging to any one state or language or region. They conveniently slipped in and out of languages and cuisines and cultures like chameleons. And when my grandfather died, leaving three young children and a young wife widowed, these captains and generals and orderlies and their families all coalesced around them in comfort. Their different colours blended in solidarity in my nana's white shroud; a temporary quiet, a necessary peace, a collective organism breathing as one.

Mythical Miyas

In India, it begins with calling you not a Muslim but a 'miya'. The word used to be lovingly added to the ends of Muslim names as a sign of respect, but in the mouth of a Hindu person who gets all their Muslim tropes from bad Bollywood movies or hate-fuelling WhatsApp groups, it's the opposite of respectful. It also becomes safe to assume this person has never sat across from an actual Muslim. They are not his neighbours, colleagues or friends; he has not listened to them speak or loved them as his own; his brain synapses are on riotous fire every time he encounters an actual Muslim, trying to place us in one of the four categories he likes to imagine all Muslims fall into:

Aristocratic old-world nawabs: All pomp, no money. Expect some fawning and exoticising of the old ways of nawabi Muslim culture, anarkali kurtas, mujra song and dance, an almost lewd obsession with biryanis and kababs.

Warmongering, barbaric Pathans: Expect that in their minds my ancestors look like Amitabh Bachchan from the 1992 parody romance *Khuda Gawah*, featuring a kohl-eyed Afghan warlord. The fear here is at fever pitch about 'love jihad'—the idea that a devilishly handsome, rugged rogue will swoop in on horseback and seduce and carry away young Hindu girls.

The fakir/mystic: Expect that those who want to use the word 'miya' but *don't want to offend you* will tell you how to them Muslims are the most spiritual of Indians, like the blind, grovelling beggar singing Sufi qawwalis outside a dargah.

The butcher: When they're feeling particularly hateful, expect that they will pull out this ultimate trope. Just talking about it will offend their vegetarianism. One day, when Misba will repress the horrors of 2002 and turn eighteen and dare to date a Hindu boy far away from this land, his mother will say to this boy: 'How could you? Haven't you seen how these miyas live, in their slaughterhouse filth?'

The Kite Flyer

Spring always comes early to Ahmedabad. One day in January, suddenly the breeze will start to shift, and while it still has some of that desert bite to it, in Gujarat we will officially declare the end of winter. This day is celebrated as Uttarayan, a day of kite flying, when warmth finally throws open the skies. Like all children, I feel this information of the changing seasons of my birth city imprinted on my skin. I don't need a calendar to know change is in the air. I need only to see the first kite in the sky. For me, Uttarayan is the day Papa, like clockwork, comes alive.

The evening before Uttarayan, Papa would always take Misba and me to the kite market. This fluctuating pop-up market would transform for Diwali into a fireworks market and for Eid into a bangles, clothes and flowers bazaar. We'd walk by the big shops with their blinding, metallic kites and floor-to-ceiling-long kandil lanterns. We'd run past manja stores and watch spools of thread being coloured and sharpened with glass fragments in the hands of young boys on the pavement. Papa would walk on and on till he found the smallest kite seller's shop tucked in the end of the bazaar. 'The small guy will pay us more heed,' he would say in that tone he used when he thought he was imparting deep wisdom to his young ones. I would hold back a smirk. My father loved a good bargain as much as the average Gujarati, whom he liked to scoff at. But I also knew my father's soft spot for those unseen, less loved.

For all his drunken meanness after sundown, Papa had a quiet way of seeing people. When Amma's mother, Nanijaan's American parcels full of Kit Kats and Snickers would arrive, he would first make us divvy out a share for Mana and her sisters. The girls had lost their dad when they were babies, and they were always first on Papa's mind on the rare occasion that he chose to notice children in his world. Once a year he would take us out for a pizza at his friend Lester's café, where he always got a discount. While we excitedly got dressed for our outing, he would take the lift down to Mana's apartment to ask their mom's permission, or rather, demand that he bring her daughters for the treat too.

Almost all my grandparents' friends had a regular visitor in Papa. He would pack us into Dada's sputtering teal Fiat every few weeks and take us to visit an elderly couple in their seventies who lived in a pale-yellow apartment that smelt of mothballs and yoghurt. I don't remember who they were, but I remember their children had settled abroad and Papa would mutter angrily, 'Selfish buggers, vamoosed off, leaving these two behind.' This way he could guilt us into sitting there for hours in the yellow apartment watching their slow-circling fan as Papa discussed politics and checked on their daily vitamin intake. This—not a movie or a park visit or a dinner—was his idea of a family outing. We hated it. It was also confusing for Misba and me that there existed this other side to an otherwise impatient, gruff and abrasive man, because he would turn into an ogre the minute we got back in the car.

But Uttarayan was different.

At dawn, the music would start before the birds. Each of the three closely packed buildings in our crowded neighbourhood—Firdaus, Royal and our own Jasmine apartments—had large open terraces overhead with an extra level for water tanks. Residents of all three buildings would climb up the tanks on rusty metal ladders, hook up supersize speakers there, and blare the war cries of the day: dhinchak, blood-thrumming Bollywood hits!

We would jump out of bed, quickly brush our teeth, pull T-shirts over our nighties, and run up barefoot to find the terrace door wide open. We would do a quick check for cute building boys. But Jasmine lagged Firdaus and Royal in enthusiasm and cute boys. That early in the morning we would only run into crows, pigeons and our rotund, moustached watchman, Hussain bhai, or the grouchy, perpetually yawning Allah Rakha bhai.

We would crawl back downstairs just as Papa was waking, eat our breakfast—omelettes with big hunks of bell peppers and green chillies and a very milky chai—then take hurried, scalding showers. We would wear light cotton clothes that would flutter in the day's windiness like flags around our bony bodies, and finally we would telephone our gang: Mana and her sisters and Amal. We were to meet on the terrace entrance at ten o'clock. That's when the cute boys arrived. At ten, we would promptly march back up and this time find the terrace chockablock with kite-flying enthusiasts. The same was true for every terrace on every building as far as we could see.

I call them enthusiasts because everyone can *want* to fly a kite. But not everyone can. I would watch fathers trying and failing miserably to get kites up in the air with their sons. They would make their boys climb up the rusty ladder of the water tank to release the kite, only to have it slump down instead. They would lean half their torsos over the parapet, staring down a dizzying nine storeys, tugging it up, and still have no luck. And the ones who would eventually get their kites up a few feet in the sky would have them promptly cut off by the rowdy but gorgeous boys from neighbouring Firdaus Apartments. Our gang of girls would only half-heartedly try stringing and flying a kite or two from the tall pile Papa had bought, then give up and instead sit in the cool shade of the water tank to gossip about how much we 'hated the Firdaus boys'.

They were a bunch of five or six notorious young chaps—we stopped counting, since they all looked very much alike—sons of the almost-mythical Khandad Khan sahab, whose legend loomed large among the three apartment buildings. The ageing Pathan had sired a whole brood of these shiny stallion men with creamy complexions, blood-red mouths and golden hair till well into his seventies. They were an utterly narcissistic band of brothers, infamous for catcalling girls on the street, especially when we crossed into 'their territory' to visit the tailor shop in Firdaus's basement or to buy chocolates at the small kirana store on the first level. If we heard a bike revving and screeching down the street after midnight, it was almost always one of the Firdaus boys.

'Saale loafer!' Dadi would yell, and spit at them from the eighth floor, the expectoration, like our teenage desires, never hitting its target.

But building pride ran strong on Uttarayan. And watching the uncles from our building lose kite after kite all morning to these beefcakes on the opposite side would get our hormones all tangled up in loyalty and lust. Misba and I would be sent down every half hour to summon the one person who all of Jasmine Apartments knew could fly a kite: Papa.

But Papa was busy in a Papa chore each time: taking a shower, taking a dump ('You know he has piles, beta. It takes him time!'), eating his lunch, drinking his chai, lying in bed reading the paper, lying on the settee watching the news; Papa was relaxing in a way only Papa could, no matter what the crisis. And when we nervously pleaded for him to come upstairs and save our side from humiliating defeat, he'd say: 'Arre abhi toh bohot garmi hai. Thoda thanda ho jaane do.' *It's too hot. Let it cool down a little.*

Mana, her sisters and Amal would watch this drama from the safe distance of our doorway, snickering among themselves. Misba and I would cringe, knowing full well what our friends and all of Jasmine said behind our backs: that our Papa was the laziest man in all three buildings.

Around five o'clock each year, the sun would start to make its way over the river and towards the new city, behind which it would eventually set in a few hours. As defeated kite warriors would start to pack away their paper armory for next year, Papa would finally stick his head out from the terrace door. In his hands he would have a giant plastic bag of twenty carefully selected kites separated from our pile that he had hand-strung himself. He would goad the sweaty, exhausted Jasmine uncles who were ceding the sky to the Firdaus boys, towering a few inches over most of them in his striped, ironed shirt, smelling like a freshly changed, napped and bathed baby: 'Kya hua, bas? Ho gaya?' *That's it? You're done?*

Then he would pull one kite out of the bag, place it on the ledge, carefully check that the kinna was perfectly tied, stretch the string from the nose to the tail of the kite. He would loop the glass-sharpened manjha through the kinna, tie it in a firm knot, and then hand the kite to Misba.

'Jaao, chhodo.' *Go. Set it off.*

She would run, barefoot and excited, turn to face him from a short distance, hold the kite overhead, and watch for the slight wobble of Papa's double chin as he would command, 'Go, beta!' *Go, son!*

Misba would jump in delight. I would watch Papa from behind, where I stood holding the spool. How he would deftly pull at it with his left hand and tug at the kite with his right. In barely a few seconds, our kite would be dancing up near the water tank, then up where most of the neighbours' kites were battling for space, then higher and farther out, until it was as tiny as a plane gliding far, far away from our tiny little terrace in this speck of a city.

The tiles of the terrace cooling my soles, I'd watch Papa stand tall against the blue sky, staring far beyond the flurry of these crazy, colourful diamonds at that boundless space where only his kite dared to go. My lazy, drunk, angry, obsolete and bumbling-through-life papa, so sure in that moment of the thread cutting into his finger, his eyes eagle-like, pulled back and fixed; a rare, beautiful smile curving his lips.

One of the Firdaus boys would eventually swoop in to break his trance. Papa would let out a triumphant hoot. He has been waiting for this. His arms moving in quick rhythm, he'd make our kite scissor across the sky and loop once, twice, thrice around the young boy's. The two kites—now intertwined—would start to pull in opposite directions until one gave. Most people think it comes down to how much glass has been used to sharpen the string. The deadliest string wins, they say. But Papa would stand there, balding pate beading with sweat, eyes twinkling as they caught the sun, knowing through forty years of kite flying in his blood that it was about how high one's kite is when engaged in this aerial standoff. He would savour every excruciating tug, with an 'Aa bachchu, ab aaya pakkad mein!' *Come on, kid, I've got you now!* The string, taut and heavy from holding a kite nearly a quarter of a mile into the sky, would bite into his fleshy palms as he'd start to reel it in with a rare gentleness. Inching backwards, kite and body in tandem, he'd bring the war right over our heads. I would move out of his way, hold my small palm to his back to stop him from toppling over the water pipes on the floor. Misba, Mana, her sisters, Amal and all of Jasmine would watch from their balconies, palms cupping our vision; bloodthirsty cry after cry would rise:

'Get them, Papa!'

'Chalo, Zaheer bhai!'

'C'mon, Zaheer uncle!'

And just like that, with one swift snap of his arm, the Firdaus boys' kite would go limp in the sky, stilling for a second and then dipping, dropping, floating on its belly, its severed string looping empty air, headed for the ground below us, where children from the slum already had their eyes on it. Unless a tree got it first. Across our terrace battlefields, Khandad Khan's precious sons and their precious red mouths would sag in disappointment as Papa proceeded to wipe the sky clean with his single kite. From our terrace there were cheers of 'Kapioche! Aye! Lapet! Lapet! Lapet!' *Reel! Reel! Reel!* Uncles, young boys, bands of girls, we would all break into lewd victory dances pointed directly at the Firdaus boys.

As the sun would bleed into the river and finally sink behind the new city, there would be no one else flying but Papa. As the Maghrib azaan went off, he would begin to bring his kite home, weathered but victorious, and pack it all neatly away. He would head back downstairs to our flat, spine a little straighter, head a little less bowed. He'd pour himself a nice highball of whisky, followed by another and another, while outside peaceful flyers would take to the terraces and string their candlelit kandils to a kite and send them floating into the night.

The war of the day would slowly melt away. On these nights, Papa would drink less and even hug us goodnight. He would sleep undisturbed, his snores ringing through the contented halls of C-8. On this day each January, the myth and legend of Zaheer, my papa, Jasmine's heroic kite flyer, was safe and alive.

Patchwork

Papa was Dada and Dadi's firstborn. Known for his twinkling, mischievous eyes and cyclonic temper, he was a brat who was allowed to be just that. He was also born in what the family would often reminisce were 'simpler times', the post-independence fifties, though simpler for whom was a question no one dared ask them.

Papa grew up among doting aunts, rowdy cousins, Parsi, Hindu and Christian childhood friends who spent their evenings racing bikes, playing cricket, going out to dances and unapologetically shattering neighbourhood windows. He went to Ahmedabad's only Jesuit college, bowled right-arm spin on the state cricket team and even wooed a future Bollywood heroine around campus.

Then in 1972, as Phupu would tell it, he arm-twisted his parents into using up most of their retirement savings to send him to Irvine, California, for grad school, since all his rich friends, sons of local textile mill owners, were going. Later he would remind us it wasn't a free ride. He mopped motel floors and scrubbed toilets and flipped burgers before he returned with an MBA and a disdain for 'America's selfishness'.

Once again, Phupu poked a hole in this patriotic tale during a fight.

'You didn't come back!' she smirked. 'They threw you out!'

Turns out Papa had gotten himself deported for overstaying his student visa. When he appeared in front of a judge in California, he was given two options: apologise, purchase your ticket and go home with no deportation stamp *or* have the US government purchase your ticket and go home blacklisted. Care to guess which one

Papa chose? Yes. He took the free ticket and the ten-year ban from re-entering the United States.

This decade-long ban also became his lifelong sentence. He would have to live in Jasmine with his parents and carry them through retirement.

Papa never spoke of it. His version staunchly remained that he wouldn't go even 'if someone paid him a million dollars'; he'd very much rather be home in Gujarat—a state that is, ironically, known for exporting many of its young men to the United States.

When I think of him now, having been that age myself and been equally if not more foolish, I wonder what was going through his mind. Was he angry at someone just then? Did America not live up to his fantasies? Did someone break his heart? Or was he simply too broke and too ridden with guilt to make one last phone call home? The parental guilt on eldest sons in India is its own unique, complex organism. Peer more closely into the foundations of our great and ancient civilisation and you'll find the fossilised remains of men who died trying to be good sons.

When Papa left India, his parents—a self-made civil servant and the daughter of a British-era magistrate—had all the comforts that being educated and upper class in post-independence India could afford them. Cars and chauffeurs to drive the family to swim lessons and rummy parties, an English education in private Catholic schools and colleges, learning to jive and savour single malts in a secular, cosmopolitan bubble, a father who stayed up each night during exam week to warm milk for his children, and a mother who coiffed her hair each morning and obsessed over crystal bowls and bleached doilies. When Papa returned to Gujarat, he even had a job waiting for him, privilege opening doors to more privilege.

He was hired at the very first place he interviewed: as a junior manager in the state-run Gujarat Electricity Board (GEB). The secretary of the board, who interviewed him, couldn't believe that a foreign-educated young man had chosen to return to his underdeveloped home country and serve in the public sector, when almost everyone else was headed westward. This was the time of the Indian brain drain. Papa didn't correct the gentleman. Instead, his big American debacle forgotten, Papa settled into the world of being an 'officer', expecting life to treat him exactly as it had his father.

Instead, he found the world as he'd known it slowly crumbling around him. Where his mouth had remained stuffed with the stainless steel if not silver spoon that upper-middle-class Indian life in the fifties and sixties could afford, other young men, with half his privilege and twice the hunger, were joining the workforce. Many of these men were angry. In those first thirty years after India's independence, prosperity had been divided up with dollops of discrimination: fairness of skin, caste lineages, the ability to speak English. Amid the abject poverty and communal divisiveness in which many Indians found themselves mid-century, many young men had also turned toward indoctrination by militant organisations like the VHP and Bajrang Dal, which had spread their tentacles into Gujarat's neighbourhoods. Later, we'd find out even Narendra Modi had grown up in the local RSS chapter of his town. Like him, Hindu boys of all ages were attending shakhas run by these right-wing groups, where they were being given militant physical and ideological training. In Gujarat, this was especially rampant because of how poorly education and social-upliftment programmes ran in the state, plus the constant threat that came with sharing a geographical border with Pakistan.

And to men like these, who ended up in government service in places like GEB, whisky-chugging, American MBA–toting, never-had-to-fight-for-a-thing-in-his-life Papa was exactly the kind of alien 'other' they had been trained to channel their systemic anger, even antagonism, towards.

By the time I was born in 1986, Papa had worked for almost a decade in GEB. And the slow violence of his job had congealed into our daily dinner-time drama. We sat around the table, eating

Amma's curries and sabzis and Gulshan's rotis, hearing about the latest microaggression. We didn't have that word at the time, of course. It was always something some 'bastard' said to him that day.

'He called me a descendant of Timur Lang.'

'He asked me when I'm moving to Pakistan. There, I'll get my next promotion sooner.'

Each summer Papa received a transfer order to a town or village where no one wanted to go. These places were called 'punishment postings' because of the lack of clean drinking water, proper schools, infrastructure and roads. Sometimes there wouldn't even be a position there for him, but one would be specially created just so he could be moved. GEB was inherently political. And Papa became one of its many pawns.

In 1995, the BJP came into power in Gujarat for the first time on the rhetoric that the Congress, Mahatma Gandhi's party, was historically pro-Muslim and therefore anti-Hindu. The Congress (and Muslims) were blamed for Hindu workers losing jobs, for Hindu girls running off with Muslim boys, for the dirt and poverty on the streets, for cow slaughter and so on.

With a brazenly anti-Muslim government now in place, people among us with pre-existing prejudices felt emboldened. Papa's humiliation at GEB became constant and persistent. The peons would mock-salaam him; his subordinates would take over his office and put a chair out for him to wait in the hallway. At events he'd be introduced as the sahab whose only job was to write reports in good English. They joked at parties about Papa's incorruptibility in a rampantly corrupt line of work.

He's so privileged, they said, he can afford to turn down a bribe.

But it wasn't privilege. It was stubbornness. Once we were travelling on the Shatabdi Express train to Bombay to visit cousins. As always, Papa had waited till the last minute to get his travel grant from the office to book the tickets. Two hours into the journey, the ticket collector came by. As he came down the carriage, casually glancing at folks as they held up their tickets for him, he 'randomly' chose Papa to check if he was carrying his ID.

Papa—talcum-powdered, dressed in his usual formal shirt and trousers, his polished loafers—was hard to miss in a crowd of scruffy passengers. After the TC saw his name on his ticket, he insisted Papa show him his ID. When Papa gave him his driver's license, the officer said, 'No, no. The one you used to book the tickets.' Papa had used his employment ID, which he wasn't carrying with him on vacation.

The TC threatened to deboard us at the next station if Papa didn't pay the fine, which was the full fare. I remember to this day that the amount was about four thousand rupees. It was more than what Papa had in his wallet for our entire vacation. The TC then nudged Papa to come talk to him in the area between the compartments, by the toilets, to discuss 'a settlement'. Five hundred rupees and he'd leave us alone.

Papa came back to his seat fuming.

'There is no such rule! Bloody liar, bastard.'

Misba and I cowered in our seats, watching our father cuss when he wasn't even drunk. He made Amma empty out her purse and poured out his own wallet. Together they counted out the full fine, including all their change. With a proud smile, he turned and handed it to the shocked TC, who proceeded to shake his head in total judgement of this very impractical man and write us a receipt. Papa hovered over his shoulder, making sure he filled in all the boxes correctly. When we reached Bombay, his cousin, a wealthy jeweller, shook his head in similar disbelief.

'Why didn't you just pay the five hundred bucks, Zaheer? You can't live in India like this!'

Papa bit into his kheema pav, grinning. 'Arre, don't worry. I'll get it back. You'll see.'

Then, because he could never resist a snide remark, he raised his double chin proudly to add, 'My money is hard-earned. An honest living. And whatever India is, aaj bhi ek system hai. I will get it back, you'll see.' *We have a system.* He always liked that. He was a part of it.

When we returned from our vacation, Papa sat down at the dining table on a Sunday morning and carefully handwrote a five-page grievance letter to the Western Railways Complaints and Redressal Office, detailing the incident in his perfect Queen's English, the kind that still triggers people but usually gets the job done. A month later he received a cheque with the full amount refunded. He was right. There was no such rule.

So how could a man like that have survived in one of the most lucrative government organisations? GEB produced and supplied power to a state of fifty million citizens, handled coal, steam and hydrological works for India's fifth-largest state in terms of its sheer size. Very few people working at the time considered it an opportunity for public service. And Papa was a constant pain in the ass with his questions and snide, smirking need to call people out.

And so, every year, juniors whom Papa had recruited were promoted ahead of him. Every year, he would be up for a promotion, and each time he'd get *superseded.* This word, 'superseding', the very act of Papa's slow diminishing, became like flaming coal on our tongues. We heard it every night as glasses flew and smashed in the living room. We stood frozen and mute in its presence.

This pattern of daily harassment lasted twenty-two years. Or rather, that's how long my father's spine bore it.

Each summer for twenty-two years, Jasmine's apartment C-8 turned into a control-tower room fighting to avert a crisis. Papa and Dada would get on the phone, write letters and pleas, go out and meet old bureaucrat friends and old acquaintances in the government with any influence to have a new transfer order rescinded. Under the building, bootleggers lurked each month to sell Papa cheap whisky and Old Monk rum. On those control-room nights, the drinking would be more intense and tempers would flare, and when the order would be overruled, Papa would fall at Dada's feet in gratitude and relief. This peace we bought with our patchwork attempts to fix and mend and hide and darn the many gaping holes through which Papa threatened to slip. This peace would last anywhere between a week and a month, basically until the next episode of workplace bigotry took place.

In April of 2000, two years before the train burning, Papa was transferred yet again, to a town I couldn't have pointed to on a map at the time. My grandfather, now almost eighty, stepped up yet again to try to have the order revoked. It seemed like his persistence to save his son would work again. That night, we celebrated. Phupu baked a cake to ring in my parents' sixteenth wedding anniversary, which was the next day. That night, there was very little drinking. That night, as we all went to bed with rare happiness and contentment, Dada woke up for his namaz, walked out onto the balcony, looked up at the sky, muttered his thanks to Allah, and slumped to the floor. His back slid down the French windows, waking Amma and us, who were sleeping on the floor inside.

Until that day I'd heard Papa's voice in only two decibel levels: one when he laughed till the house shook, and the other when he roared and raged till the house burned. I remember waking up the morning after Dada died to a third: the sound of Papa sobbing like a child.

Without Dada, the transfer order stayed. Rajkot, where he was being asked to go, was still a dusty town with severe water scarcity and very few good all-girls schools. I was nearing my tenth-grade in a year's time. I would be taking my board exams. Papa hesitantly offered to leave us in Jasmine and go live by himself until his superiors chose to let him come back home. Given his worsening mood swings, we were willing to take that choice. But Papa couldn't do it.

He stopped going to work. Every morning he woke up and instead continued to lie in his bed in his soft white kurta pajama, watching the ceiling fan above him draw circles. On the creases of his fingers, my agnostic father struggled to pray the only two Arabic ayats he knew, thirty-two times each. As the words slipped and missed his lips, he'd hiss in frustration, bite back cusswords and keep going. Perhaps he'd never learnt to pray before because he'd never needed to.

The new BJP-backed leadership of the board were pleased to finally have a real stick to beat him down with.

Take voluntary retirement and accept the measly pension or be fired for not showing up and have a long record of service ruined—that was the deal they offered this broken, shrinking man.

In late 2000, at the age of only forty-eight, Papa *retired* from GEB. *Voluntarily*, his papers insisted. He had given them twenty-one years, practically half his life.

This is why I can now see that when the train burns and the violence begins around us, Papa is hard to shock. He has already been burnt and looted by his state in invisible ways.

Four years from now, at the age of fifty-three, Papa will die. The cancer that starts in his left breast, just above his heart, will slowly chew up his spine. He will still never learn to bend. He will continue to insist Gujarat is his one true home, even in those last incoherent days. What we, his daughters, will never understand is why he didn't quit sooner. Maybe while we cowered from his angry shadow, our papa never learnt how to leave his father's. He never learnt how to fight for his own survival or his family's. His father made sure he'd never had to.

Neither the men at work who mocked him nor those in power perpetuating this hate could ever fully grasp what those twenty years of GEB did to our family. When you're eight and twelve and fifteen and nineteen and you see your home and family destroyed by a 'system', one your father so desperately believes in, the names and faces of the people in it blur into one entity. To me, 'the system' became represented by these men who poked fun at, harassed and broke the spirit of the foolish but principled man who didn't mince words and wouldn't bow down. These men didn't just take away a job; they turned his life into a twenty-year purgatory at the end of which he emerged alcoholic, bitter and yet strangely still incorruptible till the day he died.

I am thirty-one the day I start to write this story. And this right here is its beating heart, which I pluck away from my own and let bleed on to the page. I am sitting by an ocean one day, in faraway America, at a writing residency, struggling to string words together. Everything I write feels artificial to my own eyes. Until a prose poem comes. But the words don't sound like my words. Or at least, they are not in my voice as a thirty-one-year-old woman, a mother, a grown adult who has lived her share of hurt and kindness, who has run away to hide and build herself a life away from this 'system'. The words I start to write are in the voice of ten-year-old Zara, who watches her father come home shrivelled in shame each day. A ten-year-old who hates these invisible men whom she must blame for the death of her family. I say 'must' because there are others I *can* blame, including myself. But we are a people so caught in these circles of violence that sometimes I can't see where these threads end and begin. So I give you this early knot now, the poem that became this story, to hold lightly, to gaze at with love if you can. To know you are holding the hurt in a ten-year-old's heart, put there by an ancient hate. Look at it. Then put it away.

I'd like to think your kids must wait for you to come home and pick them up and sit them on your knee and tell them how your day went and ask them about theirs. I'd like to think your wife and you stay up in bed every night making lists of groceries and bills but also lists of homes you are yet to build and places you are yet to see. My papa comes home and sits alone at seven o'clock each evening. He pours himself his first glass of whisky, orders us into the bedroom, and makes these snorting noises like his breath is stuck between his nose and lip. But one chipped plate, or too much salt in his gosht, or the sight of a slipper left out of line, and he erupts. He spews out the hate he's carried all day and poured into his second, his third, his fourth glass, hate that has burned down his throat and into his belly. His insides aflame, my papa comes home and turns into a dragon. We watch from behind the sliver of our bedroom door as our home slowly catches fire: first the food. Then the air. Then our mother. Always our mother.

When he retires to bed, we sweep the ash, glass, crashed slipper and lie down our beds on the floor of his room. Some nights I awake to the sound of angry lovemaking between two charred souls. Sometimes he grinds his teeth in his sleep. It sounds like regret. 'Bloody bastard!' he spits, and rolls off to sleep. The grinding haunts my dreams. Why won't he quit? Why won't he give in? Why can't he be just a little like you? Just enough so I can sleep.

—'To the men who trouble Papa at work'
Zara Chowdhary
June 2018
Martha's Vineyard, USA

As I continue to write for the next few years, I discover that at times I am capable of becoming Papa. I am also capable of becoming those unnamed men. And to not become them, I must sever certain threads. There's a tautness in my own spine I need to let go of. My anger at injustice is my father's wound branded into my own skin. Like Papa, I tell stories over existing ones to hide my pain and frustration with the mistakes I cannot change. So, as I write, I force myself to choose parts of him I want to carry with me. And everything else I need to leave behind. So that I never fully become him or, worse, the unnamed men.

Like Papa, I am an expert kite flyer, I remind myself. I must gently and firmly measure my anger against the length of each life lost. I must unspool these messy, tangled stories handed to me. I must gently pry at each knot and peek at the pain hiding at its centre. I am here because so many troubled men crisscrossed and wove themselves to madness. I must feel their anger, let it weft and warp past me, then watch it float, rise, climb into the sky, as it tugs at my fingers, makes them bleed. I must let go till I feel the soil my feet stand on, made of firmer, softer things. I must return to the lightness and fragrance I have also known. I must dig and then bow down and breathe in the gifts of my amma.

Flowers

Gulmohar

In May 1998, India conducts its second set of nuclear tests, I finish sixth grade, and Papa is transferred to Baroda, a town two hours away from Ahmedabad.

Baroda holds better memories for Amma than Ahmedabad does. When she left her home and mother in Madras and moved up north to Gujarat and married life, Papa was stationed in this small, lush town. He was a young assistant manager at GEB. They lived there for only two years, but Amma often reminisces that those were the two most beautiful years of their marriage, the only time she got to spend outside the scrutiny of Papa's family.

Now they must return to Baroda after living with his parents for fourteen years, with two pre-teen daughters and a withering marriage. We stay in Baroda for two years as well. And like Amma's two years, these are the most beautiful of our childhood.

We've never lived as a tiny unit, just Papa, Amma and us. Misba and I finally learn what it means to not just exist as someone's unwanted granddaughters and daughters but to thrive, girls on the cusp of womanhood. In India, strangely, this phenomenon of living away from the multigenerational home is called becoming a 'nuclear family'; the wives are often blamed for 'breaking the family', as if by choosing space, independence and freedom to grow away from their husbands' parents, women are causing the patriarchy to implode and collapse on itself. The nineties were the decade when India went nuclear. All of Papa's friends moved away from the homes they grew up in to start new ones with their wife and kids. Most parents accepted this new reality as they did colour TVs and washing machines. But the Chowdharys didn't do modernity. So here we were, thrust into it by a job transfer.

Amma, Misba and I weren't complaining. We were ready for a change in our status quo, to watch it all burn down.

In Baroda, we live in Gulmohar Apartments. Gulmohar trees dot many parts of South Asia, with delicate fern-like leaves. When it flowers, a gulmohar can be spotted from a mile away. In May each year, it bursts into vivid orange-red clusters, for which it is often called the 'flame of the forest'. Some Christian communities in the South call it the kalvaripu, 'flower of calvary', touched by the blood of Christ. When I was little, I'd sit for hours, watching Amma effortlessly paint these delicate petals on small yellow postcards she would make and sell for Diwali. But we'd never really seen too many of the trees from our perch up in Jasmine.

We don't have much furniture or much of anything, really, having lived on the coattails of the senior Chowdharys, and so with lightly packed suitcases stuffed in the boot of Dada's Fiat (which he lets us 'borrow') we leave Ahmedabad for Baroda. The Fiat has no air-conditioning or radio and Papa refuses to spend money on updating the car, but we don't mind. The truck fumes swimming in and out of the windows smell of excitement. Something new, lovely. Every few miles, the silence in the car shatters when Amma spots a gulmohar by the roadside and squeals in a way that makes even Papa smile.

'Look! Another flame of the forest!'

In Gulmohar Apartments, Amma buys herself some paintbrushes and fabric paint. She sneaks off every afternoon to the fabric shop, where she picks up soft muslins in deep emeralds, fiery oranges, warm ivories, and she paints on them roses, jasmine, hibiscus, tulips and of course the flame of the forest. She sells these to our neighbours in Gulmohar: Jains, Christians, Hindus, many of them Gujaratis. These are people we aren't used to living around anymore. We learn to share food and laughter with them again and play with a mix of children. We start to pleasure in our differences again. We take an autorickshaw to school again, but now that we don't live in Khanpur's ghetto, the demographics look more like India itself: a mixed bag of Hindus, Muslims, Sikhs and Parsis, all riding to a Catholic school.

Our closest friends in town are the D'Souzas, whose apartment is on the street level in Gulmohar—Supriya auntie is a Gujarati Hindu woman who eloped with a Goan Catholic in the eighties. Supriya auntie raises their two teenage sons, Sameer and Richard, in Baroda while her husband works in Oman. The couple have mostly written off their respective families for the hate their relationship was given. In a way, Supriya auntie becomes my model for women who firebomb tradition.

Each afternoon, Misba and I return in the rickshaw to find Amma not in our apartment but downstairs on Supriya auntie's couch, watching TV. We grab plates from the kitchen and pile on a mix of our dishes and theirs, all laid out in plastic containers. We sit down on her rug, legs folded under us, laughing at Supriya auntie's expert mimicry of whiny TV actresses.

'So silly, no, Zara?' She looks at me conspiratorially and laughs. 'What is all this ji-maa-ji? Usko saas ko palat ke bolne ka na, men!' *If your mother-in-law troubles you, you trouble her back,* she's teaching me, a lesson my own amma would rather die than impart.

'Kya Zaheer bhai, aaj mood theek hai?' she would peek out through her window and ask Papa as he'd park his car in the evening. Checking on his mood was her love language for Amma and us. If he looked annoyed, she would invite herself upstairs for evening chai with him. By the time she left, his mood would usually be better, the bitterness of his day at the office smoothed away by her Johny Lever impressions.

Fragrant hope floods our life in Gulmohar.

Some evenings Papa comes home with vegetables he buys from a colleague at work who has an organic garden. He picks out squashes and gourds that Amma likes. Amma empties out her metal trunks, covers them in soft, neatly pinned cotton quilts, and makes little padded benches for our furniture-less living room. She places embroidered doilies on cheap plastic side tables, and unlike Dadi, who would never allow liquids on hers, Amma roots plants in jars and leaves them everywhere for our bony elbows to knock around. She even starts matching her saris to Papa's shirts again. Baroda's summer air, thick with flowers, traffic smog and teenage hormones, hastens our blooming.

By the end of the first year, Misba and I have stretched into lanky, awkward teenagers. When we watch a pirated, blurry copy of *Titanic* on our local cable channel, we beg our grandmother and uncles in America to send us anything with Leonardo DiCaprio's face on it. They send us checkout-lane tabloids, a two-cassette VHS of the film, T-shirts with the lyrics of 'My Heart Will Go On', and life-size posters of the man. We tape these on our bedroom walls and take turns singing Bollywood songs to him.

A few months later, *Kuch Kuch Hota Hai* is released. We convince Amma to let us get matching bobs like Kajol so we can look 'sporty' like her. We bake our complexions in Baroda's sun, learn to play basketball, handball, cricket, volleyball and any other ball we're offered in our school's plentiful playgrounds. From girls raised in the confines of Jasmine—rolling up and down in an elevator, never allowed to step foot alone on the pavement, with nowhere to hang out but the balcony—suddenly we are let out to run, to test our legs. We run across sports fields, stages, stadiums, over swings and high-jump poles; we take off breathlessly, learning to beat wings, barely touching the ground as Amma watches, glowing with pride.

As the eve of 2000 rolls around, we dance for the first time at a boy-and-girl party on Gulmohar's roof. It's the first time we go to a real party. I wear a fitted rust-brown salwar kameez and feel my newly developing curves press against its seams. I sweat and smell something new in the air; the desire to be seen. At midnight everyone holds their collective breath as the moment of truth arrives. When the clock strikes one past midnight and the world doesn't end in apocalypse as Y2K propaganda had suggested, an embarrassed giggle goes around the terrace. *Of course it was a lie. Nothing can halt our breakneck speed. Only good times ahead now.* For this country, for young girls, for my family.

Two months later, Papa is transferred again. As I go to the bathroom at night, I overhear my parents discussing this new 'punishment posting'. We're still finishing the school year, so for a few weeks he starts to commute to this new post. He spends weekdays there and weekends back in Gulmohar. While he's gone, Amma makes us grilled cheese sandwiches for dinner and lets us eat in front of the little black-and-white TV in her room. When he returns on Saturdays, he drinks more.

Dada takes the train up to see us one weekend. It's as if he's heard some desperation in his son's weekly phone calls, some plea for help. It's the first time we're seeing him in a year. It's the first time he is seeing what could have been for his son—a family not scarred by daily resentment, where children are nurtured, where a daughter-in-law isn't a slave and she smiles wide, baring all her teeth.

On the second day, he takes an evening stroll on Gulmohar's terrace, where he can watch the sunset and pray. I go up there often to spend time by myself. I like to look behind Gulmohar. There is a bungalow there with the name 'Rukhsana', my amma's very Muslim name, even though a Parsi family owns it. Next to it there's the bungalow of a Gujarati Hindu family whose son plays cricket in the gully sometimes. He has a cute friend, a boy whose name I don't know. I first spotted him at Navratri, while I danced the garba in my new purple-and-white mirror-embellished outfit Amma had stitched for me.

He and I would smile each time we passed each other in the circle.

I watch Dada pacing the terrace in agitation. He seems older and more tired than I've ever seen him.

'I'm very worried for Zaheer,' he mumbles. Papa fought with him the previous night when Dada suggested he quit his job and look for something in the private sector. Dada was the reason Papa had wanted to serve in the public sector in the first place; he had always made it sound so noble.

'It's not how it used to be in our zamaana . . . These guys will finish him. This job will finish him.'

I want to touch my grandfather's shoulder, but he never says much to me, and I don't want his words to vanish.

'And this drinking. I don't know how to stop it,' Dada says as if to himself, as if muttering a prayer.

Then he looks at me. The sun's slant lights up the pools in his eyes. It's as if he's seeing me for the first time. As his middle granddaughter, someone he speaks to the least, I've always felt like he mustn't love me, that there is nothing special about me to love. I'm not Apa—the divorced daughter's problem child, who needs all his devoted focus and care, who demands it—nor am I Misba—the cute baby of the family, who he says reminds him of his sister. I'm the child he sees only hiding behind my mother, staring daggers at whoever hurts her. Often, his inability to save her from Papa has meant my accusing eyes have found his. And my gaze seldom flinches. Perhaps why he has always looked away.

'You know, I gave him his first drink?' he continues, as if some flood of disallowed words inside him is rising.

'Zaheer was only fourteen. I gave him his first peg at a party.'

I feel my palms start to sweat, something like hatred oozing for this kind, soft man.

'I'm so sorry, beta,' he says. I hear the crack in his voice and my throat feels raw. This is the first time my grandfather has talked to me as a whole person, a part of this family. Of him. And he has given me this burden I don't know what to do with. *Where do I set it down? Why must I carry it?* All I can hear, as he cries softly in the evening sun, is the shattering of a whisky glass as it strikes the wall.

When school ends, we take down the Leo posters, we give away the plants, Amma packs away her paints. We say our goodbyes to our schoolmates, rickshaw friends and building buddies. Amma and Supriya auntie hug tearfully. There are three hearts breaking in the Fiat on the road back to Ahmedabad, as the gulmohars whiz past us. All except Papa, who is whistling through his teeth. Soon he will be home.

That night we drag our suitcases back up the lift and into C-8. The flat seems smaller, constricting around our grown bodies. We celebrate Amma and Papa's sixteenth wedding anniversary. We have never been allowed to celebrate their anniversary, because the very next year after they got married Dadi's sister died on the same date.

Tonight is special. Papa is back in the fortress his father built, where nothing can harm him. And the last two years in Baroda have helped dissolve some of the sediment built up in his marriage. Gulmohar was a glorious blip. But Jasmine is our past, present and future.

We eat a hearty dinner, sitting around the table. Dada eats very little but laughs a lot. Phupu has baked a cake. Misba and I fight Apa over a bigger slice, emboldened by our two years away. Afterwards, we put down mattresses in the living room and pass out, exhausted. This is the night when Dada wakes up for his namaz, walks past our sleeping bodies onto the balcony and slumps down by the French windows. The river breeze dances on his open palms. Amma wakes and scrambles half asleep to his crumpled body. She shakes his arms, prods his shoulders. His chin is awkwardly spilling onto his chest. She lifts it tearfully, her desperate 'Papa, Papa . . .' waking us.

His eyes don't open. His lips softly part. A breath gushes out of him, past Amma's tear-stained cheeks.

'Allah,' he whispers, and goes away.

We cry all night over his body, then pass out an hour before dawn. Over the next few days Dadi becomes insufferable as a new widow. Amma lives in the kitchen, churning out food for the crowds that throng C-8 to commemorate 'Chowdhary sahab'. Apa, Misba and I hold one another through the void. Some days Apa still tries to bully me, but now she meets resistance. I am taller, and I have learnt to argue. In Baroda, Amma pushed me to join the debate team. I would stand for hours across the hallway in Gulmohar practising the speech she wrote, honing my enunciation, lifting and dropping my voice to show I meant business; I'd won my first-ever prize for that debate, then another the next year; I'd started to write for the school magazine, edited newsletters, directed plays. Words fly out of my mouth with an air of easy command now. I've ventured outside of Jasmine Apartments. I feel unstoppable. Apa nervously backs off but continues to watch me with a mix of awe and suspicion.

Papa seems to back off too: from life, from his ability to laugh, from decisions. Phupu takes the reins with managing Dada's unfinished business, of which there is very little. She starts to visit the dargahs and water the shrines and pour flowers over the dead. She fills his empty seat on the Waqf Committee. People in Ahmedabad recognise Professor Zahida Chowdhary as his next of kin. Papa fades even more.

This is how we come back to the ghetto where everyone is too much like us. We come back to the school where 'us' is a label to be brandished against 'them'. In sharp contrast to the way our Mount Carmel Ahmedabad teachers grovelled in front of their richest students, nobody at Convent of Jesus and Mary in Baroda had ever cared which side of a river we came from. What mattered there was how much trouble we were willing to get into for our friends. We'd made real friends. We had seen what solidarity can look like. I was still hanging on to my biscuit-coloured uniform covered in 'come back soons' and 'stay in touches' and 'go make us prouds' from my Baroda classmates, who were of various classes and castes, every faith and colour.

Ahmedabad now feels like the anomaly, where hatefulness has seeped into every street, and into our bedrooms, where our fledgling lives are constantly being dismissed. Misba and I keep telling ourselves as we reminisce about Baroda each night that there is a better, kinder world out there. And someday, when we are old enough to go to college and get jobs, we will go back out and never turn back. No one can make us. Not even Papa.

It's an oppressively hot afternoon in March 2002 when Supriya auntie calls from Baroda.

The television news is brimming with reports of rampaging mobs everywhere. In Ahmedabad. In Rajkot. In Baroda. In one neighbourhood, not far from where we lived, a family of bakers, eleven members of their household and three Hindu employees—men, women and little children—are burnt alive in the largest oven of their own bakery. This story will go on to become imprinted on India's conscience as the Best Bakery Case.

Somehow, I still can't quite picture how peaceful, quiet, banyan-tree-and-flower-filled Baroda is being consumed by the same flames that are licking through Ahmedabad's streets.

'They came looking for you!' Supriya auntie tells Amma. 'They had your names on a list.'

She tells us the angry mob that came for us torched the bungalow owned by our Parsi neighbours because its name was Rukhsana. *A very Muslim name. My amma's name.*

She tells us how one evening when the curfew was lifted, her son Sameer went out to eat at a restaurant, figuring he'd get away with it. He was Christian, after all. Shortly afterwards, a mob arrived with cops, forcing shops and restaurants to shut down. They caught hold of the boys.

'What's your name?' someone in the mob barked.

'Sameer,' he answered nervously. *A very Muslim-sounding name.* The men in the mob dragged him into the street.

'They beat him so badly, men. Uska haddi aisa dikh raha tha, you know.' Supriya auntie tearfully says, describing how her son's bones protruded where they broke through his skin.

'And his friend, that Gujarati chap Arpit, you remember? Who used to live down the street? He used to play cricket, no, with Zaheer bhai and Sameer? He just ran off, men! Left my bechaara Sameer to die!'

Sameer didn't die. But he never spoke to his friend Arpit after that day.

'Last week, some rioting started again. And our upstairs neighbours—that Gujju family who moved in on the third floor, just over your old flat—unka bada beta khud talwaar leke neeche aaya.'

A teenage boy, not much older than me, wielding a sword, rushing down the stairs, wishing we had still lived there so he could have used it.

Amma hangs up a while later. Misba and I remain quiet all day. That night in bed, we whisper to each other. *Imagine if we had stayed on in Baroda. Bah, so lucky that we left.*

Later, Misba and I will pull a quilt of happier memories over these fears, we will fasten it neatly like pins hiding Amma's army trunks, repressing all the blood and death. We will return to talking about Baroda and Gulmohar the way they existed for us: lazy evenings spent wishing the earth would swallow us, so we could rise like fresh grass from the soil of a city we'd loved for the first time. How Baroda and its people had taught us to love our bodies in return, our parents' marriage, Amma's flowers. We'd fallen in love there with boys, with ourselves, with freedom.

As Misba and I grow into older women, we will learn to hold darkness alongside light in the expanse of our palms. We will wonder if our feelings about Gulmohar would have been different had we known then that the soil underneath our bare, dancing, skipping feet was slowly being poisoned. Metaphorically by hate, yes. But literally too. Chemicals from the oil and natural gas refineries around Baroda had been seeping into our water and land for years, into the organic vegetables Papa was bringing home. Just within Gulmohar four people would die of rare and painful cancers within the next five years, among them Supriya auntie's younger boy, Richard, among them Papa.

We will still never linger on the poison too long. Because Baroda, however briefly, taught us to look outside our narrow lives and seek possibility. We will laugh at memories of Gulmohar, the awkward bob cuts and the even more awkward interactions with teenage boys, the basketball games lost because we didn't want to ruin our nails, the neighbourhood uncle we could never take seriously when he questioned our loyalties during Indo-Pak cricket matches, because his name was Popat, *Mr Parrot*. Parrot does as parrot hears.

We will one day point out the strangest coincidence—how two children who grew up in Gujarat without a patch of grass to play on, who saw flaming trees only flying past on a highway, who studied flowers in microscopic detail only when their mother painted them—were raised in fact within concrete apartments named for flowers.

Jasmine and Gulmohar in all their brick and mortar, their chaotic, troubled neighbourhoods and communities, raised us. And we were indeed luckier for it. One saved our lives. The other showed us something worth fighting for.

Indefinite Postponement

Our board exams should have taken place on 11 March. But two weeks after the train burning, on 16 March, it's officially announced: the Education Board has indefinitely postponed board exams for the whole state. We watch the words come out of the local Gujarati news presenter's mouth, same as we watch news of death and blood.

I don't feel a great sadness. If anything, there is a modest certainty. I feel convinced these exams, which were made into life-changing, career-making finalities, are a joke. Young teenagers in India end their lives over a bad board exam result. Now ending Muslim lives has taken precedence over them.

My mind wanders to the invisible bodies lying just beyond the reach of my fingers, across curfewed windows, through the fog of the city's lockdown. We're living in a tower from which nothing is visible, not the mob, not the dead, not the surviving, not my school friends. There is only this idiot box, and the idiots—the BJP, VHP and Bajrang Dal—in it, given free rein to spew hate at us, their captive audience all day.

The city police commissioner's face appears on the screen. Four people stabbed in Ahmedabad yesterday. This morning in another clash one person shot and killed in police firing. I don't need exams. I'm learning right here, feet glued to this tile on Dadi's mosaic floor, how passive voice changes everything, how words cover unspeakable things. How a *clash* is really a Hindutva mob running over yet another Muslim home/business/neighbourhood, cowering, terrified innocent people. How *stabbing* means tridents, those holiest of weapons, smeared in human blood. How *killed in police firing* means shot when they resisted their slaughter. I'm learning that as I stand here safe in Jasmine, tenth-graders in refugee camps a few blocks away have forgotten what *homes* and *schools* look like. I don't give a fuck about the boards. I haven't learnt to effectively use the word 'fuck' yet. But I'm learning there are words in which this seething fever I feel must pack a punch. I need to punch something.

Apa seems oddly quiet about the whole boards-postponement news, even though it's all she has pestered me about since she and her mom moved back in with us. *What if they cancel it? All of you will get a free pass? Even the dummies! I guess we'll never know how you could have scored.*

She's only a year older, and this same time last year, in 2001, she was taking her boards. She'd spent all her tenth grade in stress-induced fevers and loosies because being a stress bucket had become her entire personality. She'd given herself mock test after mock test, crammed piles of textbooks, solved every possible math problem in every practice workbook she found. Then in January, a deadly 7.9 earthquake had struck just weeks before her boards. Thousands dead and displaced across the state. We had left Jasmine and moved in with our Hindu family friends, the Shahs, in their modest bungalow. All students statewide had gotten a free pass from school under the previous chief minister, whom Modi would soon replace. Except tenth-graders. The boards were held despite the dead. Apa, quaking from the sleepless, displaced nights, had taken her exams and gotten straight A-pluses.

When Phupu moved into Jasmine Apartments after her marriage ended, she had Apa, a tiny baby girl of six months, in her arms. In a home that didn't know how to deal with failure, especially involving a daughter, Apa was both a constant reminder of it and a reproach to the men, urging them to overcompensate for the man missing in her life. Dada was always fiercely protective of her. Especially when Dadi venomously attacked the child for bringing 'bad luck'. Manhoos, she called her. Sometimes Dada needed to protect her so much that, if Apa got into trouble, he would come looking for me to scold me and equalise the scoreboard. Papa was also similarly programmed to temper his affections towards his daughters so Apa wouldn't feel left out. He took the shortcut and ignored all three girls equally.

When we were very young, Amma would sit Misba on one side of her lap, Apa on the other, and me across, and take turns mashing rice and dal into tiny, perfect, bite-size niwalas to feed us each from the same plate. She would eat last and least at the emptied table. When I turned three, she sat me at the dining table with a plate in front of me and whispered, 'You can do this. Those two still need me. I know you can do this.'

I remember staring at the plate—dal and chawal and sabzi all swimming across the steel, melding into one another in a way I hated. I remember the exhaustion in her voice. I remember struggling to make a niwala of rice and dal, the sloppy mess slipping down my fingers, sliding down my elbow, dripping onto my dress. I remember shame at being too old to be learning how to feed myself. I remember going to the kitchen, reaching over the large sink, washing my hands and grabbing a spoon. I would never learn to use my bare hands to eat.

As she watches me now, digesting the news of the postponement, Apa simply curls her lower lip and makes a 'mtch' sound. *Mild condolences.* I know what she's thinking. Genocide totally trumps an earthquake. But our home has been quaking for years. If I don't take the boards, it will be yet another thing added to my list of underachievements. *Meet Zara. Slim, tall, convent-educated, sure. Soft-spoken, mild-mannered, yes. But probably not very smart. We can't say. She didn't take her boards.*

I leave the living room and go sit by myself in the laundry room, staring out the little window at Firdaus Apartments next door and its emptied top floors. Those who've left these old crumbling buildings for bigger cities, places in India or outside where hate doesn't define the lives of their children, will never come back. *History. English. Maths. Economics. Those would have been the first four exams. We will die here, and no one will come.* Words, numbers, dates, graphs have melted in the growing heat of the days. *We have become the data.* I'm scared I will forget because thinking is painful. Remembering kills.

In 2006, the day Papa dies will be the day of another exam. An undergraduate midterm for my television production class. I will be a sophomore then, hoping to someday become a journalist. A part of me will always want to join those brave people from NDTV and BBC who roamed our ravaged streets looking for our stories.

By 2006, I will be the girl who has won a silver medal from the state in her twelfth grade. I will be the girl who is always top of her class. In college, I will be the girl boys call *intimidating* because I walk around with big glasses and a bigger frown on my face. I will be the girl missing from every college party picture. I will be the girl who hears the news of her father dying, goes back to her bedroom, picks up her backpack, strings her college ID tag around her neck and walks out the door. In the exam hall, I will be the girl whom the teachers will watch like a bird about to take flight. They will let her write for as long as she physically can. Then the professor will see this girl put her pen down, gently pry the paper out of her hands and say, 'Go home, Zara.'

Right now, I don't know this girl. I sit in the laundry room, hugging my knees, feeling my brain start to compartmentalise, little monkeys pushing carts around, gathering the scattered furniture of my tenth-grade education and packing it away for another day, whenever it comes. For now, my brain prepares the space I need to be *this* girl.

The one who watches from behind glass doors as the Sabarmati's barren bed stretches from our side to theirs, and beyond it, I am the girl who stares at an empty future for all Muslims, for every girl like me, an emptiness where we roam the streets drugged with fear, where we hastily mumble our assalaamalaikums in public so the sound doesn't identify us, where we cut our beards and take off our caps and hijabs and dupattas, where our men are forced to drop their pants so their circumcisions can be checked before they round us up and burn us, where cows sit in the middle of newly paved roads stained in our blood.

The phone rings. It's Mana asking if I want to come down to her flat.

'Not to study, of course!' she says, giggling nervously. 'Uska toh koi fayda nahin.' What use is studying when the state is teaching us a lesson? This is going to become an inside joke, gallows humour for Muslim children.

'You want to watch *Kaun Banega Crorepati*?' Mana asks. I mull over that for a second. Who doesn't Want to Be a Millionaire in the middle of their own genocide? Behind me I can hear Apa lecturing Amma, in that precocious voice of hers, about how I shouldn't stop reviewing my lessons even with the postponement. *I will lose momentum.*

My body has been in fight-or-flight for a month now. I wake up at the slightest squeak and sleep with all my day clothes on. I'm not sure what momentum she thinks I need.

'*I'll* even help her if she wants,' she's offering, and I can hear my mother helplessly mutter, 'Thank you, beta.'

I whisper into the phone with urgency, 'Coming!' and slam down the receiver. I put on my chappals and fly out the door.

Annapurna

All ancient cultures of the world have a vegetation deity. They're what one might call a mythological trope—a powerful god or goddess whose presence makes the seasons happen, plants, trees and fruits grow, cycles flow. Their absence throws the universe into grave imbalance; everything alive starts to get consumed by hunger, starvation and deprivation. In Indian mythology, this force is Parvati, the feminine goddess of nature and energy, who brings equilibrium to Shiva's often-unchecked masculine power, with which he creates and destroys as his mood pleases.

Shiva's and Parvati's tales are filled with anecdotes of passion and all-consuming love but also illustrate their mercurial tempers, their volatile disagreements and their philosophical, esoteric debates, which sometimes last a couple eons. In that sense, they are South Asia's first marriage of equals.

One story is about an argument where Shiva insists that everything in the material plane—homes, farms, agriculture, family life—is merely maya, *illusion*. He says the food people eat to survive isn't even real. He essentially tells his wife that her work *is not really work*.

Parvati is furious. She does what all wives do when their husbands act like they are god's gift to mankind. She fumes so hard in silence that she disappears.

With Parvati gone, seasons fall out of sync. Famine and desperation pour through the void. Parents plead, gods and demons beg with sunken, hungry eyes. Shiva descends into a deep depression.

But Parvati is not gone. When she can't bear the cries of suffering any longer, she sheds her old skin and takes on a new avatar—Annapurna, a moon-faced, high-breasted goddess in red and purple robes, holding a golden bowl of porridge in one palm and a bejewelled spoon in the other. She sets up a food pantry in a mythological town called Kashi. (Later, as modern humans of the democratic nation of India start to break down mosques looking for mythological gods, many will insist Kashi is the present-day town of Banaras.)

As hungry crowds flood Annapurna's kitchen, a beggar lines up, holding out his bowl. This is Shiva, worn and humbled, come to submit himself at the feet of this mysterious goddess, ready to acknowledge that, without the feminine or food, no life, no joy can exist.

As I said: Annapurna isn't the only vegetation deity in the world. In Mesopotamia they had Ishtar. The Egyptians had Isis. In C-8 Jasmine, we had Amma.

In our new curfew schedule, after dinner we go down to Mana's apartment to hang out with the girls while their mother, Shilu auntie, watches the news, her dupatta covering half her head, the rest stuffed between her lips. The national news makes us feel as though the whole world can see Gujarat. People in the UK and the US are protesting our chief minister. Bollywood and theatre celebrities are offering platitudes of concern on talk shows. Yet somehow no help is reaching us. Nobody can end this damn curfew. Nobody can bring us back to 'normal'. We are addicted to this news of our own demise. Like a zombie, Shilu auntie stares into the blur of incidents, reports, statistics and moving images. Her sister, who lives close by, calls just then.

Shilu auntie finishes speaking to her and looks at us, worried. 'Rumour hai ke kal yeh log doodh ke packet ko poison karne wale hain.' Apparently, since the mob can't break into tightly packed and cloistered Muslim neighbourhoods like ours, they're going to poison our milk deliveries.

I giggle, imagining a highly motivated group of young Gujarati boys squatting by a milk truck, carefully injecting poison into each plastic pouch. I've often seen people at the railway station pouring polluted tap water into discarded plastic bottles like this, resealing and selling them on trains as bottled mineral water. *Typhoid by tainted water* is Papa's biggest fear and why he made me carry a canteen of double-filtered home water to every birthday party I attended, even though I wasn't three years old anymore.

Our household buys four packets of milk each day from the local dairy wala. All of it is smelly, largely unprocessed buffalo milk. Three packets are without fat, one with, so Amma can set yoghurt in her little steel bowl with a green chilli in it.

'Isn't our milkman a Muslim, auntie?' I ask.

'No, beta, he's that Gujarati uncle from the chowk behind. Anyway, he mixes in so much water with the milk!'

She sees my stunned face and chortles, as if trying to wipe away my fear. I don't want to judge this invisible man who has lived in Khanpur with us so long. I've never seen his face, only the orphan packets lying on our doormat when I grab the newspaper in the mornings. *He is one of us.*

'Pata nahin, abhi kuchh bhi ho sakta hai,' she sighs, and turns to the TV again. Indeed, we don't know. Anything can happen.

Shilu auntie is someone I adore. Her loud cackles have always knocked me out of my childlike seriousness. When her second daughter, Farha, a pale, green-eyed little cherub, got slapped by the Gujarati-language teacher at Mount Carmel one day for not doing her verbs, I remember Shilu auntie holding her and laughing, saying, 'Arre jalti hai woh. Usko sirf ek language aati hai. Tumko teen aati hai.' It was true. The Gujarati teacher was perhaps overcome to see this beautiful Muslim child who, unlike her, spoke English, Hindi-Urdu and Gujarati, who could hold so much in her little body. We all laughed at Farha's misery.

Watching Shilu auntie sitting like a statue now, legs wrapped around the foot of her table, jaw clamped down on her dupatta, the same one she wore to pray to Allah for her daughters' well-being, it really feels like anything is possible, as crazy as it sounds.

The milk arrives at dawn every day in small tempo rickshaws just after the morning namaz. Crates full of two-hundred-millilitre pouches, dewy from the ice block they are transported on, are carried into each apartment building. The delivery-man goes floor by floor, starting at the top and winding his way down the stairs, dropping each family's order into the worn tote bag they hang on their latch. If we forget to put a bag out, he leaves the packets on our doormat. Papa yells his head off about the germs when that happens. As I rush downstairs to catch my school autorickshaw, I catch a glimpse of Jasmine's inhabitants—the second-floor Parsi uncle in his white sadra and pajamas, the fifth-floor Bohri grandmother in her namaz dupatta and ridaah, the beautiful young daughter-in-law on the seventh floor with the thick, long, plaited hair, always in a frilly nightie. Wrinkled but ramrod-straight Pant auntie in her block-print sleeveless nightgown. Braless.

After our game finishes, Misba and I go back upstairs to find everyone winding down for the night. Nobody bothers to ask where we've been. The gates of Jasmine are so tightly locked now day or night, it's not like we can run off anywhere. Plus, we live in a post–school night world. No child in our building has gone to school since the day the train burned.

I find Amma in the kitchen, wiping down the counter, and barge in with this news.

'Ma, Shilu auntie says tomorrow they're going to poison the milk!'

Amma lets out an exhausted laugh. 'What! Why would they do that?'

With each passing day in lockdown, I am convinced my family is going to die of sheer denial and complacency.

She walks away to ask Phupu, whom she trusts to know the latest. Phupu is lying on Dadi's bed with Apa cuddling up next to her.

Dadi is pacing around blowing protective dua'as all over her apartment after her night namaz. She blows less on us humans and more on her chandeliers.

'Zara, just massage my legs, no?' Phupu says.

I do it. Phupu after her night shot of coffee is not someone one should argue with.

I'm pressing my fingers past her deep-purple varicose veins as Amma tells her the news/rumour. Phupu chews on it.

'Sounds ridiculous. But . . .' She shrugs. 'Abhi kuchh bhi ho sakta hai.'

It is strange to hear Phupu, an economics professor who prides herself on dealing in fact, echo Shilu auntie, who is known to relish a good rumour. But it turns out that evening Shilu auntie isn't the only one who has heard this about the milk. The family pir, Shah Sahab, telephones with a similar warning.

The next morning Khanpur's drains run white as residents from each apartment building, hundreds of little boxes in Ahmedabad's grainy sky, pour their milk down the drain, and with it, their trust.

Misba and I sit at breakfast drinking lemon squeezed in water and buttered toast. Papa, the dairy lover in the family, grumbles irritably, cheated of his daily glass of milk. He takes an extra calcium supplement from his medicine cabinet. If this apocalypse lasts all year, we might still be able to survive on his hoard of American Centrum jars sent by Amma's family.

It was probably not true—in fact very likely untrue—that anyone would try to poison a whole neighbourhood through milk. Later, when this is over, many families will switch to the boxed, pasteurised stuff sold in supermarkets. But this is how delicate the foundations of community—a broken community—become. Jasmine didn't fall in the once-in-a-century earthquake. But its inhabitants are slowly crumbling now. All it takes is one act of hate, one whisper, rumour, unchallenged bias. Little lies we've been told about one another start to circle the drain, drawing us deeper towards a dark spiral, pouring our collective lives into free fall.

After breakfast, I help Gulshan make the beds the way Dadi likes them, envelope ends folded and tucked tightly. I ask her, 'Tum log ne bhi doodh phenk diya?' *Did you all also throw away your milk?*

Gulshan looks at me with amusement and love. 'Hum log doodh peete ich nahin!' *Throwing milk away was a luxury afforded to those who could buy it.*

Later the same afternoon, Amma and Gulshan take stock of our last remaining groceries. Amma will have to divide the meat in the freezer into even smaller packets and ration how she uses it. We're down to our last four potatoes. Dinner that night is roti and a potato dish that is more water, less potato.

'Can you guess how many I used?' she asks me.

'You used all four!' I say in panic as I watch Phupu going for seconds and heaping more on Apa's plate.

'No. Just one!' She smiles triumphantly.

She tells me how she learnt to make this aaloo nu shaak from her Gujarati neighbour when she had just moved to Baroda with Papa. The kind Hindu lady across from their flat had shown her how to save on groceries by extracting maximum flavour from minimum veggies.

'And if it's too watery, besan zindabad!' Amma grins, putting away the gram flour she padded the curry with.

She is in a real mood tonight. As I grow older, I see this pattern in Amma during a crisis. When others wither in the face of hardship, she lights up. She's at her most resourceful in a disaster, as if some part of her has tucked away every bad thing that happened to her in this emotional survival kit. She becomes possessed, powerfilled.

Over the next week she continues to surprise us, once making a single potato stretch for two meals for eight people. When the potatoes finally run out, she makes kadhi and khichdi, and we eat it with pickle or papad. But Papa remains unimpressed and complains that this food is making him feel 'weak'. He scolds Amma at the table one afternoon.

'Kya hai yeh khaana? Enough of this watered-down nonsense. Find out where the others are buying their vegetables.'

Amma and Gulshan find out from the watchman network that smuggled vegetables and gas cylinders are being sold on the riverbed in the evenings. The next day the women make their way down to the front steps just as curfew is lifted for an hour. Much like I did the evening of the Godhra burning, I retreat into prayer for my mother's safety. The two women slip into the tiny lane between our buildings, weave through the narrow back alleys and sneak past the slums. Gulshan leads Amma past her own hovel and onto the sandy riverbank.

There they buy overpriced onions, potatoes, ladies' fingers, squash, tomatoes. Amma puts these in a cloth bag on her shoulder. Then they buy a black-market gas cylinder. We are running low on gas. For once Amma doesn't haggle and pays the inflated rates. She and Gulshan haul it onto Gulshan's slight shoulders, Amma bends her knees and holds up the base, and the two women, Amma a tall and stout five feet eight inches and Gulshan a petite but solid five feet, hobble back to Jasmine Apartments through the back alleys once more.

They arrive at the doorstep heaving the cylinder and supplies between them. I run to the front door the minute I hear the lift dock. Both women look exhilarated, their faces flushed. Backs hurting, they pour into the kitchen with their loot, adrenaline coursing through their veins, giggles filling the hallway.

Papa walks into the kitchen to see what the excitement is all about. He surveys all the vegetables being laid out on proud display and the shiny red cylinder sitting in the middle of the kitchen floor. Gulshan gives Amma a cup of water and fills her own steel glass. Amma's face is shining with sweat as she watches Papa process the bounty she's brought home. Not a word of thanks escapes Papa's pursed lips. Not a word of acknowledgement for what the women have done while the man of the house lay in bed rereading *Seven Habits of Highly Effective People*.

He shakes his head.

'Chalo. Abhi kuchh achha banaao. Aaloo kha-kha ke thak gaye.' *Good, make something nice now. I'm tired of the damn potatoes.*

The light dims in Amma's eyes. Gulshan sips on her water slowly till he leaves the kitchen. Then she puts her glass down and touches my mother's arm.

'Chhodo bhabhi, Bhai aise-ich hain.' *Leave it, sister. You know he's like this only.*

Amma sets her chin back up and starts scrubbing the grime off the potatoes.

Misba's Birthday

When I ask them, nobody can recall what we did for Misba's birthday in the last few days of March 2002. Not even Misba. That's how used to being invisible she became in those months after the train burned.

'There was cake,' she says vaguely when I ask if she remembers. 'I don't care, honestly. We had other things to worry about then.'

That's just how Misba shuts down anything that threatens to hurt. I count back to 2002 and realise that year was her thirteenth birthday.

Amma insists there was cake. 'I ordered it myself from Holiday Inn,' she adds proudly, which also usually means she paid for it with some tutoring or Diwali card–painting money. The same Holiday Inn across from our building, whose manager had kindly allowed Papa and our neighbours to hide our cars in the hotel's parking, had also been the way we'd afforded this tiny luxury, to celebrate this coming-of-age for our youngest. *Or was it?* Phupu couldn't have baked the cake, we agree, though she was always the star baker of the family. There were no extra eggs, butter and milk floating around during the curfew with which we could treat ourselves.

Yes, it must have been the Holiday Inn.

Yes, we were so busy recounting stories of gore and blood, of how they took everything from people sleeping in their homes, including their humanity, counting the rapes and deaths of young girls as tiny as eight and nine. Who could be bothered about a child sitting *safe* in an apartment losing only her memory, so that one day she would call these her blank years?

This was just another thing lost. She was just another forgotten daughter in a city on fire.

Uniform

It's a month since the train burned. From our balcony, if we squint hard enough, we can spot the clump of trees behind which our school lies. Other children have started to go back in through its gates. Other children who live across the river. Other children who are not being hunted. Not us.

I have been having this recurring nightmare. In it, Misba and I walk across the riverbed in our grey-and-white pinafore school uniforms. Misba and I are trying to take a shortcut to school instead of the longer, winding autorickshaw ride. They say in the news mobs stop autos and tempos and cars filled with Muslims and burn everyone inside. In my nightmare, my own two feet are all I trust. But as Misba and I put one foot in front of the other, in my dream brain, I am also mapping each way we can cut across and run back home to Amma and Papa in case a mob shows up. *Should I push her to run diagonally away from me or keep her with me so we can die together*? my dream brain asks.

In the nightmare, we're always more than halfway across the riverbed when the herd of angry men and women appears and starts to chase us. We break into a run, holding hands, abandoning the idea of school, turning back towards the slum where Gulshan lives. *Get there and you're safe*, my dream brain knows. From behind the slums, sometimes I see Jasmine rising into the sky, smoke billowing from its top, on the eighth floor. It's always too late. We are always running towards ashes.

When I wake up and reach for her baby-soft palm next to mine, I realise how silly the dream is. I don't have to go to school anymore. My boards will never be announced. But Misba will have to eventually.

A few days after the boards' postponement, Misba and I are sitting on Amma's bed, watching Phupu, who has the cordless phone pressed to her ear and is listening intently. Her face is a placid, dead river. She's listening to Sister Vimla, our school principal. Sister Vimla is new and doesn't care for the old relationships that schools like Mount Carmel once shared with families like ours. Minorities looking after minorities, missionaries making alliances with those who needed them most to break through the systems of caste and class built to maintain the status quo, where anyone not of upper-caste, Hindu birth is an outsider, someone to withhold access from, someone to keep servile. In return, we gave our schools all our hearts. Students like Papa and Phupu had continued their relationship with their schools through the decades, visiting their ageing Irish principal at the hospice where he now lived, driving home their old Scottish English teacher for Sunday lunches, and teaching us to serve them khaana and sit at their feet and listen to anecdotes.

But Sister Vimla is from a new generation of Gujarati nuns. She is from within the system. I don't like her from the day she takes the job. She has an evil glint in her eyes; she has changed all our secular morning prayers to Hindu bhajans. She mocks the poor students for their stained uniforms. It's like she knows something about surviving in Gujarat that we still don't understand. She looks and acts like someone who knows where power rests and how to align herself with it.

'I'm sorry, Zahida ben, rules are rules. The child will have to come to class, or she will fail the year.' Her snipe shoots through the phone.

Phupu's voice is lowered, respectful, the way convent girls are trained to do when speaking to our nuns. But there is a growl in it. I can tell because I know when Phupu gets like that, when she isn't getting her way.

All-girls convent schools up till the nineties were some of the last places a young teenage girl like me could briefly glimpse all the other Indias that existed for other girls—the rich industrialist India of the Hindu Gujarati Ayesha, who flaunted her 'stylish' Muslim name and mocked me for wearing a shalwar under my uniform because my mother couldn't afford expensive stockings. I remember how in ninth grade she told the teacher she wanted to study economics in London and work in 'world development'. Or the India of the Parsi Hazel, whose mother died when we were in elementary school, who protected broken birds, and whose father played the guitar for our annual concerts. Or the India of Sumbul, whose mother, a proud professor of literature, wore the burkha. Or the India of Naomi, who spoke with a strange American accent and once came to my two-hundred-rupee birthday party in Jasmine and spent all evening on Dadi's bed waiting for her parents to pick her up because at my party we didn't rent chairs. My attendees sat on the floor on a plastic mat. The India of Natasha and Nandini, of Snigdha and Rujuta, and a million Mansis and Priyankas, and Priyas, and Nehas, once even an Aplu. Of girls whose parents sent them to expensive dance classes and music tutors and who thus played all the lead parts while the rest of us got cast as trees and traffic lights. This India of girls, with their neon-painted nails and bleached hair, who sat in groups based on the brand of car they carpooled to school in, taught us autorickshaw girls from the old city that there were ways we could also pass as something else in the world if we mimicked their plastic sheen. But most of us couldn't be bothered. We sat in our India, a huddle on the same shared, broken basketball court, the smells of our chicken samosas and mutton rolls drawing groans of disgust from the militantly vegetarian Jains and Gujaratis around.

But as Ahmedabad grew from a sleepy army town to a manufacturing and industrial hub, Mount Carmel drifted from its hundred-year-old tradition of equal and quality education. It became like all the other Hindu schools in the city where our parents wouldn't dare enroll us. Under Sister Vimla, our teachers openly accepted 'gifts' from rich parents, and it showed in the grades their children got; class prefects were 'elected' on similar whims, elite Hindu children primed to sail through the system with glowing progress reports and recommendations, while our fifth-grade maths teacher, Miss Poonam, would throw my workbook across the classroom floor after learning I was Muslim. 'Good for nothing,' she would spit.

Phupu hangs up and relays Sister Vimla's decision to us. Misba, who until now has been bouncing on the bed nervously, slumps and melts into Phupu's big frame. Phupu looks a little shaken too, absent-mindedly stroking Misba's silky hair.

Like Dada, she has a soft spot for Misba. Once Papa was trying to slink out the front door to go down to the street, where in the alley between the buildings he would have his monthly rendezvous with the bootlegger. Chubby three-year-old Misba marched up to him.

'Drink lene jaa rahe ho?' *Going to get some booze?*

Papa was stunned at his baby daughter's audacity and clarity. She had learnt to recognise his grey-and-black striped duffel bag as much as the heavy guilt in his gait. He scowled at her, then, realising how she was too little to face his wrath, he slowly let out a nervous laugh and hurried away.

'She's got no filter,' Phupu hooted with joy. She had watched this takedown of her brother with fascination. She threw her head back and laughed.

That week the curfew starts to relax for a few hours every morning. The killing across the state has slowed. Now it happens in far-off forested areas in the north and south of the state. The fire has moved from the centre outwards.

Phupu announces she will go across the bridge and check on her apartment, collect fresh clothes for Apa and herself. She offers to drop Misba at school on her way and bring her back while Papa mutters in the background, 'Let her just skip the year. What is all this risk for? Not like she'll miss anything.' But in a home where Misba is mocked and bullied for her colour, her weight, her filter-less chatter, her love for chocolate, or that she might never amount to anything compared to her brilliant older cousin and skinny, fair-skinned sister, Phupu knows Misba needs school. She packs the kid in her Hyundai and takes off.

Amma and I wait all morning for our baby girl to return to us. We stare down the clock, willing time to leap ahead to 2 P.M. We stare down the phone, hoping it won't ring with any more bad news.

At two thirty, Misba returns home, hiding in Phupu's shadow. Her natural bounding delight is missing. She is quiet the rest of the day.

'It was fine,' she says with a shrug every time one of us asks her how her first day back in the classroom went. Later that night, Amma sits down on our mattress, pulls Misba into her lap, and coaxes it out of her.

'This girl . . . she's been in my class since first grade. Rich Gujju kid. I just thought since we are all under curfew, she must also be, so I asked her, "How was it for you all?"' Misba's big saucer eyes fill up.

'She just laughed at my face, Mummy. She said, "What curfew? My brother went to loot the shops."'

I don't want to push her, but I know my sister. She's always so fearless. I want to know.

'What did you say?'

'Nothing,' she replies, hugging Amma's knee. 'I just sat there.'

Next morning, Misba has regained some of her spirit. She refuses to go to school anymore. Phupu gets on the phone, calling every Jesuit brother, sister, father and mother she knows in the city.

'I'll call the pope if I have to,' she declares.

Sister Vimla finally agrees to let Misba sit out the year on 'compassionate grounds'.

We don't know then what children across Gujarat are enduring just so they can go to school. In the days after the train burning, 108 miles from us, a crowd of almost ten thousand people gathered outside a madrassa in Bhavnagar, a sleepy town in southern Gujarat. The crowd was yelling and brandishing swords, tridents and crude bombs, thirsting for the blood of the 450 Muslim children and teachers inside.

Since 9/11, the word 'madrassa', an Urdu word for 'school', had become something akin to saying 'RDX' or 'dynamite' in this modern lexicon of Islamic terror. When we watched CNN and the BBC in the months following the Twin Towers attack, it was almost comical to hear Western news presenters bite around the word, then dramatically announce 'crackdowns' on such buildings in the UK and rural Pakistan and Afghanistan.

My sisters and I studied the Quran in our homes, taught by maulanas often raised and educated in madrassas. And if you ever met them, you would know why this media obsession with these schools' purported syllabus of propaganda and terror was funny. Our maulana, for instance, would march in each afternoon, and when we placed the Quran in front of him, he'd lick a fingertip, turn the page to where the day's lesson began, and then sheepishly smile.

'TV lagaaogey please? Aaj India–Australia ka match hai.' *Could you also please turn on the TV? India is playing Australia today.*

Maulana sahab would slurp his chai on those hot afternoons, keeping one eye on our tiny index fingers scraping across the beautiful calligraphy, the other eye fixed on the match score.

Madrassas have a long and rich history dating back further than the day Western media discovered them. And in Gujarat, that history extends as far as 636 C.E., when Islam first arrived on this westernmost coast of the subcontinent. Arab traders brought the faith but also science and astronomy, medicine, poetry and literature. Under the Gujarat sultans, these schools flourished, and swathes of lands were granted to madrassas to educate the public, both Muslim and non-Muslim. But history has rarely succeeded in overpowering human bias. In our home alone, each of us had a different attitude towards madrassas. Papa and Dadi felt people like our Maulana sahab were unkempt and uneducated and gave all Muslims a bad name because they chewed so much betel nut and spat everywhere. Amma woke up from her siesta to make Maulana sahab his chai and nashta because he reminded her of the maulanas who taught her own two mischievous brothers and her in their childhood. She'd regale us with tales of the pranks they'd pull on their sleepy teacher. Dada always had a soft spot for madrassas because one had offered safe harbour to a lost, runaway boy once, and made him the Chowdhary sahab he was.

So it wasn't totally surprising that one day the world woke up and decided that madrassas were breeding grounds of hate. Hate builds in microcosmic ways. That centuries of hate had built like sediment in the blood of Gujarat's Hindus, that now they were ready to spill the blood of four hundred innocent children, this was something we couldn't have foreseen when we laughed at those news pieces.

That morning as the mob flings burning tyres into the school, District Police Superintendent Rahul Sharma arrives with a hundred policemen. He recently arrived at this posting from his earlier position supervising Godhra—the town where the train burning took place—as superintendent of police for Western Railways. Sharma and his men now find the school building in Bhavnagar surrounded by a mob of thousands. Sharma warns the crowd over a loudspeaker to disperse. When they continue to press on, trying to tear through the school gates, Sharma draws a musket and fires.

After that first shot, the mob quickly breaks apart. Many flee.

It's shocking to think it was always that simple. Sharma decides to leave the madrassa in the care of a trusted junior officer and drive downtown to reinforce other teams fighting back similar attacks on Muslims. A hotel with foreign tourists is under siege elsewhere. A factory owned by a Muslim has been burnt to the ground.

'If something happens, don't hesitate to fire,' he tells his men.

A few hours later, Sharma's junior officer calls. The mob is back and growing in numbers. Sharma rushes back in his jeep but finds the main road leading to the school blocked by burning logs and tyres. He swerves off the tarred road and onto country trails, making his way to the back of the school building.

As his small team of policemen bravely holds back the mob at the gates, Sharma loads four hundred children and their two dozen teachers into a convoy of three buses he has arranged. He jumps back into his jeep and leads the convoy out onto the main road.

He turns up his wireless to full volume so radio chatter echoes from his vehicle. He wants the mob to think there is reinforcement, even though all he has are two other junior officers with him.

His men and he cut through the smoke-filled night, leading innocent souls into the safe refuge of the Ibrahim Masjid, in the middle of a safe Muslim enclave.

For doing his duty and saving innocent citizens, Officer Sharma is transferred again. On 26 March 2002, Rahul Sharma arrives at the Ahmedabad Police Control Room.

When he sees how shoddily the massacres at Gulbarg and Naroda Patiya have been recorded, how quickly the bodies burnt and disposed of, how several complaints are stuffed into single reports to reduce the total number of reports filed, Sharma raises an alarm with his seniors. He is asked to ignore it.

In those last days of March, as we wait for this hell to end, listlessly staring out our windows, giving thanks for merely being alive, somewhere in the same city Rahul Sharma is collecting cellular phone records of BJP ministers and party members like Dr Maya Kodnani and Dr Jaydeep Patel, who armed and led these hungry mobs to screaming children, women, and men. He will document instances of police dereliction of duty, of gross failure and apathy of the state, of complicity.

He will save these on CDs. Later, when investigators question the BJP leadership and this data is declared 'lost', Rahul Sharma will offer this vital piece of evidence. The state government in return will file a case against him for mishandling or inappropriately acquiring evidence. Rahul Sharma will take early voluntary retirement, a term our family understands well. But unlike Papa, he won't give up. He will become a public defender and continue to fight the good fight.

We don't know this yet, but 26 March, the day the good cop arrives in Ahmedabad, is the first time since the violence started, and the very last time ever, that my sister will go to school in that city.

Good Cop

The curfew was supposed to end by mid-March. But it's the end of the month now, and they've put us back under lockdown. In Ayodhya—the temple town, not the bungalow—the VHP, the Bajrang Dal and officers from Prime Minister Vajpayee's office participated in a ritual where two Hindu idols were acquired to be placed on the demolition site of the Babri Masjid. It's like pushing a hot prong into an open wound. For weeks we have been nervous in Ahmedabad, worrying that a new wave of death and mayhem will find us through this umbilical cord our city seems to share with Ayodhya. Later one day, we will learn that this cord was strong because more than half of the VHP's membership was from our state, Gujarat. That Gujarat was their 'laboratory'. For now, we sit imprisoned again inside our homes, while across the river hunters roam free. For now, neon lights from theatres and restaurants sparkle and bounce off the puddles in the Sabarmati riverbed, teasing our hunger.

Misba and I are helping Amma lay down our mattress in the living room when the phone rings. Phupu is at the table drinking her late-night cup of coffee. Amma answers the phone.

'Hello! Yes. This is Rukhsana, her mother.'

Our ears all instantly perk up. *Who could possibly want anything from one of Rukhsana's daughters?* Amma beckons me to the phone receiver.

'It's your teacher, Ms Preeti!' she says, as wide-eyed with surprise as I am.

'Zara!' My Hindu Punjabi history teacher bursts through the receiver. 'How are you, beta?'

To hear her call me 'child', someone who only saw me a few hours each week; to call me 'child', all of sixteen, scared and unsure if I'll ever see her again; to call me 'child' out of the tunnel of silence where no one has called us for weeks; to call me a child with care. Something about the word makes my chin wobble.

'Fine, Miss Preeti. It's so nice to hear from you.' There is that good convent school training again.

She asks if everyone in our building is okay. I mumble something. She asks if we have enough food and milk in the house. I pause.

After the Great Milk Drama last week, we've all learnt our lesson about rumours. The Chowdharys get twice as cranky without their evening chai, and Phupu stalks around looking for easy prey without her daily dose of thick, sweet Nescafé. Our caffeine fixes have since been restored, but we are still running low on everything else. Seven people stuck indoors all day with one another, with nothing but the news to watch, has made everyone come alive with hunger at meals.

Amma, Phupu and Apa watching me carefully. Papa will probably kill me for saying this, but I swallow hard and go for it.

'Actually, no. We're running out of everything.'

Miss Preeti asks me to put Amma back on the phone. Amma makes a face at me as if I've gotten her into trouble somehow. I shrug and walk away to the bathroom. I can hear Papa in the adjoining bathroom, running the flush. I can hear Amma listing food items outside. I pray Amma will end the call before he gets out.

Papa's footsteps arrive in the hall just as Amma hangs up. I pray Phupu won't tell on us. She doesn't.

Later that night, a police jeep pulls up outside Jasmine Apartments. A police constable gets out of the jeep, crosses the road. He rattles the big metal gates that guard the building. Hussain bhai lets him in. This is the first policeman to enter Jasmine since 27 February 2002. The constable rides up in the elevator to the eighth floor, crosses the empty hallway to where only we live. He rings the doorbell to C-8. Phupu opens the door. Papa and Dadi hover in the hallway. Amma and I don't go anywhere near the door.

We have always known that Ms Preeti's husband is a top-ranking police officer in the city. Which is why I wasn't expecting a call from her. I didn't think we had any bridge left between us.

But Ms Preeti has sent her husband's constable and a jeep full of produce: potatoes, tomatoes, onions, ladies' fingers, squash, spinach, butter, milk, flour, sugar and more. Enough not just for the seven of us but for at least two more homes. Amma makes packets of everything the next morning and dispatches us to Mana's house and to a family down the stairs from us.

To this day I have no words for the sound of that doorbell. The dread in my belly as it slowly turned to hope. The police commissioner had said, 'Even policemen are part of this society,' as if to suggest their bloodlust deserved priority over their sworn duty. And yet here was this constable carrying us food, sustenance, hope.

In the board exams I am no longer waiting for, our history syllabus included chapters on the Holocaust. All through tenth grade, Miss Preeti taught me history but also compassion for the story of a young girl, Anne, who lived and died across a chasm of time and distance from me. She placed a tattered copy of Anne's diary in my hands one school afternoon. Tonight, sitting across a river that won't let me see Miss Preeti anymore, I think of her. And what she did, by placing a book in my hand then and a bag full of ladies' fingers now. She has given me something to hold on to.

Flowers in Her Hair

Every birthday cake we ever had growing up, Phupu baked it. She'd be offended if we instead bought one from Papa's friend Uncle Lester, who owned a café on the other side of the river. Papa would also be slightly offended. Phupu's cakes were free. They only came with a slice of smug superiority.

Phupu's cakes were always some combination of dark and milk chocolate with Pickwick wafers and Gems for decoration. Mostly they were simple squares or circles. Once it was a house. They were always delicious. One year, she walked into the room in Jasmine where a small cupboard stood mostly stuffed with our school things and the toys Nanijaan sent for us from America. Phupu dug through the mess and pulled out a Barbie.

This was my last surviving one. Apa had pulled off the heads or scratched the faces of all the others. Phupu had seen a Barbie cake design and wanted to make it for her daughter. She was pumped. And she outdid herself. At Apa's birthday party, I watched as my Barbie stood tiptoed in a pink swimsuit, and from her tiny waist down, an impressive skirt of little pink frosted roses umbrellaed outward, cascading in concentric spirals.

Afterwards, the cake was sliced up and packed away, the gifts opened, wrapping paper folded for reuse. My Barbie sat in her pink swimsuit on the kitchen counter, smears of icing on her legs and arms. I reached up to the counter so I could take her home and give her a bath.

'What do you think you're doing?' Phupu's voice boomed from the kitchen, where she stood.

'Taking my doll back?' I meekly asked.

'Rubbish. That's not yours.' She stood there glowering at me for a minute, as if seeing in me a brother who always took what he wanted. Then she grabbed the doll and locked it up in her closet.

I could hate her for this in the way hate sometimes arises from the childish corners embedded inside our adult bodies. But Phupu also gave me so much.

For most of our childhood, she rode a scooter. And her scooter had a sidecar attached to it. Every time she needed to start it, she'd kick the pedal hard multiple times to get it to fire; then she would tilt the scooter, lifting the whole thing with the sidecar in the air to make the fuel flow toward the engine. We kids, along with the watchmen and bystanders in the street, would watch in awe when she did this.

'She's like a man,' people would say, gaping. Phupu would grin and wink at me, giving me this gift. This pride in watching a woman's body do things nobody believed she could.

Phupu was the only one willing to take us out for fun. Perhaps because she herself needed to get out and get away. She would pile us all in—Apa and I clinging to each other on the seat behind her, Misba in Amma's lap in the sidecar—and take us for late-night ice cream in the bustling Municipal Market. We'd go to a soft-serve shop called Chills, Thrills, Frills. We hated going there with Papa. He would order the ice creams, collect them, distribute them, and then make us roll up our windows and hurriedly slurp melting cones in the suffocating heat, piled one on top of the other in the Fiat. All because the dust would get in and settle on the ice cream and give us sore throats.

But with Phupu we would sit on the pavement watching the night bazaar, all the skimpily dressed college kids from the newer side of the city, the neon lights of the market haloes around their freedoms and ours.

Phupu taught me how razors and waxing worked. She was the

first person I told when I got my period. She was the first woman I heard laugh out loud at male underwear commercials.

'That chaddi is definitely stuffed with a carrot,' she would boom while the rest of us squirmed and Papa hurried to change the channel.

In 1993, a movie called *Damini* was released. It was the story of a young woman married into a joint family who witnesses her brother-in-law rape the servant and decides to testify in court for the victim. In the process she is slut-shamed, institutionalised and declared insane.

The men in our family thought the trailer was 'too much', and my grandmother thought the lead actor was too chubby. So Phupu piled us girls in her sidecar. Wind in our hair, singing songs from the movie, we arrived at the derelict old single-screen Rupali Cinema. The movie was intense, and as I looked away from the violence, I caught Phupu's face in the dark hall, her tiny diamond nose ring glinting. Suddenly I noticed her eyes glinting too. The world called women like my phupu and Damini crazy, mainly because women like my phupu and Damini scared the world.

That night yet another fight burned through our home, Papa spitting angrily over why Phupu wasn't contributing to the house expenses, how he suspected she was saving up for her own apartment and letting him pay everyone's bills. She spat back at him, 'Why shouldn't I? They spent everything on you. What did I get?'

It was like watching a home-video version of *Damini*. Phupu ranted at this brother trying to lecture her on equality. He'd stolen the most from her. Papa barked, and she barked back louder. The next morning, he woke up with the stench of whisky in his pores, sulked his way to the bathroom and growled at Amma for his breakfast. Phupu made herself an extra-strong cup of coffee, downed it, put on a starched block-printed cotton sari, smeared on a bright-pink lipstick and walked out the door.

. . .

As I grew older, I confided more in Phupu. Before I ever told my own mother about this, I told Phupu about a family friend who had touched me when I was younger. This was a few months before the train burned. We were spending the day at Phupu's apartment. I was taller, older, braver now, but still terrified of visiting this family friend, and we had been invited to his house for dinner.

I was about to make an excuse when Misba spoke. She told Phupu that she felt 'weird' around this man. Shame rose in my belly, as did a blinding anger. I couldn't bear the thought that he had also perhaps touched my baby sister.

Phupu, who was relaxing in her bed, sat up. 'You are imagining things.'

Then Apa, who had been quietly listening from the foot of the bed, sat down next to Misba and me. 'They're not lying, Ma. I was trying to go to the bathroom in their house last time and he blocked my way.'

Phupu watched us in silence.

'Then why didn't you all say something before?' she said, her pitch rising. She drew herself up from the bed and put on her slippers. 'I'm going to call them right now'—my heart froze—'and say we're not going.'

As she left the room, we cousins crumpled into one another, arms entangled in awkward hugs. I heard Phupu repeat, 'We're never going there again.'

In March 2002, journalists find a woman named Madina Sheikh, a wounded lion like my phupu, in the Kalol refugee camp. She's from a village outside Ahmedabad.

When reports of attacks trickled in, Madina's family decided to split up and move into their neighbours' homes to hide. The next morning, the hut where she, her eighteen-year-old daughter Shabana and her niece Suhana were hiding was set on fire. Madina and the young girls ran out, heading for the fields around them.

Madina remembers the screams of her family, of the men as they were discovered, stabbed and cut to pieces one by one. She remembers the screams of children. Then she remembers watching as two men from her own village, *family friends*, pulled away her daughter.

'I could hear her screams as they passed her around, raping her.' Another *family friend* found Suhana, Madina's niece.

Madina hid within the wilting crop and watched as the young girls were raped by men they'd grown up with.

'My daughter was like a flower, still to experience life,' Madina tells the journalists. 'I heard them say, "Cut them to pieces; leave no evidence."' Madina crouched all night in the field, watching her flowers turn into flames. Madina tells anyone who will listen how Suhana and Shabana tried to save each other, that they died within feet of each other. Madina sits in the camp, an aunt and mother who has nothing left but the looping memory of how she couldn't save the girls.

'Then . . . it became quiet' is all she says.

Phupu, Amma and we girls spend our curfew nights watching journalists, outraged and shocked by these brutalities, report these stories on national television. Mothers with ghostly pale faces, women who jerk away from a helping hand, girls pushing away mics and cameras, staring blankly into hopeless futures. From time to time, it becomes too much to stomach and we stare away from the screen, letting the blackness beyond our balcony swallow us. Somewhere out there, aunts and mothers like Madina are lying awake on threadbare mattresses. The journalists have left with their stories. The survivors are left with their nightmares. At night, Misba, a child who never lets anyone except Amma hug her, allows me to hold her close, letting the warmth of our breaths remind us of the gift Amma has given us in birthing us as sisters. Phupu makes us massage her feet every night. But now she kisses our foreheads. We know she's breathing the smell of our hair in. We are still here. This is what we have.

. . .

And then there is the other Shabana, a distant cousin from Dadi's village. This Shabana and her family now live in Ahmedabad. This Shabana has milky skin, a smile full of mystery, and dark, cascading hair that falls to her knees. This Shabana looks like a girl who has waited all her young life to be married.

Phupu is known around town for her matchmaking skills. And it makes sense. As a college professor, she has hundreds of young people crossing her path. And Phupu, like her brother, has eagle eyes. She can spot them from a mile: young men and women who will make 'good' husbands and wives. Despite her own divorce, Phupu remains a consummate romantic. Her home is an open invitation for students from both sides of the river and from out of town in this small college community. She feeds them, celebrates their birthdays, holds them when their hearts break; she mentors them in their career choices, fixes their marriages, encourages their elopements. Everyone's parents owe her. She knows everyone. When she spots the soft yearning in Shabana's doe eyes, her brain whirs into motion, flipping through the phone book of eligible young men she can introduce her to.

She decides on a boy who is 'a total dream', to hear Phupu describe him. A Muslim dentist with his own established practice, and from a family full of dentists. He is educated, well-spoken, and when he meets Shabana, he is adequately besotted by her beauty and gentleness. The next time I see her, she hugs and thanks me, blushing, as if not just Phupu but I have found her a husband. Now the Chowdharys are to be guests of honour at the wedding.

'Who knows?' Shabana winks and smiles at Apa and me. 'Maybe you will find someone at my wedding!'

Apa and I smile uncomfortably. Won't that be a relief. To find one of these 'dream' boys and escape this madhouse. And so, secretly hopeful but pretending not to care, Apa and I spend a lot of time designing our clothes for Shabana's wedding. We have just sent our measurements and mountains of fabric, lace, buttons and zardozi borders to the tailor to stitch our lehengas and kurtas when the Sabarmati Express burns.

By mid-March of 2002, we have nothing to do but lie on our bellies all day, wondering if everyone else who is alive and Muslim like us is also languishing in lockdown. Apa and I talk a lot about Shabana. It has been a dramatic month for all of us, but no one more in our circle than Shabana.

On 28 February, just as Phupu and Apa moved in, the phone rang. It was T auntie, Phupu's old friend and Shabana's going-to-be mother-in-law. They were under attack. This family, who till 27 February had been busy planning their only son's wedding, were standing in their apartment, thirteen women and two men huddled together in a few square feet. As T auntie sobbed into the phone for help, a mob of four thousand angry VHP and Bajrang Dal murderers gathered outside their balcony. The mob had started by burning every Muslim car and scooter parked downstairs. Then they started to launch flaming rags into the apartment. Some police had arrived. But instead of quelling the mob, they shot tear-gas shells over the apartment gates. A stone hurled from the street had hit and injured the T auntie's husband; someone had shot a bullet at Shabana's fiancé. He was lying, gripping his chest, in the living room. His aunts visiting from the United States for his wedding were sobbing over him. T auntie begged Phupu to send help, to call whoever she knew, to do something, anything.

For long, excruciating minutes, Phupu was on the phone with them, as this horror unfolded on the other side. We listened in on ours. If Phupu could, she would have got into her Santro and driven off to their building across the river. Instead, she stood by the majoos helplessly listing cops or influential parents of students she could try calling.

'Give me a few minutes,' she said to T auntie, as gently as I'd ever heard her speak.

She called everyone in her phone book. She knew at least two

Muslim police officers. Both were hiding in their own homes with their families. The Hindu friends she called mumbled incoherent excuses.

Afterwards we didn't hear from T auntie for two weeks. Phupu sat gripping the back of her chair at the dining table every time the phone rang.

Yesterday we finally heard from them. They were alive. They were in hiding. She wouldn't say where.

Shabana's family tell us the rest. When no help arrived, T auntie's husband, a dentist and national rifle-shooting champion, took out his licensed pistol and shot at the mob. One person crumpled and fell. The mob and cops shot back at the father. For four hours, the father fought four thousand people through the window of their apartment. Ultimately, police reinforcement arrived later that night, and the crowd dispersed. Two men were arrested: Shabana's wounded fiancé and his father.

'How she must be feeling, no?' Apa is saying, eyes tinged with tears. 'This week would have been her mehndi ceremony.'

I can see how much Apa cares for Shabana. Perhaps because her mother has pointed all her affections at them. Apa always does as her mother does.

'She met Mom yesterday, when we went to clean the apartment,' Apa says.

The two men are still languishing in jail. A chatty policeman told them that if they hadn't done what they did—shot at the crowd—'they would have also ended up like Gulbarg Society'.

Nineteen cars and three homes were burnt in their community. People who'd lived there for decades fled. T auntie tried to return to the apartment to sort through their burnt belongings last week but found a man standing at their gate. He threatened her, yelled at them to never come back. The family decided to obey.

Two days later is the day Shabana would have got married. We wake up to this realisation ourselves, thinking of her, how she would have felt if the train had never burned, if our lives had never melted away with it.

'She would have been brushing her mehndi off.'

'She'd be putting flowers in all that long beautiful hair!'

'She'd be fussing over a zit.'

Instead she comes to meet Phupu, her matchmaking prophet, dressed in black, long hair pulled back in a severe plait.

'He is telling me I should move on,' she says between strangled sobs. She has just visited her fiancé in jail.

For months afterwards, Phupu will hold the girl in her arms as she mourns the wedding she almost had, refusing to let go of her newfound love. Phupu will put strong cups of caffeine in her palms, tell her in that firm but gentle voice that she needs to remain strong. This is where she becomes a woman, not in some wedding shamiana.

'You are lucky he is still alive,' Phupu will remind her. We are all lucky to be alive.

A year later, when a committee—constituted by the chief minister, which will eventually exonerate the state and minimise the pogrom—calls for victims to testify, no Muslim will show up. The boy's father will be a lone, first voice.

'People were screaming all around us, hurling threats: "Tamne jivta balvana che."' *We will burn you all alive.*

T auntie won't want him to speak up, to endanger the fragile peace they have just found—a small, nondescript home, a simple, no-fuss wedding for their son. But her husband will call this their bonus life. Their old one, he will say, ended the day a mob surrounded them. The day the police arrested and imprisoned instead of saved them. The day their frantic calls went unanswered.

'I am the secretary of the Ahmedabad Dental Practitioners Association, but no one came to help me in jail. No one has asked since how I am doing.'

Among the mob he will identify a man who was the state minister of revenue at the time, Haren Pandya. The following year, Haren Pandya will be found murdered on a morning walk near a park in Ahmedabad. Later, a committee called the Concerned Citizens Tribunal, panelled by retired judges and social justice activists, will claim that Haren Pandya had spoken to them, on condition of anonymity, about a meeting convened by the chief minister on the night the train burned, asking all the state's top officials to expect a *Hindu reaction* to Godhra, saying that *they should not do anything to contain this reaction.*

I will never see Shabana or her family after 2002, not know what happened to her beyond that shared fiery spring of our lives. All I will remember is the wedding that didn't happen.

Later, one day in 2010, Phupu will be back on her college campus. After a full day on her feet teaching, she will return to her chair in the staff room. It will have been years since either Misba or I have massaged her legs for her. At least two years since we have spoken. It will be a random spring day when a clot from a clogged varicose vein in Phupu's leg will travel up to her brain and bring this woman, thrumming with life and fight, to a thundering silence. She will crumple in her chair and never awake.

She will be laid to rest next to the father she fiercely loved and the brother she fiercely fought. Equal at last. Shabana and her family will be there to see her off. Misba will be there to bow her head before this fallen giant. Apa will be there to kiss her beloved mother goodbye. I will not be there. I will have learnt to say my goodbyes quietly, from afar, scared to be misunderstood, afraid to feel unwanted, panicked at how invisible the city leaves me feeling. I will grieve her for three days, as Allah has commanded. And then I will spend the rest of my life trying to reckon with her legacy—the teacher, the ally, the fierce mother, the unshakeable force who swept up young girls like fallen leaves in a storm and pushed them to pursue life and freedom.

Hymn for the Dead

To die a Muslim comes with specific instructions:

- The body must be covered as soon as the person passes.
    - Our dead deserve dignity.
- The body must be kept facing towards Mecca.
    - In C-8 Jasmine, we don't need a compass to find Mecca. It lies where the sun sets, beyond our balcony, across the river.
- It is permissible to kiss the dead.
    - When Papa dies, relatives will force us to touch his feet and ask for forgiveness. I won't. Misba will and won't ask why.
- The body must be washed and then covered in a plain white cotton shroud, something that can melt back into the earth.
    - I cannot tell you the number of times I will wish I could melt, shroud-like, into Ahmedabad's soil.
- If a man has died, he must be washed by men. If a woman has died, she must be washed by women. They must wash her hair and arrange it over her chest to cover her breasts.
    - When Amma's mother, Nanijaan, reaches the age at which her husband died, she stops letting Amma trim her thick, raven-black hair. She says she's growing it to prepare for her death, to meet her one true love again.
- The family of the deceased must pay off the dead person's debts with any money they leave behind.
    - Dada leaves his wife and children with everything they will need—a home, a pension, dignity. And no debt. The cleanest death a good Muslim can dream of.

- The body must be carried by four men to a graveyard. A procession of friends and relatives can follow.
    - Four years after the riots, Papa will die. I will stand on the sidewalk outside Jasmine. I will watch everyone he's known—his Hindu, Parsi, Sikh, Christian school friends; our watchmen, Allah Rakha bhai and Hussain bhai; our janitor, Daaya bhai; maulvis from the local masjids where he never prayed; old Gujarati family friends whose daughters continued to mail rakhis to Papa, a sign of their sisterly love, even if they had all stopped visiting our ghetto; neighbours he fought with in society elections; Dada's old peons, who will come wearing all the new pants and shirts he would give away to them; his friends from Ayodhya; his cousins, his relatives, and all of their sons; men of every shape, age and size—coalesce around his shrouded body. Drowned under a shower of flowers, my father the mountain will have turned into a fragrant mound. Together, this mass of men will walk his body down the main street of Khanpur. I will find myself wishing more than ever that I could have been born a boy. Just so I could walk a few more feet with my father.
- No one must sit down until the coffin is laid in the ground.
    - Amma will not get off the floor for two days after Papa's body leaves Jasmine. I will watch her, scared that she's turning into her own mother, who gave up once her husband died, or Dadi, who lost her mind. Misba and I will be lost if Amma breaks.
- The mourning period is three days. Yelling and crying aloud after this time are not permitted. Three days are all you get to mourn and weep for your dead.
    - Of course, the Chowdharys yell and cry as much in death as we do in life. There are snarky whispers at Papa's funeral, Dadi's relatives calling me names because I fought with Papa so much before he died. 'She's just cold-blooded,' they will say. 'A snake,' Dadi calls me.
- The grave must be wide and deep enough to swallow the whole body

so neither animals can reach it nor odours may emit from it. Once the body is in the ground, mourners throw dust on it three times.

  - My father is a tall, stout man. It comforts me to think that animals must burrow into his sides now, making homes in his body.

- Building concrete and mortar structures over a Muslim grave is forbidden. But a rock or piece of wood may be placed to mark it.
  - Papa lies in the gentle shade of young trees, beside his father. Phupu planted the trees. Later she will be buried there too. The road that our family took each Sunday to visit relatives, past the poet Wali's shrine, is now a road I jokingly call the 'land of my dead'. In the Musa Suhag qabrastaan or cemetery, the dead Chowdharys lie side by side. No one snores. It's a quiet green sanctum where parrots and pigeons flit from branch to branch, a crow caws incessantly, peacocks dance occasionally.
  - Musa Suhag was a thirteenth-century mystic. On the road one day to visit his mentor Khwaja Nizamuddin in Delhi, Musa came across a group of young brides in the desert. He was mesmerised by the bangles they wore up to their elbows and their embroidered, flowing skirts. By the time Musa reached Delhi, he had shed his masculine appearance and appeared before Nizamuddin in bangles, dressed as a bride. The amused saint gave him the name Musa Suhag—Moses the Bride. He asked Musa to return to Ahmedabad. They would soon need his help, Nizamuddin predicted. This town by the Sabarmati was perishing under severe drought. When the people heard of this strange new saint in town, they came to Musa Suhag pleading for a miracle. Musa broke into a mad dance, twirling in circles, his skirt flowing around him. In one hand he held a brick and in the other all his bangles, shouting to the skies, 'Send down your rains or I will smash these bangles and become a widow.' Because, in our world, that's what widows do: they leave beauty, colour and song behind. Heavy rains poured down on Ahmedabad soon after that. And for six hundred

years, whenever the river dried and crops withered, devotees came bearing flowers to Musa's shrine. His tomb in the cemetery remains bathed in incense and roses.

- To be buried close to Musa the Bride means that devotees sprinkle their leftover flowers on your grave. On my papa, dada and phupu.
- Two miles down the same road from these lucky ones lies a smaller qabrastaan, the Kalandari. Heba Ahmed, a political studies scholar, writes about the qabrastaan in 2019, comparing the graves to Nazi crematoria: 'There is a sanctity that is accorded to the mortal remains of the dead; most funeral rites involve procedures for cleansing and sometimes even adorning the body. But pogroms do not make beauteous corpses.'
- Three days after the Gulbarg and Naroda Patiya massacres, a handful of survivors bring trucks filled with body parts, shreds of clothing and what bones are left of their loved ones. For three days, Ahsan sahab's and his neighbours' homes were left smouldering so that no evidence, no numbers, no stories remained.
- The tiny plot of land doesn't have enough space for individual graves, nor is there enough of each body to fill one. The superintendent of the graveyard and his family bury these half bodies and full lives in mass graves. His sons go out in the middle of the pogrom and bravely organise the trucks to collect what pieces are left at each massacre site. His daughter-in-law prays at every grave. Three fifteen-foot holes are hewn into the earth; in two of them bodies they can identify as adult male and adult female are separated and buried. Over the third one a metal sign is placed, scribbled on which in Gujarati are the words 'Qaumi fasaad mein shaheed bachche: 50'. *Children martyred in communal violence: 50.* These bodies aren't full enough to be washed or cleansed. They are wisps of ash held together by the love of the living. The superintendent sprinkles a few drops of water on each, lays them down in rows, reads the janaaze ki namaz and buries them.

How to Grow Flowers in a Bedroom

By the end of March, there is no place to breathe in C-8. Papa has forbidden us from standing by the windows. He monitors how long we stand on the balcony, whom we look at, what we're thinking. Inside, it feels like all air is finite. We're trampling over one another for space to think, to be. Our silences have gone up our nostrils, come out our mouths, run out the door into the elevator, and fled. Our words now dance on the riverbed, mocking us from afar. We will never be free.

Every room in this home is tainted by violence. Papa and Amma's dark bedroom with its single small window, the kitchen with its deep sink and cloistered shelves, the laundry room, where I hide and write in a diary, the mori or dishwashing bathroom behind the kitchen, where only Gulshan is sent to clean our muck, Dadi's room, with a view of the street but also Dadi's fuming mouth.

My parents' room was where Misba and I hid each night during drinking time. We would hear loud, animated conversation outside—glasses chinking, something crude said, some laughter. Then the voices would always grow louder, angrier. Something would be thrown, something smashed. Then Papa would storm off to the bathroom. The door would be slammed. A moment of quiet. In my earliest memory of a night like this, when I was barely three, Amma came rushing into the bedroom, Phupu close behind her.

'Rukhsi! Don't just walk away . . .'

Amma turned to close the door on her.

'Zahida apa, please. Please.' Her voice wobbled. 'Just please let me be.'

She came around and sat at the edge of the bed. There, sitting a couple feet from my mother, I felt it for the first time: my mother's burden shifting, growing, moving restlessly inside her, welling up in her wide, honey-coloured eyes. But Amma squeezed her eyes shut and pushed it back in. I remember inching closer to Amma, placing tiny hands on her hunched shoulders, attempting an awkward hug. I remember Amma taking my tiny palms and shaking me off like a wet leaf stuck to her clothes.

'Please . . . Zara. Leave me alone.'

I felt my own burden sprout, a tiny seed of helplessness.

'Kidhar hai Rukhsi?' I remember my father slurring, demanding to be told where his wife was hiding. *Please don't tell him, Phupu*, I prayed in this, the worst game of hide-and-seek ever. I remember Phupu's deadpan voice telling him. I remember how he threw the door open, exploded into the room.

'Bitch. Come back outside!'

Then I remember Papa's eyes accidentally meeting mine instead of hers, ready to fire, locked on a target. My eyes are wide and big like hers but dark like his. And yet for the first time I see my twinkle-eyed, smiling father—who tickled me till I collapsed giggling, who scratched my knee till I fell asleep—towering over me from the foot of the bed, glaring at me and seeing not his daughter but a limb that has grown from this woman. A part of her.

He spits.

'Do your drama. Brainwash the girl against me.'

He rumbles, his mountain body barely holding back its rage. I sit there frozen between these two. The woman who won't let me touch her, the man whom I dare not approach. All I want to whimper is *I love you both*.

I remember Amma finally shaking out of her trance, then standing up and walking out of the room, hoping to draw the fire away, to spare me. I remember Papa turning to look at me one last time, hate in his eyes slowly melting into inebriated confusion.

The fire and its first victim walked away.

I remember Amma coming back later that night to call us to dinner.

'Come on, girls,' she says in that shaky voice, not letting me look into her eyes anymore. When I hesitate to leave the safety of the bed and go out where the plates will tremor like me, she looks at me with complete emptiness. There is no love there, no joy, no life, only exhaustion.

'Please, Zara,' she repeats. I quietly, guiltily get off the bed and follow her. I know then that there is no running, no saving myself. I can never leave. Not without my amma.

'Arre, no two states of this country can stand each other. Everyone is fighting over food or language or rivers. We have four in this house!' we learn to say, trying to normalise or exoticise our home's dysfunction for ourselves.

It's true. Dada is from Punjab in the North. Dadi is Gujarati. Amma's mother is from the mango coast of western India. Her dead father is from the South. We blame the diversity for the disturbance. Too many stories in collision with one another, no shared tongue. But it's also very not-true. Amma said yes to this marriage dreaming she'd learn to dance the garba, a dance she'd always marvelled at from a thousand miles away. Phupu can cook herself any cuisine in the world, but she rushes to the table first when Amma is frying dosas. Dadi hates the mention of Dada's family in Pakistan's Punjab, but she pushes Misba and me to dance in front of the guests to every Punjabi bhangra song played at weddings we attend.

'Tumhaare khoon mein hai yeh,' she reminds us. It is all in our blood.

No, the madness in our home, like the rest of this country, lies in our search for a strongman. In our home, no man is strong enough.

Dada is haunted by how he failed. Papa withers under the burden of his own mistakes. The women become dictators when they become divorced or widowed. There is no room in C-8 Jasmine for grace.

So we huddle in Amma's bedroom each night, telling each other stories, making up imaginary ones in which we live in forests by little streams, just Amma, Misba and I. There is a tape deck in the room, a wedding present for Papa and Amma from his friends the Reddys. It's his prized possession. Papa takes us every Friday to Law Garden, where in the evenings a man sells pirated and original audiotapes from the back of a converted Tempo Traveller: albums of every new and old Bollywood movie, as well as collections of ghazals, devotional Sufi and bhakti music.

Papa never buys pirated. They will spoil his deck. If ever his purchases turn out to be fakes and the tape spools out and jams the player, he goes back and fights with the tape wala, calls him a dozen names. And then buys three more tapes. He buys Nusrat Fateh Ali Khan for himself. Some mornings he plays it after his shower and raises his hands and hums 'Allah Hu, Allah Hu' as if temporarily possessed, energised, tentatively tethered to a faith he doesn't understand. This is the only grace I see. I watch him, his soft beer belly rising and falling, the depression dropping away like the seams of his semi-transparent cotton kurta suspended around his heaviness. Since the riots started, he hasn't played it.

But one Sunday, bored out of his mind, he opens the deck up and cleans the head with cotton swabs and Dada's eau de cologne.

When Misba and I shut the door of Amma's bedroom that evening, we look at each other conspiratorially. We switch on the tape deck and allow ourselves the same grace. Grace is the only language Misba and I know to speak in. It has been our shared tongue as sisters since before we ever learnt how to talk. We don't yet know what it means to save each other, but we know something happens when we dance. We feel redeemed. We have done this each evening from the moment we started to walk, from the moment we recognised our world burned like clockwork each evening.

We insert our favourite tapes one after another, hits from 2001: *Lagaan*, *Kabhi Khushi Kabhie Gham*, *Dil Chahta Hai*, *Aks*, *Lajja*, *Nayak*, *Pyaar Tune Kya Kiya*, *Zubeidaa*. We haven't watched all the movies. Papa takes us to the theatre only for the big ones. But song after song we go, moving and making the movie with our bodies. Through the moods and bhavas and rasas of each song, we make up steps and build facial expressions, we construct entire lives and love stories filled with heartbreak and mischief and sublime joy. Amma slips into the room in between dinner preparations to watch us. A few times, Dadi and Phupu peep inside too. Apa sits on the bed, arms folded, her grim mouth slackening into a smile. There is nothing to dance about right now. But in C-8 Jasmine, there seldom is. Dance is the only way Misba and I know to transcend this reality.

When Amma comes in to watch, I watch her back, as she leans her tired body against the linen closet, her smile building from her thick lips to her honey eyes. Soon she's clapping with our every shimmy and shake. She lets out a soft hoot. This is all she can do. Dance is teaching us what she can't, mustn't.

That we have power. That as long as we have each other, our souls will be okay. She watches us bloom amid all this smoke, gracefully stretching into life, grateful we are hers, thankful we are alive.

Air

Extinguished

Amma tells me her father loved her mother's dark, flowing hair so much that when she had a hysterectomy and couldn't wash her knee-length locks, he sat her down on a stool in the middle of their army quarters and washed it for her. Amma remembers giggling at this visual, which soon became the family's Sunday-morning ritual, and Amma's gold standard for a loving marriage.

Amma tells me how when her father went off to war in 1962, to fight the Chinese forces who had attacked India over Prime Minister Nehru's decision to shelter the fleeing Dalai Lama, her mother held a small portable radio to her ear each afternoon, listening for news of dead and surviving soldiers, drying her hair over a wicker basket full of steaming lobaan—that sweet-smelling resin that would smoulder on coal embers and leave the house smelling like a Sufi shrine. Like faith.

Amma tells me how each afternoon their army orderlies would clean and slice the meat, chop the vegetables, and then her mother would prepare huge vats of saalans and dals and machhi and gosht and pulao. She'd sit on the kitchen floor folding samosas and pressing together perfectly round cutlets. She was a simple woman who prayed to Allah five times a day, a legendary cook whose recipes cousins still hoard to this day and a sort of ethereal beauty whom no woman in the family was able to match up to. 'Least of all me,' Amma tells me with emphasis.

Amma has told me lots of stories of her mother. They sound almost legend-like, the way children witness every mundane act of their parent through the haloed lens of a hero. How Nanijaan, once a waif-like, motherless girl from the western coast of mangoes and clamshells, was brought to Madras by her half brother, who then raised her; how she was spotted at a movie theatre by a young army officer who insisted she would be his wife; how she became *the* army wife—neat, respectable, a great host, an impeccable, sweet tyrant. Amma speaks of her mother as someone who could conquer anything she set her mind to: how she taught herself Urdu and English despite being a seventh-grade dropout; how she learnt to knit from magazines she could barely decipher; how each summer she filled jars with homemade jams, pickles and ketchups, and baked cakes and cookies, learning from a Punjabi general's wife in one posting, a Malayali captain's wife in another. How she absorbed all of India's rich cultural diversity from every posting her husband took her to. How she hungered for perfection, for beauty, for life and learning, in a way those who have known pangs of deep, physical, painful hunger often do; how she always laid immaculate tables, packed them with produce her green fingers had raised in her garden; how she teased life out of an array of Indian soils wherever her military husband's duty took them—karewa by the Chenab River in Jammu, alluvium in the backwaters of Trivandrum, sunbaked high-plateau clay in Nagpur or Bangalore's fiery red laterite; how in her garden she grew bananas, papayas, drumsticks, chikoos, ladies' fingers, guavas, spinach, mint, coriander and chillies; how she lined their fence with jasmine, bougainvillea, daisies and asters; how Amma's own love for flowers, her own desire to conquer Jasmine's choking close-mindedness, came from this—the blazing memory of her mother, who could make life out of thin air.

Amma tells me her father, my nana, whom I never knew, was the son of a Muslim doctor in the British army. When his father died, Nana learnt to shoulder his mother's and brother's needs at an early age. In Nanijaan he found not only a partner who shared his sense of duty towards family but also a wife who filled his home and heart. Amma's cousins tell me Major and Mrs Amir Ahmed, my grandparents, always had a seat at their table for anyone who walked in from the cold, that Nana and Nanijaan were first at any funeral, praying and feeding their relatives, first at any family wedding, bringing jeeps full of army supplies, their three well-dressed children and their joint electric sense of mischief and humour.

Amma tells me that when, after two healthy, strapping sons and many stillborn daughters in the Ahmed family, Nanijaan gave birth to a little brown squiggle—my mother—with hair too fine, eyes too wide, an almost invisible nose, Nana named her Rukhsana, *of beautiful face*.

Amma tells me that, as she grew, Nanijaan and her sisters tried and failed to massage her nose out, disappointed it didn't point regally and prominently forward like their own. She tells me an aunt known for her glowing, fair complexion spent hours trying to peel Amma's darkness away with homemade remedies of multani mitti and chane ka atta. Half our lentils we eat, half we scrub all over ourselves in this desperation for beauty. Amma tells me another aunt jokingly called her 'kashmir ki kali', tickled that such a dark child had been born right when the family was stationed in the fair, snowcapped mountains of Kashmir.

Amma tells me her father chuckled too. And that it broke her heart. But Amma tells me Nana insisted on holding, lifting and mending what was broken.

Amma tells me that, at twelve, when she was her full height of five feet eight inches, starting to tower over her middle brother, and her breasts had grown, she started to hunch over in shame. Her wide, childlike grin narrowed. In photos I notice Amma smiling at that age through clamped lips, also pronounced 'too thick' by her mother's and aunts' standards. I didn't know then how deep this rot of caste, class and colour ran in our subcontinent. How this obsession with fairness had seeped in from the North, from as far as Europe and Persia and Central Asia, and slowly dripped and pooled into the South too, turned centuries of families against their own children. Taunts whispered as 'just a joke' breaking the souls of little children, telling them they are predestined by the hue of their skin to lead smaller lives. Amma tells me how at an early age she felt this sense of not belonging to her own mother. And where we come from, mothers are your first nation. A mother is the land your feet take root in.

Amma tells me then one day how she found strength in a myth. How Nana—watching his daughter cower about the house, dupatta pulled modestly over this body she was losing control of—suddenly lost his cool and bellowed.

'Why are you walking like that? Walk straight! Do you know who you are named after?'

Rukhsana shook her head meekly.

'Roxana,' he continued, full of pride, 'Emperor Alexander's wife!'

Little Rukhsana listened wide-eyed as her father told her over lunch of the breathtaking, wily daughter of a Bactrian chieftain, separated by almost a thousand years and miles from this contorted girl. Alexander's desire for Roxana drove this greatest of emperors to madness. He rode over the Hindu Kush mountains to conquer all of what we today know as South Asia. When Alexander was alive, Roxana tried to kill him twice, fighting this destiny where she was forced into marriage and bed with him. When he died, Roxana killed all his other wives, so she could finally wrest away the power that had been denied to her all her tender life.

Amma tells me how her father's eyes lit as he told the story, how little Rukhsana recognised suddenly where she belonged: in her father's darker skin, his big almond-honey eyes, his wide grin, his unwavering assertion of his belonging. She walked tall, lanky, dark and proud that day, knowing in her heart she was worth more than the sum of her skin, that her father, this son of India's soil, baked and bred in it, was telling her a story to ease her spirit, but really what he was telling her was *I made you with love. You are mine. You are beautiful.*

. . .

A year later, the family settled into what would be their final posting, by the ocean in Madras, where her father came from. A few days after they'd moved in, her father, the mountain that was Major Amir Ahmed, keeled over from a cardiac arrest and was gone. *Turned to sweet, fragrant lobaan smoke.* An invisible faith who would live only in her memory now.

Amma tells me Nanijaan, a sudden widow at thirty-eight, collapsed at the funeral several times. Amma tells me losing Nana took away her will to live. From the heroine of her childhood, this alive woman slowly turned into a fading memory too. As the older sons, left fatherless at fourteen and eighteen, struggled to become men, little Rukhsana was left to shoulder her mother. One by one, the boys fled to America, desperate to make a life for themselves, desperate to outrun their mother's tears. Nobody noticed the little girl who let go of dreams of becoming a doctor, chose a cheap, no-fuss arts degree instead, slowly became her mother's shadow—neat, respectable, impeccable. She chose never to fall in love, to instead be the kind of desirable young woman who'd find a decent match and fix her mother's blues. She let go of stories of warriors she was named after. She submitted instead to matchmaking aunties who brought rishtas. A cousin in faraway Bombay introduced Nanijaan and Amma to the Chowdharys.

A Muslim officer's family in Gujarat was asking for her hand—their handsome, US-educated son was a tad older (almost a decade), liked to drink (a lot), wasn't very religious (didn't know which way to turn his face to pray namaz) and had been previously engaged (dumped). She would belong in a diverse, modern, cultured family, her cousins convinced her. She would be free, Nanijaan told her. Based on her own marriage, she promised young Rukhsana a progressive Muslim husband would let her grow and become whoever she wanted to be. She could be anything, *after marriage*.

Amma tells me she said yes to the rishta because it gave her something concrete, a promise to hold on to after the way her childhood suddenly disappeared: safety, freedom, somewhere she'd root herself, somewhere she could belong.

When India fractured into two nations, all the bloodshed, the land-grabbing, the wrecking of women's bodies, this happened mostly along the northern, western and eastern borders. The southern peninsula, guarded by ocean waters on all three sides, saw a fraction of the trauma, even as the stories travelled. Nana's family, like Dada's, was affected. His older brother heard of the better opportunities for Muslims in Pakistan and chose to migrate. Nana chose to remain and serve in India's military. These brothers too were separated by a line drawn by a white European. But this fracturing left hardly any splinters in the Ahmed family. It was a decision made for opportunity, not for land or belonging. No homes were burnt, no farms snatched, no mothers and sisters raped. And so the South and its Muslims like the Ahmeds with their matriliny-leaning cultures, their equal access to education, their confidence in their belonging, had remained safely ensconced.

In 1984, when Amma got married, Major Ahmed's brother flew down to Madras from Karachi to give her away in place of her father. In his suitcase, he brought her a dark maroon silk kurta and a gold-and-maroon brocade gharara, its flared divider skirt falling heavily to the earth. The dupatta was a pale-rust tissue, the colour of soil, with delicate golden tassels around the borders. Amma's wedding dress. Amma tells me she picked the colours herself, because she knew, and her mother didn't, which colours brought out the gold in her dusky skin. Amma tells me she had never felt more beautiful, more like herself, than when she wore her wedding gharara.

I will grow up looking at the gharara. My fingers will touch its intricate weaves, seeking answers: was I destined to end up like Amma, always struggling to belong? Would I someday wear a dress like this and sign my life away, hoping for mere things like safety and freedom, when I knew in my bones I was worth more?

I needed to believe in the stories Amma was telling me so I could walk tall and proud in my full self. But I needed Amma to walk alongside me. My amma, who lit my imagination on fire, who painted flowers with wild ferocity onto the dull walls of my childhood, who could even on her darkest days tease life out of a dying marriage, who could take the ashes her daughters were surrounded with and make from them breath. What could I do to show her?

When would my mother remember the warrior she was always meant to be, and save herself?

Airwaves

In April 2002, one morning the phone instruments peal and toll in loud cacophony through the deathly silence of C-8. Amma rushes out of the kitchen to answer.

There is that familiar click of the cordless, someone listening in as Amma answers the corded landline. Papa. He has done this since the day Nanijaan brought us the Panasonic phone, suspicious that she will use it to plot with her family to break the Chowdharys apart.

Unluckily for all of us, it is Amma's brother calling from California. The *riots* have made it onto American cable news. Muslims in the United States are demanding that President Bush condemn the violence and chastise the chief minister, Narendra Modi. CNN has been showing them images of streets on fire. Streets where the dead Major Ahmed's only daughter and her children live. Amma is conscious of her husband listening in.

'Why don't you first say salaam to Zaheer?' she chirps.

Papa is given no choice. He must *officially* come on the line.

'Haan salaam-alaikum,' he grudgingly wishes my uncle.

'I told you, Zaheer bhai, you should have moved here when you had a chance,' my uncle is saying.

'Wahaan kaunsa better hai, yaar? Udhar humko saale terrorist ke jaise treat karenge.'

Amma's brother's voice is enough to enrage Papa. 'As if it's any better there!' he immediately spits. 'There we'll be treated like bloody terrorists.'

The year the cordless phone first arrived, in 1995, my uncle had also sent sponsorship papers for my parents and us. As with GEB,

Papa's paranoia wasn't unfounded. They did want us to migrate and live closer to them. And they didn't know why he wouldn't go back. He would die rather than tell them. Papa had held the sponsor papers in his hand like he was about to explode.

'He just wants me to come there and become his servant in his auto shop. Why should I go do that? I've washed enough dishes in that bloody country. We have dignity here. My father has worked for it.'

Then he saw me watching him.

'Gujarat is home, beta. Remember that,' he said with uncharacteristic kindness. 'We are born here. We will die here only.' Then he tore the sponsorship papers up and told Nanijaan she was not welcome in Jasmine again.

After this current exchange with my uncle in 2002, Papa is worn out enough that he doesn't care to eavesdrop anymore. Amma takes the cordless. I notice her slowly walking away from the rest of us, edging towards the kitchen. The sound of the pressure cooker muffles most of what she's saying. But she seems to be speaking only in 'hmmms' and 'haans'. Even with all the Chowdharys surveilling her, usually her voice carries a little more excitement on these calls. Today she seems to be in a hurry to shut down whatever her brother and mother are saying.

'Haan, yes, insha'allah, we'll see about that. Chalo, khuda haafiz.'

After lunch when my parents retire for their nap, Misba and I sit outside flipping channels, carefully avoiding news channels. We settle on *Happy Days*. Misba and I have recently discovered it, and even Papa doesn't mind us watching this American show, thrilled that we're watching *clean* entertainment from the good old days. He doesn't know I watch *Baywatch* after this one.

Suddenly, their bedroom door opens softly and Amma steps outside on tiptoe. She looks comical, Pink Panther–like in her skulking. In her hand she's holding the cordless, which she's pried away from a snoring Papa. Amma sits down on the settee behind us, not focused on the TV screen but instead urgently flipping through her tiny phone book. Joanie and Chachi are making out on-screen, and usually I'd be embarrassed to have my mother around. But all my energy is focused on Amma whispering into the phone. She is greeting one of her English-tutoring students.

Why is Amma sacrificing her afternoon nap to call a student? Her voice has a slight tremor.

'Beta, you said your brother works in the railway office, no?' she whispers.

She sounds like an excited little girl . . .

'Please meri help kar do, beta. I need to book tickets.'

Like an excited little girl remembering to walk straight . . .

My heart is pounding in my ears. Chachi and Joanie and their perfect, simple lives can go to hell.

'Haan, please note it. I need three tickets, beta. Yes, in May. Ahmedabad to Madras.'

Like an excited little girl realising she's named after a warrior . . .

'Yes.' Amma's voice is bright as the sun. 'My mother is coming home.'

Dancing for Durga

In my board exams, now 'indefinitely postponed', one of the subjects I am to be tested in is the language Sanskrit. I've studied Sanskrit for three years, along with Hindi and Gujarati. It's become my new favourite. Everything about the language works in neat tables and patterns. Yet it's fluid. And it tinges the air with something otherworldly, from many millennia ago. Saying it aloud makes me a part of its tangled mythology, gives me a place to belong. The stories that Sanskrit holds of heroism and oppression, people born out of dewdrops and flying mountains, these open their vast mouths and swallow me. In Sanskrit I can see the origin of our pain too. My favourite shloka is about Durga.

> सर्वमङ्गलमाङ्गल्ये शिवे सर्वार्थसाधिके ।
> शरण्ये त्रयंबके गौरी नारायणि नमोऽस्तु ते ॥

> *All good things come from her, this partner of Shiva who creates and destroys.*
> *She protects those in her refuge. And the world's wealth belongs to them whom she decides to bless.*

This state, Gujarat—the soil where three generations from my Dada's side have lived and grown—isn't the native home of the Chowdharys. Except one, whose soul is made of this land, for whom land is everything: Dadi.

When the British left and Bombay Presidency became the two states of Gujarat and Maharashtra, based on their languages, Dadi convinced Dada to choose Ahmedabad as his posting. Gujarat would always be their safe refuge, she promised. Dadi was the youngest daughter of a Gujarati landlord who had been endowed with a magistrate's title by the British. They were Muslims, but the kind for whom caste, land, blood, lineage—the reality of their feudal world—mattered more than the transcendence of the Islamic faith. Her father's colonial allegiances gave him tax-collecting powers for the whole district. Little Hawwa was born into privilege and used to having what she set her eyes on. Tennis lessons, a British education (one that she would abandon early to marry the dashing young Anwar), evenings at the gymkhana with her brother and two older sisters, both of whom were also married to men in the British police and army. When India got its independence, young Hawwa was on a train from Aligarh, a town near Ayodhya in north-central India, where she had gone to visit her brother in the police academy, and was returning home to Ahmedabad.

Halfway through their journey, a mob of angry Hindus boarded the train. It was the time of the Partition. Trains were bloodbaths. The mob was checking carriages, hunting for Muslims. Hawwa and her sister, both dressed in saris with low-cut blouses, were a far cry from the veiled women the mob was looking for. Both sisters spoke in perfect Gujarati and insisted to the mob they were Hindus. Their metal trunks were pulled out from under their seats to check the name on them. 'Desai,' they read. An upper-caste, Hindu-sounding surname meaning *landlords* the same way 'Chowdhary' did in Punjabi. It gave nothing away of one's religion. Only of one's place in the social order of caste, a diabolic hierarchical system that had ranked and turned us against our own for centuries. The sisters were allowed to continue their journey to Ahmedabad, back to the safety of their privilege.

In Ahmedabad, Hawwa and her sisters were known as the magistrate's daughters. Once her brother became a police officer, they were known as that cop's sisters. In this world, where allegiance to power meant everything, Hawwa was unassailable. And so when Hawwa met the young and charming Anwar, a government servant, an orphan with no family this side of the border, a charming man rising quickly through the ranks, she knew. She could always remain unassailable.

Dadi's land, Gujarat, believes so fervently in the Hindu goddess Durga that, for nine nights each year, every city, town and village in the state remains awake. Old and young take to the squares and streets, spinning in dizzying circles, dancing for Durga. The festival is called, quite literally, Navratri, *nine nights*. Nine nights for nine avatars of Durga. For nine nights Gujarat dances the garba as if it has lost its mind. The garba is the traditional folk dance of the Gujarati people, specifically performed for Navratri. Concentric circles of humans move around Goddess Durga's bejewelled idol. The name literally means 'womb'. People believe that when you dance the garba, your body becomes a shrine or temple for divine energy.

In her time, Dadi was quite the dancer too. We would hear stories of how she and Dada used to do the foxtrot and the waltz at parties, her eyebrows perfectly tweezed, face painted, hair dyed to perfection, little ringlets at her delicate ears. How when she was younger Dadi would drive around town in her Corvette, windows rolled down, cigarette in one hand, the wind in her immaculately coiffed hair. Of how she spent many evenings at the card tables at the local gymkhana club. But the story we heard most was of how Dadi had a metal foot. Or something along those lines.

Not long before I was born, Dadi slipped and fell and cracked her delicate left ankle. Screws and wires were inserted through painful surgery to hold her up. Since the mid-eighties, she had walked with an almost-imperceptible drag in one foot. It didn't terribly restrict her life, but Dadi didn't dance anymore. As she grew older, she would sit frowning behind me as I watched old Hindi black-and-white films on our tiny TV. But the minute a dance number would come on, her left foot would start tapping and her fingers would rap at the sofa arm with something like frustration mixed with rhythm. She was dying to bust some moves. Instead, all she could do was hoarsely sing along.

'Paan khaaye saiyyaan hamaro. Sanwli suratiya honth laal laal.' *My country boy chews his paan, brown-faced and scarlet-lipped.*

The dainty sixties actress Waheeda Rehman danced on-screen, lip-syncing to the sultry voice of Asha Bhonsle.

'Haye haye malmal ka kurta, malmal ke kurte pe chheent laal laal.' *Look at his beautiful mulmul kurta, now he's gone and stained it with betel juice.*

A young village belle teasing and chastising her man for his imperfections, dancing lithe, beguiling, an all-knowing smile on her face.

Afterwards Dadi would uncurl her pins and wrap herself in a beautiful chiffon sari, put on a pearl string and sit back on the sofa. For this goddess her sofas were her thrones, and the granddaughters were to never sit on them. We sat on the settee. But when I wasn't mad at her senseless assertions of power, I'd watch her with quiet awe. Looking after her face, hair and body was an obsession that fuelled Dadi. Again, it was that protection of what was real. Soul, spirit, moral dilemmas, she didn't bother with these. There was a self-love there that felt rare and out of my reach. I thought about how lucky she must have been, raised to love herself like that. All year I'd struggle with living in this no-man's-land, reminded that parts of me were from somewhere else. That I was born here *but not of here*. That if I didn't even speak the language of my dadi or my father, how was I theirs? It was only during the festival of Navratri, when my dancing feet would step outside the closed bedroom of C-8 Jasmine, when for nine nights my soles would stomp on the soil of this state, that I would understand what it meant to love my own body, the only real thing I can carry. And what it feels like to belong.

Phupu would pack all three of us girls, in our long, flowing skirts and chunky silver jewellery, in her sidecar for all-night garba events across the city. Later, after the 2002 pogrom, rowdy men from the

VHP would start to guard these same venues, checking ID cards, threatening to sprinkle cow urine and apply Hindu religious markings on the forehead of anyone arriving at the dance.

'No beef eater must be allowed in. Non-Hindus not allowed. This is a matter of our faith.'

But back then, we'd revel in the all-night dancing with millions of strangers. As we'd clap and move, skipping on thin air, Misba and I would lose track of time, carried as if by a power deep within us, the universe born anew with our every ragged breath. One of the nine nights, our venue would be Dadi's sister's apartment in Shahibag, where people of all faiths would gather on the lawns below. While Papa and Dada settled down to drink upstairs with Dadi's nephews, she and her sister, both elderly and limping, would bring their saris over their right shoulders and pin them the way Gujarati women traditionally wear them. Dadi's sari would drape below her blouse, exposing her cleavage. They would take the elevator down to the lawns. The aarti prayers would be finishing just as they'd arrive. Misba and I would grab chairs and watch, fascinated, as the slow beats of the music would kick in and grandmothers of every faith and size would descend, like stardust on the dusty ground, gently, often shakily, putting one foot in front of the other and clapping, once, twice, thrice. Women turned to goddesses in three simple claps.

After two rounds Dadi would hobble back to her chair, out of breath, face flushed like a little girl's, rearranging her sari to its usual left side, hiding her breasts, transforming back into the good Muslim wife, mother and woman again.

The music would pick up tempo, inviting younger feet. We would feel her eyes boring into us as we joined the growing circle of granddaughters. We'd start from the far end of the lawn and eventually come to pass right in front of her. She would be frowning and judging the sizes of these younger girls' blouses. She would spot us then—twirling, moving fluidly across the sand and past her. We'd see other grandmothers around her start to point, gape, wonder who we were, our dance practices behind locked bedroom doors paying off. Her invisible Cinderella granddaughters. People would soon leave a little gap around us and pause to watch and imitate our intricate, symmetrical moves. As we passed by her again, spinning as if our bodies were the very axis of the universe, we'd hear her hoarse voice over the music.

'Aah mari chhokriyon chhe. Mara Zaheer ni.' *Those are my girls. My Zaheer's girls.*

Something otherworldly, from millennia ago, would rise in us. Girls knowing how to love themselves because they belonged in this soil. Misba and I would continue to dance all night, long after Dadi had gone upstairs to harass her niece-in-law just as she did Amma. When Papa would ramble to her in a stupor and demand to be told where we were, she'd nod as if trying to calm an agitated pup.

'They're downstairs. Dancing. It's okay. Let them dance a little longer.'

We were not to make noise, sit on her couch, touch her chocolates, take up her son's attention or ask for sanitary pads, because we were 'that woman's daughters' the rest of the year. But on the nine nights of Navaratri, when we danced the dance of her people, and danced it so well her people stopped and gaped, Dadi would wholly claim us. She would relent for those nights that Gujarat was in our blood, that she had put it there. And perhaps the dancing too. *She protected us in her refuge. And the world's wealth belonged to us.*

Saying My Name

And then just like that, as if suddenly all guns have been silenced, all swords resheathed, all lost ones brought back to their unburnt homes, the boards are announced.

It's happening. The exams I've waited all year for are going to take place in April. A whole month, many false alarms and rumours later, many episodes of remembering and forgetting and panicking over what remembering means later, it's happening. I will have to show up, write my heart out, compete with children whose world is now the opposite of mine and somehow manage to pass. I don't have to outdo Apa. I just have to pass.

Early in the morning, as we all gather around breakfast, Phupu announces that she is going across the river to her apartment. I suspect she is trying to get used to this fear that any time you leave the house could be your last. And not even genocide can keep her locked in with her mother and brother. She promises to pick up my hall ticket for me from Mount Carmel.

Hall tickets are little postcard-sized documents that look very serious and official with the student's name and ID number and a stamp from the State Education Board—that's why the name 'board exams'. The Education Board thinks that if we take our exams in our own school buildings, we will cheat, or that the boards will somehow feel less serious than they are clearly intended to be. So to add to our terror, students are placed randomly in schools around the city. The arrival of the hall ticket is usually quite a momentous occasion in homes more obsessed with their children's education than C-8. Usually, girls from our convent school wait to see if they've been placed in one of the Jesuit all-boys schools. That way they'll know to shorten their pleated uniform skirts. In another time, I would have been excited at the idea too. I am yet to fall in love and too busy trying to stay alive to wonder about it.

Instead, I restlessly wait for Phupu to bring back my hall ticket. When she does, Apa grabs it out of her mother's hands. I'm irritated. I've been waiting to scan the school list on the document and make sure these places are even accessible under the curfew.

'I've never even heard of this one,' Apa declares, twisting her pretty mouth 'Hanumanpura? Where the hell is that?'

At this point, just the name of a Hindu god is enough to make me nervous.

'Should we go earlier and check it out? See where it is?' Phupu suggests. Papa shoots her down instantly.

'Nahin, nahin. Bekaar mein why go twice?'

He isn't wrong. The news says there will be police protection at all exam centres, but would the cops care if something were to happen to an errant family jauntily driving around an evening before? Why tempt fate?

I look at the other two centres: St Xavier's Mirzapur is Papa's alma mater. And the neighbourhood of Mirzapur is where he grew up before Dada bought this apartment in Jasmine and sold their bungalow. The family had roots there that went back decades, living with Parsi, Hindu and Muslim neighbours. Something about seeing it on the ticket, printed in blurry grey ink standing for a world when we still cared for one another, calms my nerves. I will be safe at Xavier's.

There is another school's name and address printed for the last exam, one too obscure to remember. But I don't care to think that far out. Since 27 February, I count each day I make it to my bed at night as a bonus. I'm just going to focus on the four major papers at Hanumanpura, I decide.

But there is one other thing. My name is staring back at me, printed in clear grey block letters at the very top: ZARA CHOWDHARY.

'Just tell them you're Parsi, if anyone asks,' Phupu offers as she sees me trying to rub it away, lighten it, perhaps.

As a child I'd pester Amma to repeat the story of how I got my name, even though I knew it verbatim. She was watching a Pakistani soap opera called *Tanhaiyaan* when she was expecting me, and something about the beautiful, graceful Zara in the show—who when her parents die must grow up too soon and become the fierce, self-sacrificing mother figure to her younger sister—worked for her overwrought pregnancy hormones. That was my name. But in naming me, Amma always says, she willed herself to have another daughter two years later. 'I needed you to have a sister. I wanted you to have what I didn't. Someone who will always be your person no matter where in the world you go.'

When Misba came along, a list of Islamic baby names was produced by an Urdu scholar, a friend of Dada's. The word 'Misba' sparkled off the page to Amma. The word meant 'divine light', just what Amma needed. She would remind my sister of this too, as she grew up to be the funny, mischievous brat who lit up any room with her antics, her dance, her sly humour: that she was, in fact, the light of Amma's and my lives. But mostly I loved this story because in a culture where even the right to name your child is often taken from you and given to the paternal aunt, or phupu, Amma had found a way to wrestle for herself this tiny act of agency: modern, unusual names—small rebellions.

'Zara? Haan, I only agreed because anyway it is half my name and half hers,' Papa insists. Through the years, even when Amma sometimes warps the name out of endearment, calling me Zaru, Papa never does. I'm always only Zara. And once in a rare while he adds 'my darling'.

'Don't act too proud, okay?' Apa once says when we are very young. 'It's just short for Fatima az-Zehra, the Prophet's daughter. So basically, your first name is just like "Fatima" or something.'

'Fatima' is the name of her nanny, whom she tortures so much the young woman stops showing up one day.

'Fatima, Fatima!' Apa teases me for a whole year, as if calling me the name of someone she considered her servant were a way to belittle me.

Our Maulana sahab had his own take.

'Beta, aapka naam na actually Zara nahin hai. Zehra hai. Wohi sahi Arabi hai,' he clucks his tongue like a chicken and says. Apparently, I don't know what my name is. *It is not this modern-sounding 'Zara'. No, no, in Arabic there is only 'Zehra'. The only way.* I grab my school backpack and show him the brown paper–covered notebooks with my name on all those flowery labels. Z-A-R-A. If my mother had wanted to name me Zehra, she would have. *She didn't,* I say, temper starting to flare. He continues to call me Zehra till the day Papa fires him for watching too much cricket, teaching too little Arabic. *Waste of money.*

Jhaara is what most Gujaratis insist on calling me. 'Jhaara' in Hindi means 'ladle'. Friends in school tease, 'jhaara, jhaara, shudh jhaara'. mimicking a popular jingle from a groundnut oil commercial.

'Zhara' is how our Maharashtrian friends pronounce it, as if forcing their epiglottis to wake up.

'What a lovely name you kept for her, huh, Rukhsi?' Papa's Parsi childhood friend once compliments, her tongue lightly skimming over the *r* in my name in her clipped accent, no added frills.

'Zarri, zardozi, jevu. Brilliant. Golden.'

She is right. The simple, four-letter name Amma wanted for me comes not from Arabic but from Persian. It sometimes means 'flower', sometimes 'lace', always 'sparkling golden', like the gold-thread embroidery Persians brought to our land.

When I explain all this to anyone who asks, the next question is, predictably, about my surname. That's usually a telling one. People ask so that they can quickly gauge what rung of the caste or religion ladder you come from and then know how they want to treat you.

'So your name is Zara? So, like, you're Parsi or what?'

'No. I am a Muslim,' I patiently say.

'Achha.' The person will usually start to eye me warily. 'And your surname?'

'Chowdhary.'

'But how "Chowdhary" can be Muslim?'

I choose then between two possible responses. The first: to dive into an encyclopaedic lecture about how 'Shah', 'Desai', 'Patel', 'Chowdhary', 'Chaudhari', 'Choudhary', and a million other surnames could well be Muslim because, in South Asia, we didn't all arrive yesterday on camelback; we have assimilated regionally and socially over millennia and are as diverse linguistically, aurally, culturally as Indian Hinduism. If I start to explain how my grandparents all are different kinds of Indian, a majority of the time I notice the eyes of the listener glazing over with information overload: the idea that people can have more rich and nuanced lives than their monochromatic imaginations—it's all too much. So I simply look the person in the eye and go with option two.

'We can.'

But can't Phupu see? I can't lie and say I'm a Parsi just 'cause my name sounds like it. I am not like her. Or like Papa or Dadi or Apa. I don't fit in as well as they do. I don't speak Gujarati as fluently as them; I failed the class so often I had to switch and choose Sanskrit instead. I won't get through a single sentence before I'm outed.

'But that's how Parsis speak ya!' Apa mimics my more pronounced accent, which she seems to think is not offensive at all.

'And you toh even look it. Same fair-fair, pheeka face,' she says, pulling at my pale cheeks. *Allah, someone stop her*, I groan inside. But then she puts an arm around me. She's trying to comfort me, I realise. It's true. I am scared to die for a stupid set of exams. I spend the next few days alternating between staring at my notes and staring in the mirror, practising 'Ame Parsi chiye'—*We are Parsis*—though I already know it's a lost cause. I try remembering stories from Papa's childhood growing up with Eruch uncle, Feroze uncle, Freddy uncle, the Navrojis, the Anklesarias. I try to reimagine his stories of mischief and masti with them, superimpose myself into them. Maybe if the mob catches me, I can quote verbatim from the only Gujarati lesson I ever managed to memorise—the dudh ma saakar, *milk and sugar*, story: When the Parsis fled persecution by the shah in Persia and arrived at Gujarat's coast, Jadi Rana, a Hindu king, showed them a flask of milk filled to the brim, symbolising an overfilled kingdom, no space for outsiders. In response, the Parsi priest leading the refugees smiled. He took a pinch of sugar and added it to the milk. 'Like sugar, we won't cause your cup to overflow,' he insisted. 'We will make your lives sweeter.' It is said Rana offered them not only refuge but also protection and freedom to practice their faith freely.

Some of our Gujarati Hindu friends love telling this story. But to hear it from our Parsi friends, whom Papa lovingly calls 'our long-lost cousins', it is an example of Zoroastrian diplomacy, learnt from a long, hard history of oppression.

As the days wear on, I study less and practise saying this chant more—'Ame Parsi chiye, Ame Parsi chiye'—how I will explain away my name. If the examiner asks which religion I belong to, I'll tell him the true story of my name: I'm Zara, 'gold' in Persian. I'll explain it isn't Muslim enough. It is certainly not the Muslim Prophet's daughter's name. I'm different, I'll explain. I'm my mother's Zara, born from her desire for sisters. I'll promise that I'll blend like dudh ma saakar. *I am a Chowdhary, see? How can 'Chowdhary' be Muslim?* People in a mob are usually in it because they're stupid. They won't know that I am shape-shifting, as I have done all my life. For now, I must believe my name can, will, save me. If I live to tell the tale, I'll find a way to forgive myself for all the erasure with this linguistic sleight of hand. I'll kiss my mother's feet for the gift of a name that could save my life.

Metamorphosis

The evening before the first exam, the phones ring incessantly. First up is Shah Sahab, the family priest.

'You're making a mistake, Zaheer. This a trap,' he says in that measured, annoying, all-knowing tone.

Most Muslim children across the state, especially those who are displaced from their homes and surviving in camps, are either refusing to take the boards or being coaxed not to appear for them by adults around them, for fear of fresh attacks.

Papa hangs up eventually and comes to me where I'm sitting at the dining table with my books and says, 'You can always take them next year, you know?'

I know. In a home that has cared only that I make a good match and am taken off their hands, I know. But when I look at Papa's eyes, there is no unkindness with which he is offering me this out. Only a father who would like to see his firstborn child live. I look at him silently. Then at a plate behind his face, where the ayat-ul-qursi hangs on the wall. Nanijaan brought it for us the last time she visited Mecca. It's the only thing in our living room that says out loud, *We are people of faith*. I will learn this about myself later, every time I feel the glare of the world on my face, decisions, opportunities, choices ticking away in bated breath. I will look away from the world into the glistening, thin places between our reality, just past what's troubling me. I will look in these in-between planes for signs, for answers, for the sound of my own voice.

'No. I want to take them this year only,' I look at Papa and simply say. He doesn't argue. Just shrugs and calls back Shah Sahab and asks him to pray for me. Then, out of nowhere, he comes back and places his hand on my head for a whole minute.

The boards don't start as early as regular school. Even then, by 7 A.M. C-8 is a flurry of activity. Papa is showering and dousing himself in his talcum powder; Dadi is praying and has a whole forest of incense lit at the table. Misba and I lie in Dada's bed hugging. I'm shaking slightly in my jeans and T-shirt as my sister hugs and repeats.

'You're going to do great, Zaru.'

Amma comes out of their room. She is dressed in a lovely, starched cotton block-print sari, a big bindi drawn on her forehead. Dadi turns her neck to check her from head to toe, then violently starts shaking her hand around Amma's neck, still mumbling her dua'as.

'I think she's asking you to wear your mangalsutra,' I say to Amma, laughing.

The mangalsutra is mostly worn by Hindu women, but not exclusively. Again, we're counting on a mob's stupidity. Amma takes hers out of a small jewellery box in her cupboard and puts it on. Papa sees her all dressed and smiles.

'Very nice.' Then, because he can't help it, he adds, 'Proper Tamilian you look.'

I see his hand trembling slightly too as he grabs the car keys from the majoos.

'Chalo, ready, beta?' he asks. I pick up my cloth pouch with my pen, pencils, eraser, two books to review in the car, and look at my family. We are stepping outside our cage. We are dressed to camouflage. We have practised the sounds we must make to survive in the wild. I don't know how to be more ready than this.

There have been outbreaks of violence in the chowk behind Jasmine Apartments recently. After a few weeks of no curfew, this morning our area has been put back under it. Papa goes downstairs to bring the car to the front, and Amma and I follow.

Dadi blows dua'as on me and waves incense in my face, still muttering god knows what. We reach the front steps of the building to find Papa sitting in his Hyundai Santro, drenched in sweat, the AC running at its highest setting. We stop by the police blockade, where Papa shows them my hall ticket. They let us pass. We drive around our street corner and out of Khanpur for the first time in two months. Entire neighbourhoods are deserted even at nine in the morning. Bustling markets are graveyards; cows sit lazily chewing their breakfast in the middle of the empty roads as Papa drives around them.

As we get out of the 'Muslim areas', life seems to course slowly back onto the streets. Scooters whiz scarily close to the car, as if all the city's daredevils are out to claim the streets. I sit in the backseat, morning air on my face, unsure whether to delight in this sudden aliveness or fear it. We are moving farther out of safety.

Hanumanpura turns out to be worse than what I've pictured in my head. Short and squat buildings, dull concrete and everything suspiciously empty. An industrial ghost town with very few trees, a police station to one side of the road, dust-covered cars and scooters on the other, looking like they haven't been moved in weeks. We stop a few times to ask for the address. Every person we ask peers into our car in a way that feels violating. I try to talk loudly and fearlessly to Amma, trying to be just another child, 'one of theirs', ignoring the suspicious eyes at the window, speaking over our thumping hearts, while Papa asks for directions in Gujarati.

We finally find the school. All our faces shatter. It is a two-storey row of classrooms with flimsy wooden doors, *which could be easily broken through*, we all are thinking.

In the throng of parents and students outside, I spot a few more Muslim faces. Saba, one of my classmates, walks up to me quickly and tightly grips my hand.

'You're okay?' she asks.

Yes, I nod, tears in my eyes just to see her alive and here. 'And you?'

She hugs me quickly, for the first time in all my years of knowing her, then returns to her corner to study.

We've all been told not to call one another's Muslim names out loud and accidentally spill who we are. I quickly scan the perimeter to see if there is the promised police bandobast, *cordoning*, at this school. I spot a single potbellied constable leaning by the gate. It's as if they didn't expect any of us to show up.

'Saba!' somebody suddenly shouts from across the veranda. It is another girl from Mount Carmel, a Hindu girl, bustling her way towards us. I watch Saba freeze, the colour drain from her face. I see parents with their sons and daughters look in the direction of this frozen girl as if recognising there are others, camouflaged, hidden among them. Papa mutters 'Bloody idiot' under his breath. I feel his body tense next to mine. The bell rings just then, thankfully, and the kids all disentangle from their anxious parents and start to walk away to the classrooms.

'You just keep your head down and keep writing, okay?' Papa tells me, putting a hand on my shoulder to steady me. I am properly shaking now. As I walk away, I turn to look at Amma and Papa standing under the tree one last time. He stands there, expressionless, hands held behind his back, belly sticking out into the world. Amma smiles as if with her smile she's trying to send me all her strength.

Later all I will remember of that three-hour exam is how I covered my hall ticket with my hand every time the proctor walked past me in the aisle. *Ame Parsi chiye* my brain keeps repeating, as if trying to build scales over my body. My hand writes furiously of its own volition. I am holding Nanijaan's old fountain pen, one that has a silver cap, inscribed almost invisibly on it 'Mjr. Amir Ahmed'.

I keep looking at the clock to see the hour hand move closer to noon. One privilege of going to an elite school was that, in the months before our genocide, teachers had prepared us, almost robot-like, with a series of mock exams to time ourselves to finish each paper within two and a half hours and leave a half hour for reviewing. I spend my half hour quickly skimming the pages, then tying them neatly together with a thread. I collect my pens and pencils in my hand, pick up my paper, walk to the front of the class and submit it to the examiner with five minutes to go.

Phupu has told me not to leave the classroom before that. My true colours might show if I stand out in the sun too long. She can come get me only at noon. At twelve exactly, I rush out of the dark, cold room into the hot afternoon sun and blink hard. Phupu isn't here yet. Then at the corner of the street I see her red Santro kicking up dust. I run to hug her tightly. Only then I realise there is someone else driving her car. Giri, her Hindu student, who is some sort of minor royalty from an old princely state, has come along as her bodyguard. Giri's loyalty to Phupu is unquestionable. He chauffeurs Apa around, runs her errands, once even punctured an abusive neighbour's car tyres for this teacher he worships. Apa keeps saying that Giri is a little dim, but she seems to have a minor crush on him, like all the other women in our family. He looks at me full of care.

'You're really brave, dude,' he says as I slip into the backseat and Phupu into the passenger seat next to him.

'See!' Phupu turns around to grin as she thwacks Giri on his bicep. 'I brought muscle power.'

I also notice the big wooden baton on her dashboard.

This is how I get through the first four exams. Papa, Amma and Phupu alternate dropping me off and picking me up in different cars, in different clothes, different routes each time. My exam at St Xavier's feels like a welcome break. Our bones are turning to salt.

• • •

'Yeh to apna area hai,' Papa proudly says as he drops me off in the Xavier's compound. He knows this neighbourhood; it's a biome he grew up in. He ran around these grounds, chased friends, kissed girls, played cricket, troubled old Irish principals.

As I wait to take my English exam, I sit on the steps of my father's school, soaking in the morning sun. I watch Xavier's boys walk past, thinking of what life could have been if I had gone to a mixed school instead of an all-girls one. *Would I be the way I am? Scared of touch, frightened to speak my mind?* I sit there wondering if life will ever offer me another path. I watch two boys pushing each other into the ground playfully. They're my age. But perhaps not from my side of the river.

On his way back home from dropping me off, Papa whistles to himself, feeling lighter than he has in days. The fresh air is clearing the mould in his heart. Then, just at the edges of his Mirzapur, his Hyundai is flagged down by cops. Papa speaks carefully, in pure, clear Gujarati, his bubbling rage under his skin threatening to show his true nature. The cops see his licence, read his name. Papa forgets to pretend like he is Parsi or Hindu or anyone but himself. He snaps in annoyance at these public servants. They order him out of his car to stand helpless, humiliated, on the street. Passersby mock. His car is searched. They poke and prod at his brand-new Hyundai. They smirk at the plastic covers still unremoved. Papa lets them. As he has let this state poke and smirk at him for thirty years. Once, this was his bike route to Xavier's, every day for twelve years. Once, he could walk this road in his sleep. Once, he would have punched anyone who stood in his way, making him feel like he didn't belong. Today he doesn't. He doesn't even go home and tell anyone. He tells us many years later. Almost at the end.

The road I am seeking to freedom appears after lunch. I am tired after the morning's exam and want to lie in front of the TV and doze. But Amma comes and wakes me. In her hand she's clutching the cordless.

'You know my student? The one from my English-speaking class?' I stiffen, thinking something terrible happened to them.

'Her brother just called. He was able to find tickets!' she beams.

Misba, who has been pretending to nap on the settee all this time, bolts up. 'For Madras?' she exclaims.

'Shhhh!' Amma and I immediately say.

'Yes!' Amma whispers, sidling up between us. All three of us hug.

'But how will we go?' I ask.

'No chance he will allow.' Misba nods, gesturing to Papa's bedroom.

Amma touches my cheek softly.

'I've seen you out on the balcony. I know what you have been thinking.'

I'm scared suddenly of how much my mother knows of how empty my insides feel, how ready I have felt to jump some days. Her touch seems to ground me.

'I have to try,' she says, and just like that she gets off the settee and heads for her bedroom. Misba and I look at each other. *Now?*

We follow her but stop outside their door, shamelessly eavesdropping, hands clasped with each other.

'Zaheer, I need to tell you something,' we hear Amma bravely start.

'Hmm. Kya hai?' he says. I am betting Papa hasn't even opened his eyes to listen.

'Mummy is coming to Madras next month.' I hear her voice wobble. She struggles to keep it steady. 'I want to take the girls to see her.'

Silence.

'Zara is depressed, Zaheer. And Misba, she won't show it. But they just need to get out of here for a bit, Zaheer. Please.'

More silence.

'It's too late,' Papa finally says. 'It's peak vacation time. I used to get the GEB quota, but no chance you'll get tickets now—'

'I already got them,' Amma jumps in. 'My student says her brother can bring them tomorrow if I can confirm now.'

Heart in my mouth, I peep around the edge of their door to see Papa's face.

'How many can he get?' Papa asks. I can see him now, propped up on one arm towards Amma, watching her like a hawk. She seems to be holding her ground.

'Three.'

'Only three?' He raises an eyebrow.

'Yes.' She meets his gaze. And doesn't flinch.

Papa lies back down flat and stares at the fan. Misba and I stand outside the door chanting prayers under our breath.

'Hmm. Kaafi kharaab ho gaya iss time,' he quietly mumbles. *This time was like never before.* He pauses again. Then finally, there it is, the path.

'Jaao.' *Go.*

Misba and I look at each other. Did he really say *go*?

Before our brains can process, our bodies fly inside their room, jump on the bed and crash on our father in a hug he didn't see coming. He awkwardly pries us away from his body.

'So you're going to go without me, huh?'

I remember us making some appropriately sympathetic noises. *So sad, no tickets. Only three. We will miss all of you.*

But *yes*! we yell inside our chests, *we are going!*

Radio Silence

Amma's eyes have held me spellbound since the moment I first saw light strike them. I remember the exact moment. Standing on the balcony, Amma was looking directly at the sun as it set across the river. She wasn't really blinking, as if trying to inhale all its heat and life, urging it towards her magnetic gaze, asking it to warm her darkest, coldest secrets. As the sky over the Sabarmati burst into a riot of ochre, violet and gold, her eyes caught flecks of it. They turned molten. Something alive moved there. Dreams passed before I could catch them. Blink. Gone. Then Amma turned to look at me. Her eyes when she would first notice I was beside her always looked empty. Then slowly recognition would fill. Her daughter. Her Zara, whom she named for that same sun-like brilliance. *In the eyes of the world, her firstborn.* Soon a wave of unbounded love would start to flow again, a dying river come back to life. But for a split second there, we'd both known a truth. I was not her firstborn. There was death before me. There is always death in Amma's eyes before she sees me.

Amma got married to Papa weeks before she turned twenty-two. In her wedding pictures, Amma reminds me of night flowers, a honeysuckle or cereus. A young girl still on her way to full bloom, grown used to coming into her own when no one's watching. I think of her as unnoticed because both the darkness of her skin and the death in her childhood seemed to weigh on her shoulders. In the pictures, she—the bride—seems to shrink from all the attention. All she seems to want is to get away from the bright lights, settle into her happily ever after. This is in May 1984.

. . .

Five months later, India's first and only woman prime minister, Indira Gandhi, is assassinated in Delhi. In Baroda, Amma finds out she's pregnant. A girl never shown how to love her body, who had no experience of men before her husband, no lessons in birth control or consent, no idea that pleasure and love are marital rights promised to her by the faith she so devoutly embraces, married to an imperfect stranger she's still learning to love, now finds herself hurtling towards womanhood. When I ask her today how she went so quickly from being at the precipice of art and self-discovery in college to suddenly just the body meant to bear this man's children, Amma simply shrugs.

'I was just doing what was expected of me. Yes, it's hard to believe, but even for an educated girl, I was mostly clueless.'

There are things we just aren't taught to ask for in our homes, including that love can be the reason to birth children. We're told two people being married is enough.

In her seventh month, just before she was to leave for her mother's home in Madras, where she would birth the baby, the obstetrician in Gujarat told Amma the walls of her uterus had loosened. A procedure to tie them up and hold the foetus in was performed, and Amma was put on the train back to her mother. Papa insisted he wouldn't take off from work till the baby arrived. He was still new at it. In Madras, Amma's best friend gave her Benjamin Spock's *The Common Sense Book of Baby and Child Care*. Amma immediately read it from cover to cover. An aunt recommended she see Dr Neela, one of the finest obstetricians in Madras. Dr Neela scanned her uterus for fault lines and found that the foetus's head wasn't as developed as it needed to be by eight months. Amma was given extra doses of supplements, more bed rest; her mother cooked her fresh broths and ghee-laden rotis.

Finally on 6 April 1985, a month shy of her first wedding anniversary, Amma gave birth to her first child, alone in the delivery room with Dr Neela and a midwife. These two strange women urged her on to do things with her body she had never done, to rip from it a part of her own flesh and blood and make it anew, give it its own first breath. No husband to rub her back, no mother to whisper prayers in her ears, she lay in that room there, a brave twenty-three-year-old woman-child heaving and pushing this child who had lived inside her for nine months, who had already started to feel like her own, whom she had come to love more than the man she'd made it with. She passed out the minute her son was born.

When she woke up in her hospital bed later that morning, her brother, mother and maternal uncle were standing in the room. Her brother looked like he'd been crying for hours. Through the post-partum fog she remembered she had birthed a son, the ultimate gift a woman can offer an Indian family. She was gold! *Why then*, she remembers asking herself, *are these silly people crying?*

Next to her a big bouquet of flowers took up all the space on a nightstand. Not from her husband, who was still a thousand miles away in Gujarat, but from her friend who'd lent her the Spock book. Finally, Dr Neela came in and sat by her bed and held her hand. Amma couldn't understand why everyone looked so sombre. Then she knew.

'Your baby isn't going to live very long,' she remembers the doctor mouthing.

'How long?' Amma asked. A few hours. A day or two at most, she was told.

Amma wanted to see and hold her child. They brought him to her. As he lay on her chest, a little piece of tape on his upper lip hiding his cleft palate, head full of silky brown hair, he opened his eyes for a moment. Her heart stopped.

'He had my eyes,' Amma tells us, always choking on the words, thirty-six years later.

. . .

Her brother with his deep baritone voice in which he often sang Frank Sinatra songs she loved, now sang the azaan, the Islamic call to prayer, into the baby's ears. He looked around the room for a name. *Should we even name him?* Amma could hear her family wondering. For now, he was still here. So Amma insisted he have a name. *Mohammad Yusuf.* The first part for the Prophet, the second for her grandfather.

Nobody thought to ask Papa. He was going to have no part in this child's short life, not even in the choice of name.

Little Mohammad Yusuf was taken back to the nurses, and just like that, bare-armed, empty-wombed Amma was brought away home. Her uncle frantically telephoned Papa, asking him to fly out immediately instead of waiting to take the thirty-six-hour train scheduled for two days later.

'Things are not okay with the baby, beta,' her uncle said. 'And Rukhsi needs you.'

Papa's plane landed in Madras the next afternoon at three thirty. Just as his only son softly breathed out one last time, alone in a hospital at the other end of the city.

My mother, when she tells this story, usually skips ahead to the part where Papa ranted and yelled at her mother and her, blamed them, packed her up and took her to Bangalore to his friends, where he drank and drank until he forgot all about what had just happened; she tells how she was simply patted on the back when she returned to Ahmedabad and told by Dadi, 'Chalo, try again,' that her womb would fill again in no time. And how it did, with a daughter; how she was never again given that most basic of care while pregnant, not allowed to ever go back to her mother's for her deliveries. Amma skips ahead to all the bigger, louder, visible wrongs because she needs the spectacle of the great Indian family tragedy to hide her unease with the senselessness of loss.

But I pause in that moment the last time I ask her the story. I ask her, 'What was the first thing Papa did when he walked in that door in Madras and saw you there? A mother with no baby?'

Did he see your empty eyes the way I have all my life? I want to add but don't. She looks at me like I'm a fool, to think a man could ever understand what that means, to have your child wrested away from you, whether it is by human bloodlust or a birth defect.

'He came in and hugged me,' she hesitantly relents. 'And he stroked my hair and said, "It's okay. It happens." That's when I broke down. Wept and wept.'

So strong is her rage for everything that came after, she skips over this sliver of time when he tried. This time of two people quietly grieving what they'd lost; this moment of guilt a young girl felt, as if her body had failed the family she was supposed to make, this moment when a hole punctured its way through a young man's heart—a man who despised pain—for a son he would never hold, never teach to play cricket, never ruffle his hair, pinch his cheeks, arm-wrestle. All the things he'd later half-heartedly try with me.

Being as stubbornly plain and honest as he was, Papa knew he had failed his wife and child by his absence. And guilt didn't sit well with him. Guilt made him a monster. In that moment the only window of light that had shone on their marriage slowly started to close. From that day, it would start to suffocate them both and the children born of them. He would never again speak of the child he never saw, nor would he ever fully see the daughters he had. She would never again want to be touched by him, and yet she would let him. The silence between them ended that day in his rage. She stopped being a girl whose heart could be broken. She was a mother now, that most charged of roles a girl can take on. She would take all the love she was once going to give these two men and empty it out of her eyes, her heart, her memory of her own girlhood. She would make it smoke and fire and pour it into two young girls instead.

One day, during our lockdown in 2002, Papa will come out of the shower and go into his bedroom, parading past all of us first in his towel, which he wraps all the way around his abdomen like a dress. He will be getting changed into his soft kurta pajama as he has done every day since he 'retired' from GEB. He has nowhere to go, and now especially so, in more ways than one. Amma will go into the room just then to grab a fresh kitchen towel from the linen cupboard.

'Rukhsi . . . ,' Papa will softly say, and Amma will walk over to him. He will take Amma's hand and put it on his heart. His big, beating heart under the white muslin. From there he will guide her palm to his left breast. He will push her fingers into his skin until she can feel a pea-sized lump.

'Do you feel it too?' he will ask, voice never more filled with self-doubt than in this moment.

Amma will push around his breast feeling for other anomalies, a deep frown on her brow.

'Yes . . .'

'I'll go see Glen when all this finishes,' Papa will say. Always in a hurry to shut down what he cannot bear to think about. Glen is our Christian neighbours', the Ferros's, son. He's a general physician. Papa likes to go to him because he rarely charges him.

'Insha'allah, yes,' Amma will say. Then silence will settle between them like sediment again. And she will go off to the kitchen. And he will walk out to the balcony to watch over this burnt city.

Mother Tongue

Over two weeks I've written six exam papers. Through scattered stabbings in the old city, some more curfew, more police vans blaring warnings in the middle of the night urging us to 'maintain the peace', and with Papa threatening to cancel our tickets, I have written exams. He has discovered that our Amma sort of lied, that our tickets are technically not 'booked' but 'wait-listed for confirmation', and he's looking for an excuse to take back his word. We must not give him an excuse.

I study each evening for the next day's exam, sometimes with Mana, mostly by myself. Amma keeps calling the automated railway booking line to check our booking status on the waiting list. We are seventh, eighth and ninth on the list. Six people ahead of us must move out of the queue, cancel, change plans, give up, before we can get those tickets. Misba, who is the least prayerful of the three of us—once she hears this latest update, how close we are—takes to the jaanemaaz. Now every time we look, we find Misba curled up in a room, in sajda pose on the prayer mat, chubby palms open to the heavens, begging, pleading Allah to cause the other six to cancel.

I have one last paper left: Sanskrit. It's the one I am most confident about. I've been scoring a full one hundred out of one hundred on all my mock tests. Apa has been competing with me about her Sanskrit scores for the past two years. She has done very well in it too. But this is the first time I've outdone her in a subject other than English.

'Yeah, but it's an easy subject. Anyone can score a hundred,' she argues. I don't respond. As I pull on my jeans and grab my stationery to go to the last school for my last board exam, I am confident I will do it: score the hundred that is almost muscle memory for me now. I will redeem this chance I almost lost to show the world what I am made of, how hard I can work, who I can be.

When Papa and I arrive at the school designated on my hall ticket, we realise it is not really a school. It is a three-storey building within a temple complex. We park outside its gates. Papa walks in with me through the redbrick-walled compound with its iron gates, its looming idols, and 'Jai Hanuman' and 'Jai Shree Ram' written across the walls. He keeps a firm hand on my wrist, muttering under his breath, 'Arre re. Arre re,' every few steps. *Oh no.*

This isn't just a blatantly Hindu school. We notice the school workers all dressed in saffron kurtas or robes watching every student and parent with suspicion and an almost mocking glee. They greet one another with loud, boisterous 'Jai Shree Rams'. This is a school clearly looking to pick a fight, to pick out a Muslim who dares walk through its gates.

Papa deposits me outside the classroom and lingers. I can see he doesn't want to leave me here for three hours.

'Kuchh nahin hoga,' he finally says. 'Just keep your head down, don't talk to anybody, and keep writing.'

Then he leans in to my ear.

'Don't worry. *God* is there.'

We both know we dare not mention *Allah* within these walls.

The exam starts, and for almost three quarters of it, things seem as normal as our new normal can seem, even if I'm wound up like a spring on the inside. I hide my name on my hall ticket as usual. I keep checking the faces of strangers in the seats around me, hoping to spot a familiar one, someone from the world outside who may know and recognise me, some comfort. But it seems like I am the only kid from my class of sixty girls who has been placed in this centre.

An hour before the exam is supposed to end, a man walks into our classroom. He's dressed in a scruffy kurta and looks like some of those people we have seen on the TV screen running amok on our streets, hunting, looting, burning. It looks like he and our room's proctor know each other. I notice the big saffron tilak mark on his forehead and feel my palms begin to sweat. I pretend to keep writing, but my whole body is measuring the distance between this man and me.

The stranger tells the proctor in Gujarati, 'Come, let's get a cup of chai.'

The proctor looks sheepish and gestures towards us, students writing our exams. The man with the saffron mark grins and nudges his arm. 'Haan, let them also relax, have some fun.'

The proctor laughs at this. And as I watch in shock, both men leave the examination hall and walk away. The class of fifty-odd unsupervised students around me erupts. Young boys and girls rise out of their chairs, start to boldly roam around, peeping into other students' papers, chatting loudly, throwing pens and pencils at one another across the room. The law has left us to vent it out. Figure it out among ourselves.

I sit there horrified, melting into my desk, unable to believe this is a state-level exam, the same one I was told all year my whole future depends on. I can't believe these students and their bold entitlement to this moment; how normal it seems to them, to race ahead like this, grab an unequal advantage when handed one by the authority, to take what they want, override the system, a moral free-for-all.

A new anger builds inside me. Or perhaps it has been sitting in me all these weeks. Here I am, struggling simply to recall everything I've studied, everything my teachers and books taught me before that damn train was burnt, before the hell of the last two months.

I am risking my life, my family's lives, to just be here. And here are the rest of them, revelling in the freedom they take so easily for granted, stomping it and rubbing it into the ground, into my face.

The proctor and his saffron friend return. They look amused as students scamper to their seats. Everyone pretends like nothing happened, even as some students continue to giggle. Everything is 'back to normal'. Then the man with the saffron tilak walks up to the first desk in the row where I am seated halfway down. He picks up the question paper from the student and starts to read out the first set of objective questions, opposites, meanings and so forth. I don't understand what he's doing.

Then he starts to call out the answers. He *is* the Sanskrit teacher at this school, I realise.

I try to shut his voice out, screaming inside my head, *No, I've studied for it. I don't want it this way. I want to do it the right way.* My mind struggles on for a few more minutes before I open my eyes and look down at the one question I am feeling unsure about.

My eyes tear up as I find myself checking the answer against what he reads out. I was right. I answered correctly. But I gave in. Now I am one of them. Sanskrit is something I take so much pride in being good at, a language I love, I want to be part of. Now I'll only be the Muslim girl who got the extra mark by cheating in a Hindu language. A severing of me from my tongue, more unbelonging.

All these months of fear, confusion, isolation, of holding out with sheer willpower against these forces that willed us to corrupt ourselves and become like them, to respond with violence, are boiling up in my belly. These are the young boys and girls I am to grow up with. It is starting right here, the country they and I must live in and share. People feeling wronged and being allowed by the law to right things as they see fit. This is the cycle of hate and imagined vengeance that is going to burn through India faster than any amount of pain and shock that can be found in relief camps across the city, where little children are still crying for lost mothers. The power is here. The privilege these boys and girls enjoy, to be safe in their names, safe in their gods. This power has always rested in their bodies, in this land. It has always been theirs to take. And now someone has come along to show them it's okay to flaunt it, to dare the system to try to stop them. And for one tiny moment, I've become one of them. And it feels terrible.

I know I am being noticeably quiet when Papa returns to get me in the afternoon. He's puzzled because all my life when he and Amma have come to get us on our last day of exams before a summer break, I have flown through the gate and hugged them in excitement. But this is no ordinary exam or summer. This has been the summer we've lost everything. He tries half-heartedly.

'So, excited now about your trip?'

When I don't respond, he gives up and we ride back the rest of the way home in silence.

Hung Up

The exams are done. The end of April is here. It's Papa's birthday. He's forty-nine.

'Chalo, now I'm fifty,' he repeats all day, as if convincing himself his 'retirement' makes sense. He has no job to return to, no interview calls from the many applications he has half-heartedly sent at Amma's and Shah Sahab's insistence. Forty-nine and nothing, in his mind, to look forward to. He may as well be seventy.

He's distracted, so Misba and I steal the cordless every few hours from him to call the automated Indian Railways number. We are down to one, two and three on the waiting list. *So close.* After Papa sees the birthday shirt Amma saved up for, bought for him and has been hiding since December in her cupboard, he disappears into his room. From his monthly pension money, withdrawn and stashed in his wallet, he pulls out the cash for our tickets. He asks her to keep it, even if the tickets don't come through.

'But I'm not letting you go, haan, if you don't get confirmed,' he warns, and walks away.

Phupu and Apa have returned to their apartment. They show up in the afternoon. Phupu has baked a simple chocolate cake. We gather around and decide we have so much to celebrate. Papa's birthday, Amma's and Papa's eighteenth wedding anniversary, Dada's memorial, but most of all we celebrate what we're hoping is the end of the violence. Modi and the state and national BJP administrations have come under intense scrutiny for how Gujarat has burned. A new human rights group has arrived in Ahmedabad every day; there are calls for criminal investigations into the state's complicity.

Human and women's rights activists and organisations from across the world have condemned the atrocities that are slowly coming to light each day.

There's no way they are going to get away with it, we tell ourselves, munching our slices of chocolate cake, sprinkled at Misba's request with Cadbury Gems.

Already, I realise, looking around at my crazy family, we are trying to tell ourselves what happened was normal. *This has always happened. And it always becomes okay.*

Dadi hovers as I am packing my suitcase the next day. She's loud enough for Papa to hear outside.

'Itne kapde kya pack kar rahi hai? Wapas aane ka plan nahin hai?' *Why are you packing so many clothes? As if you're never coming back.*

Papa sees Misba standing on the balcony at the same time as Khandad Khan's son, who is on his deck too, smoking a cigarette. He starts yelling at her for unnecessarily 'tempting boys'. *Nothing is normal,* I mutter to myself, and continue to pack. I throw in one diary and pen along with mostly only shorts and T-shirts. Madras is hot and humid. Madras is by the sea. Madras is not Ahmedabad.

On 1 May, I get a phone call. It's from a girl called Aisha who has been in the same class as me at Mount Carmel for two years. She and I have become friends over the last few months, and our parents have invited each other over for dinner a few times. Her mother thanks me every time she sees me for helping Aisha focus more on her studies and less on boys. I haven't really done much except share my notes with her, tutor her occasionally, but mostly be her only friend in class because everyone else thinks she's a bit ditzy and overeager. To me, Aisha has seemed mostly nice and harmless, even though she randomly says things like 'My dadaji hates Muslims because of the Partition' to my face and then quickly adds, 'But of course you and your family are not like those guys.'

I've listened to her rant and ignored it mostly, too afraid to lose this one Hindu friend willing to visit me within our ghetto, someone whose parents can bear to sit around and drink with my dad and it somehow hasn't ended badly. Maybe it is because her parents are as ditzy as she is and just moved to the city a few years ago and don't have too many friends either. They live across the river from us in a fancy new town-house development, and sometimes give me and Misba a lift home in her dad's black SUV. You haven't heard of Aisha so far because from 27 February until 1 May, Aisha hasn't called me once.

'Heyyyy!' her high-pitched voice now squeals through the receiver. 'Kaisi hai, yaaaar?' she drawls, in the way Americans ask, *What's up?* They're not asking to find out how you are. It's just words.

'So, how did you do on your papers? Duuuuude, I think I might even get like 70 or 75 per cent this time!' she rattles on when I don't respond.

'Hi, Aisha,' I say. In my voice I can hear the same icy formality Phupu sometimes uses with anyone who has messed with her. 'How are you doing?' I ask. I am modelling for her basic human decency. Something I have waited to hear for three months.

'Me?' she seems a little confused at my tone. 'I'm toh great, yaar. Might go to Hong Kong soon to see my cousins. I really need a break, man! You know, na? All this has been too much.'

My heart skips. *Maybe she isn't as dense as I thought her to be.*

'Yes, it's been tough,' I say, embarrassed my voice is wobbling.

'Yeaaaah man, I don't want to give another exam for the rest of my life!' She giggles. *Oh, she means this year of the boards.*

I ask curtly, 'So do you need something, Aisha?'

'Arre tu toh bohot serious ho gayi hai exam de de ke!' She's mocking my seriousness. It must be all the studying!

She chirps on. 'Chal! Let's go for a movie. I'll call Nandini and Natasha also.'

These girls are all part of a new group I've hung out with in the two years since we returned from Baroda. Again, names you haven't heard as much as Mana's because none of them have called me in two months. I'm done pretending.

'How can I come for *a movie*, Aisha?' I bark. 'My whole area has been under curfew for three months.'

Then she says the words that will continue to ring in my ears anytime I look back, anytime I am asked what school was like for me growing up in India, anytime my child wants to hear a fun childhood story. These are the words that tell me I've been living in a dream.

'What rubbish, yaar! There's been no curfew for months!'

It's as if our pain hasn't registered for anyone except us. Our loss doesn't exist. Our horror isn't real, it never happened. Their malls still brim, their restaurants still fill with chatter, their theatres still ring with music and dance, while we live hunkered in our own homes. We have sat beside one another for years, learning from the same books, fighting for the same half grade, dreaming of secret crushes and future careers and someday weddings. But we have also lived across a river that drew the line between 'us' and 'them'. And unlike the river, changing with the seasons, this line has become permanent. We live in two different Ahmedabads, two different Gujarats, two different Indias. And she isn't willing to fight for mine. Bloody hell, she doesn't even see mine.

She is still babbling on about the movie, breathlessly gasping, 'Don't worry, I'll buy your ticket too,' when I press 'end' on the cordless Panasonic and hang up on her.

Water

A Train to the Ocean

The Navjeevan, Hindi for 'a new life', is a dark-blue train with a strip of aquamarine running down its middle. It starts before sunrise from Ahmedabad Junction in Kalupur and winds its way through 1,891 kilometres of the subcontinent, all the way from the belly of India's westernmost state, with its flying dust and drying rivers, to the beautiful old Gothic Revival Madras Terminus, on India's southeastern coast. You alight from the train, you step outside the station in Madras, and you can literally smell the ocean. It's a mile down the road.

All through our childhoods, the only time Papa agreed to let us meet Nanijaan was when he could club it with trips to Ayodhya, in Bangalore, to visit his friends Ila and Rishi and their families. The whole family—him, Dada, Dadi, Amma, Misba and I—would be booked in six adjoining berths of a two-tier, second-class AC carriage. Amma would cook for two days in preparation for the thirty-two-hour train journey. She'd pack kheema and peas rolled in chapattis, fried garlicky cumin potatoes, chicken salad sandwiches, boiled eggs, mint chutney sandwiches, shaami kababs and fresh mangoes.

The household would wake up with the Fajr azaan just before the crack of dawn. Papa would call Babu bhai, the taxi guy from the slum across the way, to bring his large Omni van and pile all our suitcases and handbags in. The food bag would get special care and attention. Amma would cradle it in her arms like a baby. Papa would pack enough Bisleri mineral water from the pharmacy for the whole carriage.

Then we would reach the station, four grown-ups and two children, and we'd stand at the platform, where he wouldn't let us squat or sit, even as we bent over and leant sleepily against Amma's hip, until the train rolled in from the yard, smelling of fresh sheets and Dettol-wiped compartment floors. The next forty-eight hours would be the best part of my summer. I'd climb up to the topmost berth with a bunch of Famous 5s, Tinkle comics and later Jane Austens, and be lost to the world, descending, like the other passengers with train gymnastic talent, only at mealtimes. It was the one time nobody cared to hover and bother us, because if we came down too early, the lower berths would have to be folded up and everyone would sit huddled uncomfortably. As the sun would rise, we'd watch from the window as Gujarat's cotton fields gave way to Maharashtra's sugarcane-lined horizon. Amma would always take the smaller berth across the aisle from the rest of the family. I'd curl up by her feet and we'd stare silently at the changing landscape. She would look like she was wishing she had her brushes. I was always wishing I could jump off the carriage and run through the wide-open lands and into the horizon.

In Andhra Pradesh we'd wait for Vijayawada station so Papa could buy us all a treat even he couldn't resist. Sugary, sticky aam papdi, fresh mango pulp candied and beaten into flat sheets that we'd peel apart to make it last longer. We'd spend two train nights giggling as Dadi's snores competed with those of strangers in the carriage. She remained unbeatable.

Every time we'd go over a bridge, I'd think of how most of our railway infrastructure was as old as the British Raj, and how in old Hindi movies a convenient plot device was these rusted, rickety bridges collapsing and dragging entire trains into mighty Indian rivers. I'd close my eyes the minute we'd get on a bridge—you could tell by the changing hollow sounds of train wheels over the slats—and pray until that hollow sound went away. Till we were on firm ground again.

The Navjeevan usually ran seven to eight hours behind schedule. This was an accepted fact, and Papa would keep track of the shifting ETA. He'd roam through the carriages looking for the ticket collector, whom he would then hound for the arrival time. He wanted to be sure we were packed and ready to deboard with efficiency, with minimal touching of the toilet walls near the exits. As the train slowed to a stop at Basin Bridge Junction, just outside Madras, waiting to be assigned a platform, he'd look at Amma, who was peering longingly outside, and smirk.

'Aha! There is that smell! Now we know we're in Madras.'

He wasn't wrong. The smell that would squeeze through the AC carriage doors and windows and strike us with all its putrid pungency was from the Buckingham Canal, which ran through and around Madras, again British built, and reduced to a city sewer. The Navjeevan stood waiting over this bridge for a whole twenty minutes before it finally arrived in the city.

'Do you see your mother?' Papa would tease. 'Even this smell is okay, as long as it is from Madras.'

Dadi would frown and peer through the tinted, scratched-up windows too. The language in her ears had gone from her own Gujarati to the unintelligible Tamil. People seemed darker. The women selling fish and fresh coconuts looked freer. She liked nothing about this destination we were nearing.

But Amma didn't care. She would sit with her face pressed into the window, taking in the sea breeze tinged with the smell of shit. Even if for a short week or two, she was home. And she was going to belong.

Game of Telephone

On 27 February 1933, the Reichstag was burnt down. The Nazi Party claimed this was an act of violence by communists—one of the bogeymen of their world. They claimed emergency legislation was needed to counter uprisings. The Reichstag Fire Decree was swiftly passed. The regime could now suspend any right to assemble, to speech, to the press; it could arrest and incarcerate anyone without specific charges, confiscate property, dissolve political organisations, overrule the law.

On 27 February 2002, when the train burned in Gujarat, the BJP–VHP–Bajrang Dal, all branches of the European Fascist–inspired RSS, transmitted a unanimous message: the burning was *an act of terror.* Fingers were explicitly pointed at Gujarat's bogeymen: the Muslim citizenry. The burning train set Gujarat and India on a new path. First the curfew, the violence, the open, widespread brutality and sexual depravity towards Muslims, their total dehumanisation and disenfranchisement. By the end of 2002, more than fifty thousand Muslims became refugees/escapees/survivors in their own country. The government slowly pinched and squeezed the number of dead, as if forcibly closing a glaring wound. From more than 2,000 dead, the number slipped to 1,800, then to 1,040, and finally to a shameful ambiguous 'between 700 to 900'. Hundreds of mass graves—women, men and children, chopped up, burnt and hurriedly piled into their own land—hundreds of dargahs and mosques demolished, whole villages emptied of Muslims by the truckload, these tell a different story to anyone still bothering with facts.

In July 2002, Modi asked for the state assembly to be dissolved and for fresh elections to be held.

In December 2002, as voting began, voters said things like 'Only Modi can protect us Hindus'. The VHP leader, Pravin Togadia, declared that 'now politics in India will be based on Hindutva'. In his campaign speech on the eve of the state elections, Modi told an adoring crowd, 'You decide whether there should be Diwali in Gujarat or whether firecrackers should burst in Pakistan . . . When you go to vote this time, if you press your finger on [the Congress symbol], you will hear the screams of Godhra!'

On Election Day, a BJP ad in the local newspaper read: 'Pay your homage to Godhra's martyrs. Cast your vote.'

BJP won 127 seats out of 182, a majority unlike any it had seen in two decades of political machinations. Modi remained Gujarat's chief minister for twelve years.

. . .

A few weeks before the train burning, I had walked across the living room and overheard my name on Dadi's lips.

'. . . was saying that Zara told her that she prays you and Rukhsana get a divorce.'

My heart sank. I knew what she was referring to. That morning Dadi had been on the phone with her relative from Bombay. Over the summer, we had visited this relative—an aunt who was a known gossip. She had made us kids sit in a circle one evening and share stories of Dada. We were each narrating our fondest memories of him. Suddenly this aunt asked me what I thought about my dad, who, in contrast to my softspoken Dada, yelled so much. 'Tell me, beta,' she coaxed in her sugary voice.

I hesitated to trust her, but I wanted so much to be heard, for our silent screams to mean something. I told her, in tears, how I trembled when Papa screamed, how I couldn't bear to see my mother's eyes. I didn't know what to expect from this woman, except to be heard. But here were my words, passed through the cordless phone from Bombay to Ahmedabad, from Dadi's ears to her lips, and, warped into a hurtful untruth, they were reaching my father.

'Don't talk rubbish, Mummy,' Papa bitterly scolded Dadi. 'My Zara would never say that.'

My Zara, he was saying. My heart lifted. But Dadi rubbed it in harder.

'Why would I lie to you? I heard it myself this morning! I am also shocked,' Dadi said.

I sneaked out of the kitchen and ran to the laundry room, heart racing. I heard Papa's slippers smack across the tiles as he walked over to the laundry room.

I will obsess all my life over that brief silence between when he told his mother to shut up and when he decided to come find me. I will ask myself if that was his conscience weighing my truth against these whispers. If he knew in his heart, even as he rumbled down the hallway, that I was *his Zara. I would never hurt him.* I will ask over and over if he just couldn't help it, if all our lives we had always been hurtling towards this moment.

He threw the bedroom door open so hard it hit the wall. I still tremble at the sound of doors crashing.

'Why would you say that? Are you trying to kill me?' he thundered at me. 'Your mother has fully brainwashed you.' Then he moved towards me, hand lifted in the air.

'Zaheer!' my mother yelled, and sprang out of nowhere, a tigress from thin air.

He wasn't even drunk that afternoon, as he stood there glaring menacingly at his bogeyman, his own daughter, severing blood and trust between us, taking the violence that had infiltrated his home and marriage and making it mine to carry.

I watched Dadi standing there. She was holding back a smirk. Something broke loose inside. I'd never heard my voice this loud.

'She's lying,' I boomed. 'They're all lying.' If I'd known how to build a Molotov cocktail, I would have lobbed one into the doorway where he stood. My whole being was shaking. This was my home. I should have been safe here. I should have been believed. Instead, I had been given this lifetime of fear. I was done fearing either of them.

Papa looked at me, confused. I could feel the tears burning my eyes. In one afternoon, the slow poison that had distilled through our lives exploded as if someone had thrown a lit match down our throats. Dadi had done this. But I hated my father in that moment the most for not believing in us enough to fight for us.

That day is the first time I've ever raised my voice so loudly at my father, mere days before the Godhra fire. Afterwards I run into the bathroom and sit on the toilet shaking, hiding till the storm outside and the one raging within me pass. But they don't. I fear I am becoming him. I hear him breaking a glass outside. I hear him striking my mother. I hear my sister softly crying on the other side of the bathroom door. The fight is leaking out of our bodies, like gasoline, in the days before the train burns.

'It's okay, Zaheer.' I hear Dadi's voice. It's soothing, syrupy. 'She's a child. Children say foolish things.' I hear someone sweeping broken glass in the back, perhaps Gulshan. I know she wants to protect us, but this is what she can do: clear the debris of our hurt.

I hear Papa run off to the bathroom to hide too. We are now on two sides of the same wall, father and daughter both hiding in bathrooms. I can hear him clear and empty his throat. I pray he is emptied of words for the day.

I sit in the bathroom awhile longer. In my heart, I want this to end so badly that I'm wishing C-8 had crashed with all of us during the earthquake. I'm wishing C-8 could explode into the night sky with a leaking cylinder. Or that a plane would crash into us. Anything is better than this life of being a second-class citizen in this home. I don't know then, as I sit in the bathroom, all of sixteen, thinking my life is hard and that it should end, that the annihilation I am asking for is not one I want. I don't know that my days in C-8 are numbered. As are Papa's. A countdown has begun. I don't know yet that greater annihilation awaits out there, on the streets of my country, and I will ache for even this scrap of safety and belonging once that monster is unleashed.

. . .

In May 2014, I am twenty-eight years old and working in Mumbai when Modi wins the national elections and becomes the prime minister of a billion-plus Indians. I stopped telling people I am from Gujarat long ago; I know the truth of who he is. I know what the RSS is capable of. I am a product of those capabilities. People around the country have forgotten Gujarat's 'macabre dance of death', as one inquiry committee called it. There is no Nuremberg for us. Voters seem impressed instead by how Gujarat is a shining example of strong governance by a strong man. A nation we've long called our motherland will now have a strict, disciplined, principled father. Nobody questions the fact that there is no real opposition left in Gujarat, that law-and-order institutions have become an extension of the state machinery, that Muslims in the state now live ghettoised. After he wins, it starts with beef. Whispers of Muslims carrying away holy cow mothers in their trucks. Innocent Muslim cattle traders lynched in broad daylight. Homes of dissidents bulldozed by the state calling them illegals. In 2019, he wins an even greater majority and is re-elected a second time. All opposing forces are shut down. Only one voice speaks. And the response is a resounding 'Har Har Modi'; a chant fashioned around a religious phrase usually ascribed to Shiva rouses millions of Indians, who now swallow his every word like holy diktat, unquestioning.

In August 2019, after Modi's re-election, the country's Supreme Court finally decides the Ayodhya–Babri Mosque demolition case, which has plagued India for seventy years. Acknowledging that Muslims have a legal claim to the land but that Hindus and baby Ram (they have a trust representing the mythological infant) have a spiritual one, the land where Babri Mosque stood for five hundred years before its illegal demolition in a modern, independent nation is granted to the VHP- and RSS-backed Ram Birthplace Trust. The same Supreme Court in 2004 called Modi a modern-day Nero who had looked away while Gujarat burned. Times have changed. Lord Ram's temple construction begins with much fanfare. Hindus fill trains and planes from all over the country and across continents to attend the ceremony. All of BJP's and RSS's leaders join the massive celebrations. Modi himself lays the inaugural stone. Meanwhile, Indian news channels and publications are slowly bought out by the party's cronies. Those who hold out are raided and harassed. Meanwhile, Kashmir, the occupied territory with a Muslim majority caught in a seventy-year tussle for its independence between Pakistan and India, is divested of the special status that grants it autonomy; it is stripped of its statehood and people of Modi's choosing are installed to govern it without democratic elections. Meanwhile, in major Indian cities, homeowners and gated neighbourhoods openly say no to renting to Muslim tenants. Muslim food delivery workers are beaten up. The violence is now dispersed among town, village and city equally. Nothing is left burning so long that the world notices. Just long enough. Meanwhile WhatsApp becomes our new whisper network. Inflammatory lies wake people up each morning, rousing India's middle class against their Muslim neighbours, vendors, grocers, friends. *Muslims are spitting in your food to spread COVID-19. Any Muslim electoral victory is celebrated in Pakistan. Muslims are having multiple children to increase their population and convert India to an Islamic state. Their boys are trying to steal and impregnate your girls through love jihad. The Taj Mahal is built on the demolished site of an ancient temple. Cow urine will cure your cancer.*

Voters, hungering for a father's love, in our raped and looted land, drink in the lies.

In December 2019, the second-term Modi government forces through two important bills with its supermajority. One, called the Citizenship Amendment Act (CAA), grants citizenship to refugees from neighbouring countries based on religion, all religions except Islam. On its own, this shouldn't apply to India's two hundred million Muslims per se. But the second bill, the National Register of Citizens (NRC), empowers local officials to cast doubt on whether you might be illegal, to decide that you should be sent to a detention camp or deported if you cannot provide documentary proof of your belonging. Together, these bills put the burden of proving citizenship on anyone who may not have this proof of belonging. When Muslims protest this nationwide, taking to the streets, the government uses the Unlawful Activities (Prevention) Act (UAPA), to imprison for unspecified amounts of time anyone it considers anti-national. *A terrorist.* Dozens of educated, bright young Muslim activists in Mumbai and Delhi and elsewhere are imprisoned.

In April 2023, a special court in Ahmedabad acquits sixty-seven people accused of participating in the massacres, including Dr Maya Kodnani, Dr Jaydeep Patel and Babu Bajrangi.

In August 2023, a schoolteacher encourages a Hindu middle schooler to slap his Muslim classmate as the child sobs helplessly. Someone captures this on a phone camera. Around the same time on a train elsewhere, a Hindu cop shoots Muslim passengers and walks away. This is also captured on a phone camera. Young girls in hijab are banned from entering their own schools. A young boy is stripped and paraded naked and made to chant 'Jai Shree Ram' before they are lynched on the street, all captured on phone cameras. Lone wolves, street mobs, the whole might of the state—it works like a well-oiled machine, it looks scintillating on phone cameras. Our genocide wasn't captured on mobile phone cameras, which is perhaps why a new generation of Hindu Indians looks at these scattered stories of our cleansing intrigued, unable to draw lines between cause and effect. They don't remember where the whispers that made us 'the other' started.

A Prayer by the River

On 7 May 2002, nearly three months since our lives disappeared in an endless curfew and the world across the river forgot us, we wake up. The azaans from all six mosques around Khanpur ring in the air. It's time for Fajr namaz. I get up from the floor mattress where Misba is still snoring softly. I wash my arms, my feet, scrub water into my face and scalp. I pick Dada's favourite jaanemaaz from the table and lay it down on the balcony floor where he died. Then I step onto it, wrap Amma's dupatta around my head, making sure I cover every inch of my skin except my palms and fingers. Today I need to make sure Allah sees and hears everything I have to say.

The stars are still pricking through Ahmedabad's black velvet sky and there is a bite in the morning breeze.

'Allah miya bas humko idhar se sahi salamat le jaao,' *Allah, please just carry us safe and sound from here*, I utter as I bring my forehead to rest on the mat, spread my palms out to the sky, loose tears spilling from my eyes to the mat, instantly absorbed, accepted.

'Take care of my papa, Allah miya, and take care of Dadi, and my phupu and my apa. And take care of my dada who lies in this city, and my nana and my brother already in your refuge.'

Last evening, I went downstairs to see Mana's family. The girls' faces have been sunken for days, ever since they heard Misba and I are leaving. That they must continue to live through this nightmare. We hugged and held each other for long minutes.

. . .

I name all three sisters. 'Take care of my Mana and my Shilu auntie. Take care of my Amal, Allah miya. She taught me to love you.' A sob escapes my lips.

Gulshan will show up soon, having crept through the curfew yet again. She will help us load our stuff into the van. She will be happy for us. But she is afraid too of being left behind with Dadi.

'Take care of my Gulshan, Allah miya, and her children and all her neighbours.'

I rise from the mat, and down past the balcony's parapet I can see the little pricks of yellow lanterns starting to come on in the slums, and kitchen lights in Firdaus and neighbouring buildings.

'Take care of your people, Allah. Take care of all your people. Take care of everyone we are leaving behind.'

I hear Amma open the door for Gulshan. I hear Papa go into the bathroom. Phupu and Apa have stayed over in Dadi's room and are stirring too. Amma lies next to Misba, hugs her small body and wakes her. We quickly get dressed: jeans, loose T-shirts, canvas shoes, Amma in a loose short kurta over track pants. Normal, non-Muslim clothes. Apa hugs me from behind as I'm filling our water bottles in the kitchen.

'Have a nice time, okay?' She smiles through her braces at me. 'Exams are done. Forget all this here. You deserve it.'

Phupu helps us carry our bags to the lift, where Hussain bhai is waiting. Phupu taps my shoulder.

'Don't worry about your results, okay? I'll collect them. Let me deal with it now.'

I let go of the suitcase and wrap my hands around her waist, letting her bushy hair tickle my cheek, letting her strength be the thing I carry with me. Dadi comes out in her nightie with her namaz dupatta still tied around her head, mouth muttering dua'as.

She prays and blows on Misba's and my heads. She barely hugs Amma. Amma smiles. It is okay for now. I take Dadi's hand in mine and place each of my closed lashes on her hand, then kiss it, like we are taught to kiss our elders.

'Allah nigehbaan,' she shouts through the metal gates as the lift starts to sink down the shaft.

An afterthought of care. *Allah be your guide.*

'Eh aao jo!' Apa yells, trying to make me lighten up one last time. This phrase was an inside joke about an annoying Gujarati family friend from our shared childhood. This woman had a funny way of saying 'Come back again' that almost sounded like 'Do not ever visit us again'. Apa's voice rings through the shaft.

Downstairs, our night watchman, Allah Rakha, as usual is snoring away in a chair as we walk noisily past him. In front of the building, Babu bhai, the van guy, waits for us. He is a Muslim, but he has brought his most trusted Hindu driver to take us to the station. The man has even attached a PRESS sign to the windshield.

Papa and Hussain bhai load the car up and we get in. Gulshan, her face streaked with tears, grips both Misba and me in a hug so hard I can feel her rib cage. Like she's giving us all her jazba, *courage*, like she's saying, *Go and don't look back.* Hussain bhai waves to his bhabhi and bachchiyaan, the sister and children he has helped safeguard and raise for over a decade. He closes the van's back door for us.

'Khayal rakhna haan?' *Look after yourselves.*

We take off.

The van slowly makes its way across the sleeping city. Some stray dogs chase the van, others let us be. Cop vans and constables at blockades eye us warily. Papa stares ahead. He seems to be muttering something under his breath. I look at his fingers, placed in his lap on the front seat. He is counting the tazbeeh as he usually does each morning after his shower, dressed in his white kurta pajama. It's the only prayer he knows. Today he sits sweating into the shirt Amma gifted him on his birthday. The sky outside is turning a soft violet.

The shapes and shadows of my childhood pass by. Shah Wajiuddin's dargah—the last saint my dada prayed to the evening before he died. Sidi Saiyyed ki Jaali—*will I see the light filter through those filigreed windows ever again?* I wonder. Teen Darwaza passes. Misba's laughter and mine as we tried on different Eid bangles there as children rings in the dark night. We cross Relief Road, where all of us piled into the Fiat and go to the cinema to watch *Hum Aapke Hain Kaun*. We pass by the last relic of the Ahmedabad I've grown up in, the Jhulta Minara, the Shaking Minarets. *My home is this place of magic*, I tell myself as I look one last time at the dark, ornate silhouettes of the minarets cutting into the early-morning sky. The four mysterious minarets were part of an old sultanate monument. If you shook one, the other three also trembled, confounding the world. The British dug one up to see what alchemy lay in their foundations. They couldn't tell. The minarets were simply . . . connected.

My home is a place of magic, I chant to myself.

We arrive at Kalupur Station. Papa gets our stuff out of the car and leads us to our platform. He has timed it with all precision today so we won't be caught waiting alone on a platform. The Navjeevan Express already stands, shuddering, on the tracks. He checks for our names on the passenger list on the sheet pasted outside the carriage. We are still wait-listed: *1, 2, 3*.

'Still no confirmation? No. I can't let you go like this . . . ,' he is feebly muttering, just as Amma's student's brother, the boy who booked us these miracle tickets, arrives.

He brings the ticket collector along, convincing him to confirm our tickets. Papa watches them from a distance. Then he decides to walk to them. Misba is in tears.

'C'mon, Allah miya, please,' she's pleading under her breath.

Amma laughs nervously. 'Misba has never prayed to Allah miya so much in her whole life!'

I watch my father come back to us. In his hand he holds the little white slip that is our ticket.

'Chalo. Chadh jaao. Ho gaya.' *Climb on. It's done.*

Papa smiles broadly then. For the first time in weeks, and it's as if the sun has risen, even though an owl still hoots somewhere. Misba and I throw our arms around his neck. He holds us close, tight, these daughters he was given after losing a son.

Then he bends and kisses Amma.

'Udhar reh mat jaana,' he teases, though his eyes look scared as they never have. *Don't stay back there.* As if to say, *I can't bear losing anymore.*

Amma smiles back nervously.

We don't know then that we will never come back together to live in Ahmedabad; that by the end of summer, Papa will collect the few books and clothes we've left behind, put them in his Hyundai Santro, and drive across the country, following us to Madras, where Rishi uncle and his Reddy friends will employ him, rehabilitate us, give us a new life in Madras.

Or perhaps we suspect it. Because suddenly Amma throws her arms around her daughters and husband as the train hoots its whistle. Papa quickly whispers, 'I love you, beta. Don't ever doubt that.'

This morning will not guarantee that my father will change. He will still drink. He will still curse. He will continue to be bitter and difficult to love. He will find out he has cancer six months from this day, just as we settle into a new life. He will fight Amma for it, blame Amma for it, and he will come back to this same city to die, four years from this day.

. . .

But in that moment, as he watches us board the train, I know he is telling the truth. He loves us despite everything he's been taught about loving daughters. He loves us in the only way he knows how.

We wave vigorously at him, and he walks along the train, peering through the foggy windows till we leave the platform. And then, practical man that he is, he turns away and leaves before he is caught standing there alone for too long.

A middle-aged Hindu Gujarati couple and their teenage son take the seats next to us as the train picks up speed. They ask us our names. I can't remember the fake Hindu names we agreed on this morning for all of us in case someone asks. Except mine. It's Seema. The couple asks if we are from Ahmedabad or from Madras.

'From Madras,' Amma tells them, trying to end the conversation.

They take over more than half of our seats eventually, putting their feet up and playing cards with their son. We wait for the ticket collector, nervous that he might call our names out loud. Our eyelids are heavy with exhaustion, but Misba and I sit up waiting with Amma.

Around late afternoon, the TC finally arrives in our carriage. Amma asks him how far to go before we have crossed the Gujarat state border. Misba and I have fallen asleep by the window and wake to see the sun high up in the sky, burning over the fields.

'Arre Gujarat toh kab ka chala gaya. Abhi apun Maharashtra mein hain.' *We left Gujarat hours ago! We're in Maharashtra now.*

I see Amma biting back an urge to smile as she gives him our full names to check the tickets—our real names.

'Zara Zaheer Chowdhary, Misba Zaheer Chowdhary, Rukhsana Zaheer Chowdhary.'

The Gujarati Hindu family sharing our compartment flinches visibly, the father especially staring daggers at our grinning faces.

We don't care anymore. We have left one home behind. We don't know if there is a home ahead. And we don't care. We let out a whoop and hug one another as the TC moves away. Home isn't on our mind anymore. Only one thing is, as we sit in front of those who watched our oppression and smirked, who sit in uncomfortable silence now at our joy.

Freedom.

Ashes on Water

I wish I were a river
I'd skim both shores with reverence.
A daughter touching the feet
Of both her parents.

When Papa dies in 2006, I, a tall and wispy nineteen-year-old girl with Nanijaan's colouring and eyebrows and hair, sit in my amma's lap, wiping away at her cheeks. *You have cried enough for a lifetime*, I whisper to her. Then I take her finger and place it on my dimpled chin, showing her how a part of Papa lives on through me. This makes her smile. The dimple I've inherited from my father deepens as I cradle her sobs and hold myself together.

In the years that follow, I draw a deeper line between her and Dadi. Dadi decides to keep us from accessing Papa's retirement savings, which he has mysteriously left in her care. I write a letter. In it, I disown Dadi and anyone who tries to hurt my mother. I send it to everyone whom Dadi or her family know. Everyone whose opinions of them matter. I never see Dadi after that letter. Amma knows in that moment, as she reads the letter I am about to mail, that her daughter hasn't grown up to be like her. I'm harsher. Angrier. Madder at the world than she is. Perhaps because the deaths of my childhood weren't as quiet and bloodless as those of hers. Mine were laced with the slow-burning poison of alcohol, with exploding cylinders. My childhood was a pogrom in progress.

She looks at me as she reads the letter with equal parts dread and awe. *It is not about the money*, I explain to her, rage filling my bones at Amma's easy forgiveness. *They don't get to have us if they don't know how to love us.* At twenty-one, I need justice to be served with swift immediacy. At twenty-one, I am capable of drawing boundaries to guard my loved ones from those who promised to love us and reneged. At twenty-one, Radcliffe's Line dividing this subcontinent has nothing on mine.

What forgiveness I am capable of I have already given. One stuffy summer night in 2006, I am back in C-8 Jasmine, but only briefly. Papa is still alive, but now we are counting the days we have with him. The teardrop lump became a breast full of tumours that became a body riddled with malignancies. I have come away from an internship to see my dying father for a week. I spend the week doing the same thing each day. He wakes up. A nurse helps him get dressed and use the bathroom. He lashes at her. Then Dadi tries to help him. He lashes at her. Finally, he sits in an armchair in the living room, doused as he always likes to be in talcum powder. And he sips from a smoothie the nurse has made and listens to me read the news for him from the paper, drinking in my voice. He is fifty-three; he has lost all his teeth. I am nineteen. I am about to lose everything. All day, I sulk around the empty corners of C-8 while he mostly sleeps. Dadi keeps out of my way. Papa has warned her to. We are mired in silence like this because when Papa first got diagnosed, Dadi left her precious Jasmine Apartments to come live with her dying son in Madras. And there she did what she always did best. She spread disinformation. Based on which Papa slapped Amma. And our temporary, peaceful refuge in the south of India caught fire. Misba and I were sitting in our bedroom when Amma came into the room the next morning, worn and weathered from caring for a sick and abusive husband, and looked at us with deadened eyes.

'Chalo we're leaving,' she said. And just like that, with her daughters following her, she put a few sets of clothes in plastic shopping bags, wore her house slippers and the three of us marched out to the living room.

'Where are you going?' Papa barked, shocked to see all three of us marching out. His mother hovered in the shadows.

'I heard Mummy telling you I am the cause of your illness. So . . .' Amma shrugs.

'So? So what?' He gets up, wobbling now on his unsure, sick feet.

'And you listen and . . . do what you do,' Amma says, hand on the doorknob.

Dadi pounces. 'See, I told you. She wants to leave you. Won't think about the children also.' This preying on a weak man's insecurities, this was always the secret to starting a fire. My mother, who never looks at her mother-in-law, now holds her in her razor gaze.

'I did it all these years for the girls.'

And before either Papa or Dadi can say another word, the three of us walk out of the apartment into the street and hail an auto-rickshaw. Afterwards we stay in Nanijaan's apartment for a few days. Afterwards Amma, alive again in a crisis, finds herself a job, finds us a little apartment of our own, and puts up plants and quilts on trunks and makes us a home in Madras out of nothing. Afterwards Papa tries to convince her to come back. Shah Sahab calls from Ahmedabad, Phupu calls and writes letters, each warning us that the breaking of a family brings everyone's ruin. Nobody apologises. We remain in this in-between place until Papa relents; he has lost his wife and children. Dadi and he close the apartment in Madras and return to Ahmedabad, to C-8 Jasmine.

I have come back one last time to see him because the doctors have given up. Because Apa tells me he doesn't have long. Because Amma told me I must do this for his soul, and my own. I don't tell anyone I am back in town. I want to remain forgotten. I only want my father to know me. I lie each night on the bed in the tiny room with the tiny window where we spent our entire childhood, restless like I can't wait to run away. Papa stopped sleeping in his own room after the cancer reached his spine. He wants to sleep in his father's bed. So Dadi has been moved to the laundry room while I am visiting. When Amma visits twice that year, she still sleeps next to him. She wakes up every few hours to check on him, clean him, change him, give him his medication, pray by his side. We all come and go like trains in the night, our carriages burning, no one to see them.

On what is my last night of this visit, I get up and tiptoe ghostlike through the quiet halls of C-8 to my father. I watch him from the doorway, flat on his back, his tall, broad frame not seeming as broken as it does during the day. He has lost all feeling and use of the lower half of his body. I enter the room soundlessly and walk to the iron grille of their window, through which as a child I spent hours watching the cars and cows, Eid and Muharram processions, then one day mobs and police jeeps, army trucks, Dada's funeral procession. A black, velvet sky hangs heavily above us and stars prick through its thickness. I can smell the Sabarmati's stagnant water, but I can't see it. My father's loud, thundering snores fill the room. I kneel on the floor by Papa's bed.

In Islam they say, 'Maa ke pairon mein jannat hai.' *Heaven is at a mother's feet.* I've kissed my mother's feet all through my childhood as a way of centring myself, of finding my home. Now I kiss my father's dead, unfeeling feet. His breath still moves through his chest, aware and alive to the touch of a daughter he has been primed all his life to misunderstand. But his feet are my shrine, my dargah. I can bow my head and kiss and pray and be. I have prayed for years for freedom from his tyranny. But to lose him entirely is not the price I ever wanted to pay. I need him to know I love him. I need him to love me back. I can do neither of those. So I forgive.

. . .

Tears fall on my cheeks, my fingers and slip onto his toes; I can feel them. He can't. Soon it will be daybreak. The time for feeling and knowing will be past us.

He stirs, restless in whatever dreams this disease shows him. I'll never know if he ever dreamt of his daughters. Or perhaps he dreams of seeing his son someday again. I kiss his feet one last time, whisper, 'I love you; I forgive you.' Then I get up and leave the room on the dying river, carrying with me wisps of a short life shared with my father. Someday I will come back to immerse these wisps in this river. But not tonight. Tonight, I hold these wisps close and go back to sleep in C-8 for the last time, a home where I will always be *his Zara*, just never his enough.

Daughters of the Sea

When Prophet Muhammad's persecutors plotted to murder him, he fled the violent, capitalistic city of his birth, Mecca, and migrated to the peaceful settlement of Medina. Witnesses say he wept as he put distance between himself and the only home he'd ever known. He is quoted as saying that nothing could have got him to leave except this requirement to fulfil Allah's call.

What was Allah's call for me when I left Ahmedabad? It has taken me almost twenty years to answer this question. My call was to take what this city, this family, had given me—an intricate legacy, multiple languages, a privileged education, an ability to see people in all their complexities, to carry memory. My call was to flee. And to someday put these things I carried along to good use.

If Ahmedabad was the centre of my being for sixteen years, Madras is my Medina. Its ocean and people embraced our broken hearts and made us whole again.

When we first arrived in Madras, Rishi uncle came to visit us in Nani's house. Rishi uncle had watched the pogrom unfold on TV. Now he heard it first-hand from us. When we finished speaking, Rishi uncle telephoned Papa.

'I'm not sending them back, Zaheer,' he simply said.

He offered Papa a job in his company. He knew it was the only way his broke and stubborn friend would accept aid. Another old friend of Papa's, the Muslim Uncle A, visited us every day that summer too. He would sit for hours in silence with Misba and me, waiting for us to speak whenever we were ready. I told him about my last phone call with Aisha.

'What a warped religion she has. It made her so blind that she couldn't see me,' I said, still brimming with anger.

'No religion is inherently bad, beti,' Uncle A gently pushed back. 'People do terrible things sometimes. And they use religion to justify it. Look at it this way,' he said. 'The man who brought you here to this new life, Rishi, is a Hindu.' I drank every word of hope in.

In Islam, when the story of Prophet Muhammad's exodus is told, all the text before it, from when Muslims lived in Mecca, says of Allah, 'God is *with* those who are patient.' But once they arrive in Medina, the language shifts: 'God *loves* those who are patient.' The references sparkle through the text once the oppressed arrive in a place where freedom still exists.

Madras offers us this dignity. It heals us, holds us and shows us an India we've known only from a distance. Our shoulders relax. Our smiles widen. We start to say our names out loud again. We go to the ocean each evening and repeat 'Subhanallah' like our Dada did looking at the sky from the balcony in Jasmine. *Allah is great, and this is beautiful.* We go from a place where our vision was impoverished, where we weren't seen by family or society, and where we couldn't see ourselves, to a place where the self finally becomes seen and understood.

At the end of the summer of 2002, Apa collects my board results from Mount Carmel and immediately calls me in Madras. I have scored 84.16 percent.

'Exactly the same as me, down to the point, Zara!' she squeals into the phone.

It is uncanny, even beautiful, to hear her gush on the line. I'm pleased with the result. A solid A+ can open doors for me wherever I want to study next. Slowly my confidence builds. I do exceedingly well in my last two years of high school, even get two state medals for acing my final year. I get into a competitive visual arts programme in an all-men's college, where on average only ten women are admitted each year. I top the class at the end of three years.

We never discuss news about Gujarat or 2002 in the house. We have the privilege of doing so. There are those who have lost everything—Ahsan Jafri's children and widow, Madina Sheikh, Bilkis and Yakub, hundreds of other families and loved ones of the dead. They continue to fight, and twenty years later, some are still fighting, reliving every wound, struggling in their dreams. But families like ours and girls like me remain silent, scattered, pretending 'nothing much' happened in 2002. We insist for a long time that *everything is fine. Of course we know we belong. India is changing so much.* But in our dreams the struggle continues. Mobs break past our eyelids and vandalise our souls.

For the next decade, every time Ahmedabad calls me back, it is for death. I go back when Papa dies. I go back when Mana's brilliant younger sister, on her way to becoming a doctor, is mistreated for swine flu at a state hospital and dies at the age of twenty. The city continues to take from me. I rush back each time to the sea and to Madras, letting the waves cleanse my wound, allowing myself to drown in the pain, until the Indian Ocean like a mother lifts me and deposits me back on my feet. The faces I recognise as my people in Jasmine slowly move away. Some leave the country, if they are lucky enough to have people on the outside. Others move into smaller, cramped apartments in Juhapura and Bombay Hotel, now Ahmedabad's biggest ghettos, ignored by the city and state administrations, often mocked and called 'mini Pakistan'. I never see Gulshan again. I hear of her from Phupu and Apa for a while, but one day she and Dadi have a huge fight, and she disappears.

The last time I go back to Ahmedabad is for a quick work trip in 2012, two years before Modi becomes our prime minister. One evening, while my colleagues rest in the hotel, I stop an autorickshaw and tell the driver, 'Bhaiya, Khanpur chalo.'

Suddenly, at twenty-eight, I find myself standing across the road from Jasmine Apartments, staring up at it. It looks like it has shrunk in the years I've been gone.

The city administration, bent on the narrative of Gujarat's 'development', are trying to beautify the Sabarmati's banks. They have started bulldozing and clearing the slums where Gulshan lived. A promenade for people to stroll on and drink coffee on is being built. *They are trying to forget the blood that spilt here.* The Sabarmati now flows perennially and artificially, after Modi's administration diverted waters from the mighty river Narmada and brought them to his dry state. Like everything else that has been altered, erased and manipulated, the river too now hides the stain of our sins.

I walk up the front stairs, through the metal gates, and into the dimly lit lobby. I stop to look at names on the board. It is still there: M.A. Chowdhary, C-8. The hall feels like it is pressing in on me, a fully grown woman. I realise what is rushing back up my throat is fear, even though those who could scare me are long gone. I press the button to take the lift. I almost hoot with delight to see Daaya bhai, our old janitor, commanding it. He is seated on a wooden stool, holding the lift door open for me. He has lost most of his teeth.

'Kya Daaya bhai, tambaakoo nahin chhoda,' I say, remembering how much betel nut he used to chew. I can tell he doesn't recognise me from the way he's studying my face.

'Hmmm. Tamne toh odhkun choon . . . ,' he slowly says, taking in the details of my eyes, my hair, my dimpled chin. *I recognise you.*

Somewhere in this lifeless hull, someone still remembers.

I nod, tears in my eyes. 'Main Zaheer bhai ki . . .'

He completes my sentence for me: '. . . Zaheer bhai ni dikri!' Dikri, beti. *Daughter.* I am Zaheer's daughter.

We smile tearfully up eight storeys. I disembark and wait for the lift to leave. Then I walk up to the ornate door of Dada and Dadi's pride and joy: C-8 Jasmine.

In her last years, Dadi has added a thick protective metal grille door outside the original wooden one. More ways to lock in whatever she held dearest. More ways to lock out 'the others'.

No sounds come from within. No plates and slippers flying and crashing. No loud voices. No blaring news on the TV. No Hindi songs to which little Misba danced, every strand of her hair dancing to its own tune. No Mana, Amal and a gang of little girls giggling and wrapping saris over their skirts and T-shirts on a sleepy afternoon while the noisy snores of Papa and Dadi fill the halls. No prayers whispered by a little Zara on a flying carpet, no birthday songs.

Nothing.

I stand there thinking of how far we've gone from here. I learnt how to ride a bike at nineteen, careening down a village trail in the mountains as two friends hooted and shouted encouragement at me. I've jumped off the side of a boat into the Bay of Bengal. I've climbed trees. I've danced, protested, made speeches, written stories. I've fallen in love with people and life despite this start I had.

Where I grew up isn't who I have become, Amma. I smile. As I linger outside the door of C-8, memorising its wooden flowers, tempted to reach through the metal grille and touch Dada's name one last time, I know that my bravado will soon give way. I will turn into an eight-year-old, wishing for the door to open and embrace me, to call me its own. Instead, I call the lift and let Daaya bhai take me away.

The next morning, after spending barely twenty-four hours in the city, I am in a hurry to escape. I jump into a cab for the airport early in the morning. As the cab winds its way through the city, I look up from my phone and notice the divider where Wali's shrine once stood. *Musa Suhag's qabrastaan must be close,* I realise. As the gates flash past, I tap my driver's seat urgently.

'Bhaiya, ek minute rukenge?' *Please can you stop?*

I walk through the cemetery's gates. The scent of incense immediately hugs me. The place is empty; the afternoon namaz crowd hasn't arrived. I find Papa's grave easily, then Dada's and Phupu's next to him. I kneel and hum the first prayer of the fatiha. Then my voice starts to crack. Then sixteen years of anger, pain, hate, yearning for acceptance and love come pouring out in a flood. I smile at this deluge of tears, love and regret that Musa Suhag now brings upon his beloved city. *It must rain in his courtyard every day*, I smile.

I want to say I stop at Kalandari qabrastaan too, where the unnamed dead of 2002 lie in mass graves. It is less than five hundred metres from me. But I don't. I can't wait to get away. As the plane takes off that morning, I watch the city drop below me—a blur of ageing stone and modern chaos. Ahmedabad's soil is magnetic, I think. It has claimed all its lovers, its brides, its fathers. Its most ardent disciples refused to leave. Their remains beneath me slowly turn to dirt, becoming one with a land that denies their belonging. I gulp in big breaths as the city vanishes from my view. I was never its daughter. This is not my home. Mine is elsewhere.

The Lucky Ones—an Epilogue

When Farida Abdulkadar Khalifa, one of the witnesses to and survivors of the Naroda Patiya massacre in 2002, is questioned in court about her ability to identify members of the mob in fading daylight, she says, 'Ujaale mein khada insaan dekh nahin sakta; jo andherey mein khada hai, usko dikh jaata hai sab.' *A person standing in broad daylight is often blinded. It's when you're standing in the dark that you really begin to see.*

I've often asked myself if perhaps it was the unbelonging within my own home that so attuned my moral compass to authoritarian nation-states, joint families, patriarchy and other systems that offer you belonging or security but in return demand your unquestioning loyalty, your total acquiescence. I want to believe the darkness of 2002 sharpened the clarity with which I can discern the oppressor from the oppressed. And it has emboldened my refusal to live a life as either.

Amma would often get complimented by relatives who simply saw two shy, young girls and didn't realise how scared and closed off our lives were. 'You've done a fantastic job with these girls, Rukhsana,' they would blindly say. 'They have such good tarbiyat.' These people thought they were praising an oppressed housewife for the good *upbringing* of her daughters, who would someday also make oppressed housewives.

But you see, 'tarbiyat' doesn't really mean an *upbringing*. In Islam, it means a cultivated ethic, a *code of conduct* from where one begins an uprising. Like the Battle of Badr—the first war the Muslims fought, when Islam was not yet a major global religion but simply a band of three hundred rebels in the desert. The Muslims were fighting the Quraysh, the Prophet's own tribe, the merchant class of Mecca who had come to hate him for disrupting their capitalist society with talk of social justice. The Quraysh had an army a thousand strong. Yet the Muslims won. When prisoners of war were taken, the code dictated that their dignity be maintained. The Prophet's companions clothed the half-naked prisoners in shirts off their own backs. In a world defined by land, clan, tribe, Islam created a political unit out of faith—an agreement to follow the law despite our tribal affiliations, a clear rejection of the human impulse to take sides only with our own kind. The Prophet insisted we always reflect within first. That's where the real jihad, the real contestation, must start with one's own.

Amal, my half-Yemeni building friend, half-jokingly once told me when we were kids that ultimately all Muslims should aim to live in Islamic countries like Saudi Arabia or Dubai or Yemen. It was the only way we could have dignity and belonging, close to the home of our Prophet, close to Mecca, the centre of our faith. I refused this vehemently as a child, even when I understood nothing of geopolitics. My whole body refuses this vehemently even today, two decades later. The Islam of an Indian Muslim is one of good tarbiyat. We have lived for centuries in this nation as a minority, across the ocean from Mecca, across the border from Pakistan, maintaining our dignity. My faith is not anchored by geography. Just as my belonging to my father is not measured by my distance from his grave.

In the Chapter Al-Rahman, Allah asks children like me, 'Fabi-ayyi-ala-i-rabbikuma-tukkaziban?' *Which favours of your god will you deny?*

I cannot deny. Our idea of India and being Indian Muslims, as we learnt it through Dada, Papa, Phupu, Amma, through blood, land and spirit ancestors, through teachers who taught us and strangers who saved us, gave us a code to live by: the pursuit of justice at all costs. My home is in this memory I hold of India, of who we once were. And my uprising is to keep this story writ into history no matter how much erasure stamps over it.

Some days, when it feels like my motherland is forsaking me, telling me I am not hers, she is not mine, and my soul wants to cry like an orphaned child, I remind myself that my belonging was bequeathed to me by the best of mothers: my amma. She lost a child, a chance at love, a life of freedom. But she chose Misba and me to empty herself into. We own everything that is great and beautiful and redeemable about our country—its humour, its refuge, its magnanimity, its humility, its ability to bend and absorb every shard of grief thrown its way, and from it to grow flowers, to make life.

Acknowledgements

My gratitude to my editor Madhulika, for holding my hand and helping write these lost stories into India's history, for shaping these words with her sharp eye, and for her deep sense of care. To the entire team at Crown and Penguin Random House. My deepest thanks to Karthika, Ajitha and the whole team at Context in India. It takes publishers of integrity and a village of book lovers ready to reckon with themselves to bring a book like this, with the bravery it demands, into the hands of readers to whom we owe such bravery. This India edition is this story's homecoming, and I've felt safe and ready in their capable hands. To Arsh, for the gift of this gorgeous cover.

To Anjali, my agent, sister and ally, and the fiercest advocate a girl could ask for.

To those who spoke to me about 2002 and lent me their courage: especially Nishrin apa, Dionne and Father Cedric Prakash. To Avni, Mohit, Percy, Vamsi, Iqra, Varun, Hussain, Aamir, Nabiya, Nisha, and all my other fellow makers of good trouble. To the journalists and citizen voices that continue to speak truth to power. To every brave witness. To Umar, who speaks to me through his resilience, though we've never yet spoken. And to every dadi and nani who took the streets for our farmers and for us in 2019 and 2020.

To the First Nations on whose stolen land my body committed these stories to the page, who for centuries have stewarded this land's stories, and who continue to carry its resilience and memory.

To my MFA thesis advisor K.L. Cook for his unwavering guidance which brought this book from a scattered collection of essays to a full breathing memoir. To the members of my thesis committee: Charissa Menefee, Jeremy Withers and Brad Dell.

To my cohort: Jack, Brendan, Mike, Kartika, Kate, Crystal, Keygan and Jon, whose devotion to the natural world, crackling sentences, goofy puns, DnD and fierce authenticity taught me that sharing stories and listening to each other is our one sacred duty. To Allison, Hagan, Emily and Bathsheba whose writing orbits crossed with me, and whose kindness was nurturing. To Tessa and Margaret from my Depressed Memoirists Club.

To Debra Marquart, who insisted a book hid behind the half-poem I wrote in her class.

To Kazim Ali, who chose 'Slow Violence', the essay that would become this book, to be part of Red Hen Press's beautiful *New Moons* anthology alongside some of America's most stunning contemporary Muslim voices. And to Alex Chee who picked this manuscript from a pile of entries for the 2020 AWP prize and gave me the gift of a blurb and his championing voice when I didn't have much else.

To the women who have carried me for sixteen years and never once let me doubt: Lalita, Noureen, Pra, Sandy, Pri, Shaggy, Hana, Nida, Naaz and Sneha. To Pooji, Sidhu, Raam, Bhavi and Bin. And the humans who made them, and made Misba and me. To Chacha. To my Jasmine gang, CJM girls and Loyola rowdies. To Azhar. To every aunt who has made dua'a. To my village of mothers led by Shannon and Christina but including so many others. To Shruti who is my biswa for life.

To Sarah, Will and Cait—for the pandemic family and for every day since. We carry a piece of our Jeni St utopia wherever we go.

To the men who bookend this story: Papa, who now lives where all stories are perfect and complete; Sufi, who in Gibran's words, is 'life's longing for itself'. And Matt, in whose quiet strength I have found my sukoon, *my place of rest.*

And finally, to the two women, who generously allowed me to speak for them, even though each have their beautiful way with words. To have held my version in their palms, to have walked this road of loss, anger and forgiveness with me, and to have allowed it to heal them too, takes a special kind of mother and sister. I am the luckiest of all to have these two.

Notes

p. 26: *Nathuram Godse's connection to the RSS*

Although Nathuram Godse had always held that he had left the RSS, there are several sources contradicting this. See, for instance, this interview with senior journalist and Godse's biographer, Dhirendra K. Jha: 'India: Gandhi's killer Godse never left RSS, claims new book', *Al Jazeera*, 30 January 2022.

p. 38: *Modi speaking to Jafri on the phone*

Suhas Munshi, 'Ehsan Jafri called Modi for help, I heard Modi abuse him: Gulberg survivor', Catch News, 10 February 2017, https://www.catchnews.com/india-news/ehsan-jafri-called-modi-for-help-i-heard-modi-abuse-him-gulberg-survivor-1464888144.html.

p. 55: *Babu Bajrangi boasts to undercover journalist*

Ashish Khetan, 'Had good police support because of Modi: Babu Bajrangi in Ashish Khetan's Undercover' (book excerpt), *The Caravan*, 17 January 2021.

p. 56: *Suresh Chhara to undercover journalist*

Ashish Khetan, 'The Truth: Gujarat 2002', *Tehelka* magazine, 7 November 2007. Also see: Rajiv Shah (quoting from the *Tehelka* story), 'Story of a foot soldier of Gujarat riots coming from a vulnerable community, Chharas', *Counterview.net*, https://www.counterview.net/2019/01/story-of-foot-soldier-of-gujarat-riots.html & Harsh Mander, *Fear and Forgiveness: The Aftermath of Massacre*, Penguin, New Delhi, 2009, p. 49.

p. 57: *Babu Bajrangi boasts to undercover journalist*

Ashish Khetan, 'Had good police support because of Modi: Babu Bajrangi in Ashish Khetan's Undercover' (book excerpt), *The Caravan*, 17 January 2021.

p. 134: *love jihad*

For an explanation of this concept read: Mohan Rao, 'Nothing fair in this war on love', *The Indian Express*, 1 December 2020, and Shwetha Desai, 'The "Love Jihad" Conspiracy Theory', *New Lines Magazine*, 21 December 2020, among other pieces.

p. 189: *Rahul Sharma's role in collecting evidence*

Manoj Mitta, 'How Maya Kodnani was convicted and sentenced to 28 years in prison, before being exonerated' (book excerpt), Scroll.in, 20 April 2018, https://scroll.in/article/876344/how-maya-kodnani-was-convicted-and-sentenced-to-28-years-in-prison-before-being-exonerated.

p. 266: *the Sangh Parivar's fascist beginnings*

See, for instance: Parmal Chirmuley, 'Foreign hand in the Sangh', The Indian Express, 31 March 2018, https://indianexpress.com/article/opinion/columns/foreign-hand-in-the-sangh-rss-hindu-society-muslims-christians-5117648/; and Dhirendra K. Jha, 'Guruji's Lie', Caravan magazine, 1 August 2021, https://caravanmagazine.in/history/rss-golwalkar-links-nazism.

p. 270: *Muslim cattle traders lynched*

Delna Abraham and Ojaswi Rao, 'Cow-Related Violence: 86% Dead Since 2010 Are Muslim; 97% Attacks Reported After 2014', *The Wire*, 28 June 2017.

p. 271: *Modi as modern-day Nero*

PTI, 'Modi modern-day Nero: SC', *The Times of India*, 12 April 2004.

p. 271: *Kashmir and Article 370*

For an explanation of the ramification of the abrogation of Article 370, see, for example: 'Article 370: What happened with Kashmir and why it matters', *BBC*, 6 August 2019.

p. 271: *WhatsApp and Islamophobia in India*

See, for instance, Soma Basu, 'Manufacturing Islamophobia on WhatsApp in India', *The Diplomat*, 10 May 2019.

p. 272: *Muslim activists imprisoned*

For more on the UAPA and CAA, see: 'India Activates Discriminatory Citizenship Law', Human Rights Watch, 15 March 2024; 'India: Arrests, Raids Target Critics of Government', Human Rights Watch, 13 October 2023.

p. 272: *Teacher encourages students to slap Muslim classmate*

Rhea Mogul et. al., 'Outrage in India as teacher tells students to slap classmate who is Muslim', *CNN*, 28 August 2023.

p. 272: *Hindu cop shoots Muslim passengers*
Bureau, 'Killing of Muslim passengers by RPF constable termed 'hate crime' by family of victim', *The Hindu*, 1 August 2023.

p. 272: *young boy forced to chant Jai Shree Ram*
News Desk, 'MP: Muslim boy stripped, forced to chant "Jai Shri Ram", "Pak Murdabad"', *Siasat*, 14 April 2023.

Bibliography

The 2002 story remains contested and developing even after twenty-two years, with several cases still being heard at various levels in the Indian judicial system. This bibliography is updated as far as December 2023. Many online published resources have gone missing, offline or have been moved to archives, and may require additional inquiry if found unavailable at the mentioned URLs.

Ahmed, Heba. 'Burying the Massacred: In the Shade of Kalandari.' *Firstpost,* 28 February 2019. www.firstpost.com/long-reads/burying-the-massacred-in-the-shade-of-kalandari-6169061.html.

Amnesty International. 'Justice, the Victim—Gujarat State Fails to Protect Women from Violence.' AI Index: ASA 20/001/2005. https://amnesty-indien.de/wp-content/uploads/208/Justice-the-victim-asa200012005en.pdf.

Ansari, Ghulam Mohammed. 'Madrasas of Gujarat in the Middle Ages.' *Kashmir Reader,* 16 March 2023. kashmirreader.com/2023/03/16/madrasas-of-gujarat-in-the-middle-ages/.

Ayyub, Rana. *Gujarat Files: Anatomy of a Cover Up.* Self-published, CreateSpace, 2016.

Balaji, R. 'Gujarat Riots: Parading of Bodies Triggered Conspiracy, Zakia Tells SC.' *Telegraph Online,* 11 November 2021. www.telegraphindia.com/india/gujarat-riot-parading-of-bodies-also-part-of-conspiracy-kapil-sibal-tells-supreme-court/cid/1838356.

Banerji, Annie. 'Indian Nationalist Lawmaker Gets 28 Years for 2002 Massacre.' *Reuters,* 31 August 2012. www.reuters.com/article/us-india-riots-sentencing-idUSBRE87U0EX20120831.

Bhaskar, Ira, and Richard Allen. *Islamicate Cultures of Bombay Cinema.* New Delhi: Tulika Books, 2009.

Bhatt, Sheela. '"India Is My Country. I'll Live Here and Fight Back."' *Rediff News,* 21 June 2003. www.rediff.com/news/2003/jul/21spec.htm.

Bunsha, Dionne. *Scarred: Experiments with Violence in Gujarat.* New Delhi: Penguin, 2006.

Cartlidge, David R., and J. K. Elliott. *Art & Christian Apocrypha.* New York: Routledge, 2001.

Celan, Paul. 'Poetry: Death Fugue.' In *Art from the Ashes: A Holocaust Anthology,* edited by Lawrence L. Langer, 651–52. Oxford: Oxford University Press, 1995.

Chandoke, Neera. 'Civil Society in Conflict Cities: The Case of Ahmedabad.' Crisis States Working Papers Series No. 2, Working Paper No. 64, Crisis States Research Centre, 2009. https://www.jstor.org/stable/25663739

Changoiwala, Puja. '"They Raped Me, Butchered My Child. 17 Years On, I Have Justice—and Faith in Indian Law."' *South China Morning Post,* 19 May 2019. www.scmp.com/week-asia/people/article/3010554/gujarat-riots-they-raped-me-butchered-my-child-because-we-were.

Chauhan, Ashish. 'No One Razed Wali Gujarati's Mazaar?' *Times of India,* 16 December 2019, timesofindia.indiatimes.com/city/ahmedabad/no-one-razed-wali-gujaratis-mazaar/articleshow/72703885.cms.

Chenoy, Kamal Mitra, et al. 'Genocide in Gujarat: Report by SAHMAT Fact Finding Team to Ahmedabad.' *Counter Currents,* 10–11 March 2002. countercurrents.org/sahamat1.htm.

Concerned Citizens Tribunal. *Crime Against Humanity.* Vol. 1, *An Inquiry into the Carnage in Gujarat.* Citizens for Justice and Peace, 2006. https://www.sabrang.com/tribunal/tribunal1.pdf.

Court of Sessions for Greater Bombay. Judgement. *State of Gujarat v. Accused.* 13 August 2009. https://cjp.org.in/bilkeesbanojudgement2008/.

———. Judgement. *State of Gujarat v. Rajubhai Dhamirbhai Baria and Ors.* 24 February 2006. https://cjp.org.in/judgment24feb06/.

Davis, Marni. 'Ghetto: The History of a Word.' *Journal of American History* 107, no. 4 (March 2021): 978–79. academic.oup.com/jah/article-abstract/107/4/978/6157124?itm_medium=sidebar&itm_source=trendmd-widget&itm_campaign=Journal_of_American_History&itm_content=Journal_of_American_History_0&login=true.

Desai, Bharat. 'Board Exams Postponed in Ahmedabad, Vadodara.' *Times of India,* 16 March 2002. timesofindia.indiatimes.com/india/Board-exams-postponed-in-Ahmedabad-Vadodara/articleshow/3958508.cms.

DNA Web Team. 'Time-line of Ayodhya Dispute and Slew of Legal Suits.' DNA, 28 September 2010. www.dnaindia.com/india/report-time-line-of-ayodhya-dispute-and-slew oflegal-suits-1444808.

Dugger, Celia W. 'Ahmedabad Journal; in India, a Child's Life Is Cheap Indeed.' *New York Times,* 7 March 2002. www.nytimes.com/2002/03

/07/world/ahmedabad-journal-in-india-a-child-s-life-is-cheap-indeed.html.

Dutta, Prabhash K. 'Bilkis Bano Case: Story of Brutality and 15-Year-Long Wait for Justice.' *India Today*, 23 October 2017. www.indiatoday.in/india/story/bilkis-bano-rape-murder-case-gujarat-riots-2002-bombay-high-court-975229-2017-05-04.

Express News Service. 'Phone Records of Ehsan Jafri Missing, Admits SIT in Court.' *Indian Express*, 9 September 2009. indianexpress.com/article/cities/ahmedabad/phone-records-of-ehsan-jafri-missing-admits-sit-in-court/.

FP Explainers. '2002 Gujarat Riots: Who Is Maya Kodnani, Former BJP Minister, Now Acquitted in Naroda Gam Massacre?' *Firstpost*, 21 April 2023. www.firstpost.com/explainers/2002-gujarat-riots-maya-kodnani-former-bjp-minister-acquitted-naroda-gam-massacre-12485042.html.

Frank, Anne. *The Diary of a Young Girl*. Translated by Susan Massotty. Edited by Otto H. Frank and Mirjam Pressler. New York: Bantam, 1997.

Gottipati, Sruthi. 'A Conversation With: Zuber Jafri.' *New York Times*, 24 April 2012. india.blogs.nytimes.com/2012/04/24/a-conversation-with-zuber-jafri/.

Gujarat High Court Order. *Mayaben Surendrabhai Kodnani v. State of Gujarat*. 29 January 2013.

———. Judgment. *Sheikh Madinabibi Mustafabhai v. State of Gujarat*. 12 October 2004. https://indiankanoon.org/doc/845201/.

———. Judgement. *State of Gujarat and Anr. v. Babubhai Bajrangi*. 4 July 2011.https://www.casemine.com/judgement/in/56e0ff4e607dba389660b933

Haidar, Suhasini. 'Ruling Party Wins Gujarat Poll.' *CNN*, 16 December 2002. edition.cnn.com/2002/WORLD/asiapcf/south/12/15/india.gujarat/.

Hameed, Syeda, et al. 'The Survivors Speak: How Has the Gujarat Massacre Affected Minority Women.' *Outlook*, 2 May 2002. www.outlookindia.com/website/story/the-survivors-speak/215433.

Harding, Luke. 'Frantic Search for British Sons Lost in Gujarat Riots.' *The Guardian*, 24 April 2002. www.theguardian.com/world/2002/apr/24/india.uk.

Human Rights Watch. '"We Have No Orders to Save You": Hindu-Muslim Violence in India.' In *Human Rights and Religion: A Reader*, edited by Liam Gearon, 294–300. Liverpool University Press, 2002. https://doi.org/10.2307/jj.4418201.25.

Hussain, Nishrin Jafri. 'Bless Us, Abba: 2002 Gulbarg Victim Ehsan Jafri's Daughter Writes.' *The Quint*, 17 June 2016. www.thequint.com/voices/blogs/bless-us-abba-2002-gulbarg-victim-ehsan-jafris-daughter-writes.

———. 'Ehsan Jafri's Daughter Nishrin Jafri Recounts the Event.' Breaking News Express. 25 July 2017. YouTube video, 28:28. https://www.youtube.com/watch?v=sdhPvKwA5ps.

IANS. '2002 Gujarat Riots: Despite Request to CM Modi, Army Lost a Crucial Day Waiting for Vehicles, Says Lt. General (Exclusive).' *Business Standard,* 5 October 2018. www.business-standard.com/article/news-ians/2002-gujarat-riots-despite-request-to-cm-modi-army-lost-a-crucial-day-waiting-for-vehicles-says-lt-general-exclusive-118100500898_1.html.

Jaffer, Amin. 'The 16th-Century Design That Inspired the Logo of IIM, Ahmedabad.' *Architectural Digest India,* 3 November 2022. www.architecturaldigest.in/story/the-16th-century-design-that-inspired-the-logo-of-iim-ahmedabad-mughal-jalis/.

Jafri, Ehsan. 'Zakhmon Ko Mere Dil Ke Sajao to Bane Baat.' Rekhta.org. www.rekhta.org/ghazals/zakhmon-ko-mere-dil-ke-sajaao-to-bane-baat-ehsan-jafri-ghazals.

Jaggi Vasudev, Sadhguru. 'What Is Navratri? Nine Days of Navratri Explained.' Isha Foundation, 19 January 2022. isha.sadhguru.org/us/en/wisdom/article/what-is-navratri-nine-days-of-navratri-explained.

Khan, Ayub. '"Ahsan Jafri Was Not a Muslim Fanatic."' *Outlook,* 27 April 2002. www.outlookindia.com/website/story/ahsan-jafri-was-not-a-muslim-fanatic/215350.

Khetan, Ashish. 'Had Good Police Support Because of Modi: Babu Bajrangi in Ashish Khetan's Undercover.' *The Caravan,* 17 January 2021. caravanmagazine.in/conflict/had-good-police-support-because-of-modi-babu-bajrangi-in-ashish-khetan-undercover.

Klüger, Ruth. *Still Alive: A Holocaust Girlhood Remembered.* New York: Feminist Press at the City University of New York, 2012.

Laul, Revati. *The Anatomy of Hate*. Chennai: Context, 2018.

———. 'Gujarat Riots: Rapist Who Attacked Me While on Parole Is Out Again.' *The Quint,* 30 November 2016. www.thequint.com/voices/blogs/2002-gujarat-convicted-rapist-out-on-parole-raped-women-attacked-wife-court-police-unaware-revati-laul-journalist#read-more.

Levi, Primo. *Survival in Auschwitz: The Nazi Assault on Humanity.* Translated by Stuart Woolf. New York: Collier-Macmillan, 1969.

Mahurkar, Uday. 'Gujarat Riots: As Death Toll Rises, CM Narendra Modi's Image Hits a New Low.' *India Today,* 20 May 2002. www.indiatoday.in/magazine/states/story/20020520-gujarat-riots-as-death-toll-rises-cm-narendra-modi-image-hits-a-new-low-795273-2002-05-20.

Mander, Harsh. 'Barefoot—a House for Sparrows.' *The Hindu,* 21 March 2012. www.thehindu.com/opinion/columns/barefoot-a-house-for-sparrows/article2981161.ece.

———. 'What Bilkis Bano Survived That Day in Gujarat, 2002.' *The Wire,* 26 April 2019. thewire.in/books/bilkis-bano-gujarat-2002.

Mitta, Manoj. 'Questions the Special Investigation Team Probing Gujarat Riots Did Not Ask Narendra Modi in 2010.' *Article 14,* 28 June 2022. article-14.com/post/-questions-the-special-investigation-team-probing-gujarat-riots-did-not-ask-narendra-modi-in-2010--62ba6436b3e84.

Munshi, Suhas. 'Ehsan Jafri Called Modi for Help, I Heard Modi Abuse Him: Gulberg Survivor.' *CatchNews,* 10 February 2017. www.catchnews.com/india-news/ehsan-jafri-called-modi-for-help-i-heard-modi-abuse-him-gulberg-survivor-1464888144.html.

'"Muslims, They Don't Deserve to Live."' *Tehelka,* 3 November 2007. https://web.archive.org/web/20151017003148/http://archive.tehelka.com/story_main35.asp?filename=Ne031107NarodaPatyaMassacre.asp.

Nagarathna, B.V., and Ujjal Bhuyan. 'Early Release of Bilkis Bano Gangrape Convicts: Bilkis Yakub Rasool v Union of India.' *Supreme Court Observer,* 26 October 2023. www.scobserver.in/cases/early-release-of-bilkis-bano-gangrape-convicts/.

Nanavati, G.T., and Akshay H. Mehta. 'Report by the Commission of Inquiry.' 18 September 2008. www.sacw.net/DC/CommunalismCollection/ArticlesArchive/NanavatiReport1.pdf.

Narendran, Thyagarajan. 'The History of Gulbarg Society Litigation.' *LawBeat,* 5 November 2021, lawbeat.in/top-stories/history-gulbarg-society-litigation.

Nayadu, Ujjwala. 'My Husband Is a Goon, Not a Rapist.' *Indian Express,* 1 September 2012. https://indianexpress.com/article/cities/ahmedabad/my-husband-is-a-goon-not-a-rapist/.

Niewyk, Donald L. *The Holocaust: Problems and Perspectives of Interpretation.* Boston: WadsworthCengage Learning, 2011.

Pathan, Fayeza. 'I Survived Gujarat 2002 Riots: This Is What Our Life Looks Like Today.' *DailyO,* 7 June 2016. www.dailyo.in/politics/gujarat-2002-riots-ahmedabad-ognaj-indian-muslims-modi-amit-shah/story/1/11051.html.

Prakash, Fr. Cedric. Interview by Zara Chowdhary. November 2019.

Press Trust of India. 'Naroda Gam Riots: Kodnani Was Present at Spot for Around 10 Mins, Says SIT.' *Business Standard,* 3 August 2018, https://www.business-standard.com/article/current-affairs/naroda-gam-riots-kodnani-was-present-at-spot-for-around-10-mins-says-sit-118080300866_1.html.

———. 'Pandya Was Among Rioters: Victim.' *Rediff,* 17 July 2003. www.rediff.com/news/2003/jul/17guj.htm.

Rankine, Claudia. *Citizen: An American Lyric.* Minneapolis: Graywolf Press, 2014.

Sagar. 'After the Release of a Naroda Patiya Convict, His Wife and a Journalist Fear for Their Lives.' *The Caravan,* 6 December 2016. caravanmagazine.in/vantage/release-naroda-patiya-convict.

Satrapi, Marjane. *Persepolis: The Story of a Childhood and the Story of a Return.* New York: Vintage, 2008.

Sattar, Nazura. Interview by Misba Chowdhary. June 2019.

Sethi, Avni. 'The Muse Who Shed His Masculine Identity and Adopted the Bridal Attire, Lived in Ahmedabad.' *Counterview,* 9 May 2017. counterview.org/2017/05/09/the-muse-who-shed-his-masculine-identity-and-adopted-the-bridal-attire-lived-in-ahmedabad/.

Sethna, B.J. *Aamer Yunus Bhavnagri v. State of Gujarat.* 8 July 2002. https://indiankanoon.org/doc/1111307/.

Shankar, Soumya. 'My Pain Is Nothing Compared to That of the 2002 Riot Victims: Former Guj Cop Rahul Sharma.' *CatchNews,* 14 February 2017. www.catchnews.com/politics-news/my-pain-is-nothing-compared-to-that-of-the-2002-riot-victims-former-guj-cop-rahul-sharma-1454157500.html#google_vignette.

Sharma, Rakesh. 'Final Solution—Film by Rakesh Sharma.' Citizens for Justice and Peace. 26 February 2018. YouTube video, 2:22:12, www.youtube.com/watch?v=P6yY8DFSnfw.

———. 'Gulberg: When No One Responded to Ex-MP Ahsan Jafri's Distress Calls (an Excerpt from Final Solution).' *NewsClick,* 4 June 2016. www.newsclick.in/gulberg-when-no-one-responded-ex-mp-ahsan-jafris-distress-calls-excerpt-final-solution.

Sherwani, Arfa Khanum, and Zameer Uddin Shah. 'Watch: "While Gujarat Was Burning, Army Kept Waiting for Vehicles."' *The Wire,* 11 December 2019. thewire.in/video/video-gujarat-burning-army-vehicles-former-lieutenant-general.

Smith, David James. *Hinduism and Modernity.* New Jersey: Blackwell, 2003.

Special Court, Designated for Conducting the Speedy Trial of Riot Cases, Situated at Old High Court Building, Navrangpura, Ahmedabad. Common Judgment. Sessions Case No. 235 of 2009. 29 August 2012. cjp.org.in/wp-content/uploads/2018/05/Naroda-Patiya-Trial-Court-Judgement.pdf.

Suhrawardy, Nilofar. 'Slain Minister Led Mob Attack, Gujarat Riot Victim Testifies.' *Arab News,* 18 July 2003. www.arabnews.com/node/234489.

Supreme Court of India. Order. *Bilkis Yakub Rasool v. State of Gujarat and Others.* 23 April 2019. https://main.sci.gov.in/supremecourt/2003/17411/17411_2003_Order_23-Apr-2019.pdf

Tejpal, Tarun J., ed. 'Gujarat 2002: The Truth.' *Tehelka,* 7 November 2007.

'The Truth in the Words of the Men Who Did It: Gujarat 2002.' *Tehelka,* 3 November 2007. web.archive.org/web/20140527212851/http:/archive.tehelka.com/story_main35.asp?filename=Ne031107safehouseofhorrors.asp&page=2.

TNN. 'Oldest Indian Mosque: Trail Leads to Gujarat.' *Times of India,* 6 November 2016. timesofindia.indiatimes.com/city/ahmedabad/oldest-indian-mosque-trail-leads-to-gujarat/articleshow/55270285.cms.

———. '*Shila Daan* Concludes Peacefully in Ayodhya.' *Times of India,* 15 March 2002. timesofindia.indiatimes.com/india/shila-daan-concludes-peacefully-in-ayodhya/articleshow/3860369.cms.

———. '2 Killed in Vatva, Curfew in Himmatnagar.' *Times of India,* 22 March 2002. timesofindia.indiatimes.com/city/ahmedabad/2-killed-in-Vatva-curfew-in-Himmatnagar/articleshow/4497303.cms.

Udayakumar, S. P. 'Historicizing Myth and Mythologizing History: The 'Ram Temple' Drama.' *Social Scientist* 25, no. 7/8 (July/August 1997): 11–26. https://doi.org/10.2307/3517601.

United States Holocaust Memorial Museum. 'The Reichstag Fire.' encyclopedia.ushmm.org/content/en/article/the-reichstag-fire.

Vardarajan, Siddharth. 'Nothing New?' In *Gujarat: The Making of a Tragedy,* New Delhi: Penguin Books, 2002, 224–5.

Weisman, Steven R. 'As Sectarian Attacks Go On, India State Is Puzzled.' *New York Times,* 3 August 1985, https://www.nytimes.com/1985/08/03/world/as-sectarian-attacks-go-on-india-state-is-puzzled.html?smid=url-share.

Wiesel, Elie. *Night.* Translated by Marion Wiesel. New York: Perfection Form Co., 1988.

Wikipedia. 'Gulbarg Society Massacre.' en.wikipedia.org/wiki/Gulbarg_Society_massacre.

'Zakia Jafri #8: SIT Argues Jafri's Case Is Inconsistent and Accusations of Omission Are Unfounded.' *Supreme Court Observer,* 24 November 2021. www.scobserver.in/reports/zakia-jafri-protest-petition-gujarat-riots-hearing-report-day-8-oral-hearings/.

About the Author

Zara Chowdhary is a writer and teaches language and South Asian culture at the University of Wisconsin. She has an MFA in creative writing and environment from Iowa State University. She lives in Wisconsin, USA.